The History of Custody Law

Tom James

Second Edition.

Copyright © 2014 Tom James

Printed in Charleston, SC, USA

Cover: *"The Child's Caress" by Mary Cassatt, ca. 1890*

Library of Congress Control Number 2014907586

ISBN: 1499182031
ISBN-13: 978-1499182033

CONTENTS

Preface to the Second Edition

This book is for general educational purposes only. It is not intended as legal advice for a particular case or a particular fact situation. It should not be used as an alternative to retaining an attorney.

Child custody laws vary from state to state in many important respects, and new laws are passed in every state every year. Moreover, judges issue new interpretations of statutory law on a regular basis.

Citations in the text and footnotes are for illustrative purposes only. A reference to a particular statute or case does not imply that other relevant statutes or cases do not exist.

Throughout this book, and unless the context clearly requires otherwise, the use of masculine, feminine or neuter gender is intended to include the other genders.

Citations to sources within the text are in the standard *Bluebook* format for legal citations. New to this edition: revisions and additions to several chapters; a new chapter on the rights of gay, lesbian, and transgendered parents; table of ancient law codes; survey of no-fault divorce legislation in each state at the end of the twentieth century; and a bibliography.

ACKNOWLEDGMENTS

I wish to express my gratitude to the University of Minnesota for allowing me access to their historical collection; my family, for putting up with the many hours of research and writing that have gone into this project; and Mary Hendrickson, for helping me keep firmly in mind that an accurate history is important for reasons that have nothing to do with political or commercial viability.

INTRODUCTION

"You must always know the past, for there is no real Was, there is only Is."
–William Faulkner

This book explores the evolution of child custody law from ancient times to the present day, with a focus on the underpinnings and development of Anglo-American law.

Most people today think of custody as one of the issues that is addressed in a divorce proceeding. It is true that custody issues can arise in that context. They can also arise in other contexts, too, such as disputes between the parents of children born out of wedlock, or between a parent and a relative, or between parents and the state.

Historically, custody disputes were more likely to arise upon the death of a parent than in a divorce. Although these kinds of cases may not seem directly relevant to the determination of custody in a modern divorce case, they provide useful information about the legal relationships among parents, children, and the state, and the nature and limits of their respective rights and powers. At the same time, it is important to acknowledge that some different issues arise when a dispute is between parents rather than between a parent and a non-parent., and to understand the nature of those differences.

For the past fifty years or so, the history of custody law almost universally has been presented as a linear progression from a primitive system that treated children like the property of their fathers and therefore forced them to endure a harsh and cruel existence, to an enlightened approach that treats the best interests of the child as the paramount consideration, and for that reason places them in the loving, nurturing care of their mothers.

Professor Hendrik Hartog summarizes the current state of legal scholarship as follows:

> Nearly all recent scholarship on the legal history of American marriage … begins with a demonstration that traditional legal rules…were bad, like slavery. The narrative tells of a titanic struggle against coverture, one in which good (egalitarian law reform) is always pitted against bad (the patriarchal common law)….[1]

The traditional account typically begins with the *patria potestas* system of ancient Rome, under which fathers had an absolute right to custody of their children; asserts that this was carried forward, unchanged, into eighteenth and nineteenth century England two thousand years later; that colonists brought it to America; and that it remained the rule of decision in custody cases until the Great Enlightenment, i.e., modern-day America. It was only because American women mobilized to overthrow patriarchal rule, the story goes, that courts finally started caring more about children's

---

[1] HENDRIK HARTOG, MAN AND WIFE IN AMERICA: A HISTORY 3 (2000); *see also* Danaya C. Wright, De Manneville v. De Manneville*: Rethinking the Birth of Custody Law under Patriarchy*, 17 LAW & HIST. REV. 247 (Summer, 1999) (describing the argument that "a linear progression from patriarchy to egalitarianism in family relations occurred in the early nineteenth century and that once mothers were accorded a presumption in custody disputes, all was right in the family" as "too simplistic.") For an example of a work that follows the described approach, see MARY ANN MASON, FROM FATHER'S PROPERTY TO CHILDREN'S RIGHTS: THE HISTORY OF CHILD CUSTODY IN THE UNITED STATES (2d ed. 1994).

interests than fathers' rights. The account typically concludes with an observation that it was only relatively recently that courts began to acknowledge the superiority of maternal child care over patriarchal control as the right and proper means of promoting the best interests of children.[2]

In truth, the history of custody law is neither a linear progression nor an opus on the triumph of motherly care over harsh male control. The historical record supports a theory that the maternal preference in custody law stems at least as much — and probably more — from a desire to confine women and men to rigidly defined sex roles as it does from a quest for recognition of women's superiority as parents.

---

[2] *See, e.g.*, 1 JEFF ATKINSON, MODERN CHILD CUSTODY PRACTICE § 4-4 (2nd ed. 2004) (asserting an ancient Roman paternal right to custody continued throughout Europe until the middle of the nineteenth century, and that "[t]he common law rule that a father was entitled to custody was carried over to the United States"); HARRY D. KRAUSE & DAVID D. MEYER, FAMILY LAW IN A NUTSHELL (5th ed. 2007) ("At common law, the father ... 'owned' his children and had the primary custodial claim....Paternal preference gave way in the late 1800s"); MASON, *supra* note 1 at x ("For most of our history, well into the twentieth century, ...[f]athers...were granted paramount rights to custody and control of their children. Mothers...had no right to custody as long as the father was alive..."); WEBSTER WATNIK, CHILD CUSTODY MADE SIMPLE: UNDERSTANDING THE LAWS OF CHILD CUSTODY AND CHILD SUPPORT 42 (2000) ("Up until the mid-1800's, children were considered the property of the father, who was usually awarded custody following a divorce....Today, laws in all states require judges to consider what is in the best interests of the child when making a custody decision"); Ralph J. Podell et al., *Custody-To Which Parent?*, 56 MARQ. L. REV. 51-52 (1972) (crediting Justices David Brewer and Benjamin Cardozo, while sitting as state court judges in 1888 and 1925, respectively, with establishing the "best interests of the child" as the rule of decision in custody cases); Allan Roth, *The tender years presumption in child custody disputes*, 15 J. FAM. L. 423-61 (1976-77). Sarah Pinkerton's account of the development of early American custody law is fairly representative of the modern canon:

> Until well into the nineteenth century, the English law on child custody treated the child as the father's chattel. Before the English, the Romans in custody matters had followed *patria potestas*, a doctrine that originally gave complete power over children to the father....The American Colonies inherited and implemented the English common law on the subject of child custody, meaning that children belong to their fathers...and mothers were legally irrelevant.

Sarah Pinkerton, *Custodial Rights of California Mothers and Fathers: A Brief History*, 16 J. CONTEMP. LEGAL ISSUES 155 (Spring 2005)

Even the notion that custody of children should be decided on the basis of what is in their best interests rather than parental rights is not a recent invention. It was part of the Roman law codified by Justinian more than a thousand years ago, and there is evidence that the idea was around long before then. Contrary to the popular view that the history of children is one of deliverance from the cruel tyranny of fathers into the loving arms of mothers, it appears that from earliest recorded times, parents of both sexes have cared about their children; and judges, to varying degrees at different times in history, have shared that concern. Sometimes they have used it as a justification for favoring fathers, sometimes for favoring mothers, and sometimes for favoring one sex while purporting to favor neither.

The book comprises four parts. The first two parts trace the development of custody law from the earliest times for which there are records to the nineteenth century. Next, the development of the law in colonial and nineteenth century America is explored. The remainder of the book chronicles the various changes in American custody law that occurred over the course of the twentieth century -- from a maternal preference, to an attempt at gender neutrality, and finally, gender polarization. Twentieth century developments in the areas of child protection, unwed fathers' rights, third-party rights, the rights of non-heterosexual parents, visitation, and joint custody are also discussed.

I have included a chapter on federal welfare and child support enforcement programs. Although these things do not directly relate to the substantive law of custody, it is impossible to comprehend the current state of child custody law in America without an understanding of these programs and how they may affect custody outcomes.

In researching and writing this book, I have relied upon legal enactments, judicial decisions, and treatises, along with other primary and secondary sources from each period, to the extent available. Full citations to relevant documents are included.

It is said that you cannot know where you should go unless you know where you have been. It is my hope that this book will help facilitate that journey.

PART I. ANCIENT CIVILIZATIONS

1. NEOLITHIC MATRIARCHY?

Once upon a time, the many cultures of this world were all part of the gynocratic age. Paternity had not yet been discovered...Childbirth was mysterious. It was vital. And it was envied. Women were worshipped because of it, were considered superior because of it.... Men were on the periphery—an interchangeable body of workers for, and worshippers of, the female center, the principle of life.

The discovery of paternity, of sexual cause and childbirth effect, was as cataclysmic for society as, say, the discovery of fire or the shattering of the atom. Gradually, the idea of male ownership of children took hold....

Gynocracy also suffered from the periodic invasions of nomadic tribes.... The conflict between the hunters and the growers was really the conflict between male-dominated and female-dominated cultures.

[W]omen gradually lost their freedom, mystery, and superior position. For five thousand years or more, the gynocratic age had flowered in peace and productivity. Slowly, in varying stages and in different parts of the world, the social order was painfully reversed. Women became the underclass, marked by their visible differences.[3]

The foregoing account was penned by Gloria Steinem in 1972. The theory of a Neolithic matriarchy, though, did not originate with her. Swiss philologist Johann Bachofen advanced it over a century before her in his 1861 book, *Das Mutterrecht*.[4] It was popularized in the United States in the mid-twentieth century by psychologist Erich Neumann, then by Marija Gimbutas, and then, of course, by Gloria Steinem.[5]

The principal evidence for the theory consists of primitive artifacts depicting feminine shapes and images. The reasoning is that since people created female figurines during the Stone Age, it may be inferred that they worshipped goddesses.

Scholars recently have begun to question the soundness of this reasoning. Professor Lotte Motz, for example, has observed that Stone Age images of men and animals are just as numerous as images of women.[6]

Moreover, there is no evidence that Stone Age female figurines were created for the purpose of goddess-worship. It is possible they were fertility symbols, sexual objects or simply artwork.[7]

Finally, even if goddesses were worshipped in the Stone Age, that does not necessarily mean that women enjoyed higher social or political status than men. Examples of artistic exaltations of femininity and motherhood in patriarchal societies are plentiful.

According to Motz, "there clearly was ... no imposition of a patriarchal system...."[8]

---

[3] Gloria Steinem, Introduction to WILLIAM M. MARSTON, WONDER WOMAN (1972)

[4] JOHANN J. BACHOFEN, DAS MUTTERRECHT (Stuttgart, Krais & Hoffmann 1861); *cf.* LEWIS H. MORGAN, ANCIENT SOCIETY (New York, H. Holt 1871)

[5] MARIJA GIMBUTAS, GODS AND GODDESSES OF OLD EUROPE, 6500-3500 B.C. (1974); ERICH NEUMANN, THE GREAT MOTHER (Ralph Manheim trans., 1955); STEINEM, *supra* note 3.

[6] LOTTE MOTZ, THE FACES OF THE GODDESS (1997)

[7] *See* GERDA LERNER, THE CREATION OF PATRIARCHY 29 (1986)

[8] MOTZ, *supra* note 6 at 35.

There certainly are reasons to question the assumptions underlying the theory. For example, the recent archaeological discovery in Peru of an ancient matriarchal society known as the Mochica casts considerable doubt on Steinem's assumption that woman-ruled societies would be peaceful ones. According to project director Luis Jaime Castillo, women governed in Mochica society between 2,000 and 1,200 years ago. Illustrations from this period, though, depict the Moche engaging in brutal bouts of ritualized combat against each other. This discovery tends to lend some credence to Women's Studies Professor Cynthia Eller's assessment of the Neolithic matriarchy theory as a myth driven by ideology, an inversion of antifeminism.[9]

Of course, *matriarchy* does not have the same meaning as matrifocality, matrilocality, matrilineality, matristicism, or gynocentricism. *Matrifocality* relates to the degree of importance that a society assigns to mothers. It connotes nothing about the nature or extent of the power, political or otherwise, that women possess. *Matrilocality* relates to the greater proximity of a married couple's residence to the wife's family than to the husband's family. It, too, says nothing about women's power, political or otherwise, relative to men. *Matrilineality* simply means that rights of inheritance are traced through the mother's lineage. It does imply greater economic power for women, but it does not necessarily entail greater political, judicial or legislative power. *Gynocentricism* refers to a singular or paramount concern with women and their interests, usually to the exclusion of any concern about men and their interests. At times, it is also used to describe ideologies that ascribe central importance to stereotypically "feminine" qualities like peacefulness, cooperativeness, benevolence, and so on (basically, anything more like "sugar and spice" than "snips and snails.") *Matristicism*, like gynocentricism and matrifocality, involves the assignment of central importance to females and/or stereotypically feminine qualities. As used by Gimbutas, though, it connotes an extraordinary level of exaltation, i.e., worship of all things feminine. To the extent Bachofen, Gimbutas and others intended their arguments to establish the possibility that ancient civilizations were matrifocal, matrilocal, matrilineal, matristic or

---

[9] CYNTHIA ELLER, THE MYTH OF MATRIARCHAL PREHISTORY: WHY AN INVENTED PAST WONT GIVE WOMEN A FUTURE (2000). Meredith Bennett-Smith, *Ancient Priestess Unearthed in Peru; Tomb Suggests Women Ruled Mysterious, Brutal Culture*, HUFFINGTON POST (August 24, 2013)

gynocentric, they are possibly more defensible than claims like Steinem's that women once ruled the world. A society may be patriarchal in the political sense, where its leaders and national policy-makers are principally male, while at the same time being matrifocal, gynocentric, matrilocal, matrilineal, and matristic.

Whether the first human social organizations were matriarchal, patriarchal or egalitarian may never be known. It is possible that they were matriarchal. It is equally possible that they were not. Without written records from the period, we have no real knowledge, and can only speculate.

Even assuming, for the sake of argument, that a Neolithic matriarchy existed, it is far from certain that women's superior political and/or social position would have ensured them a superior right to the custody of children. Social hierarchical position and political power do not always correlate positively with child custody rights. In fact, the correlation sometimes is an inverse one. In patriarchal cultures it is typically women, not men, who possess superior rights to the custody of children, when the contest is between the mother and the father of a child. It is entirely possible that in a society ruled by women, responsibility for child-care could have been delegated to men. That certainly would have afforded women the freedom and time they would have needed to go about the business of ruling the world.

2. THE FIRST RECORDED CUSTODY LAWS

While no one really knows how custody rights were allocated in Neolithic times, we do have some record evidence about how several ancient civilizations dealt with the issue.

The Laws of Eshnunna

Written laws dating to about 2,000 years before the Roman Empire have been discovered in Mesopotamia, a region sometimes described as the "cradle of civilization." These laws, the Laws of Eshnunna, ca. 1930 B.C., contain what is believed to be the earliest custody law in recorded history.

Eshnunna was a city on the bank of the Diyala River. An earlier legal code is known to have existed in another part of Mesopotamia, namely, the city-state of Lagash. That code is believed to have been enacted by King Urukagina sometime between 2380 and 2360 B.C. Unfortunately, very little is known about its content. The Neo-Sumerian Code of Ur-Nammu, ca. 2050 B.C., is believed to be the oldest extant record of a legal code, but what exists of it deals primarily with crimes and punishment, not custody law.[10]

---

[10] O.R. Gurney and Samuel N. Kramer, *Two Fragments of Sumerian Laws*, 16

So far, Eshnunna is the earliest known legal code to address the custody of children directly and specifically.

The Laws of Eshnunna specified that if a husband divorced the mother of his children and took a new wife, then he "shall be driven from his house" and his ex-wife (the mother of the children) was to get everything – the house, the property and the children.[11]

The code was silent about what was to happen in the event the father was not guilty of any wrongdoing, or if it was the wife who divorced and took a new husband. One explanation could be that only husbands were permitted to divorce their spouses. It is also possible that the law was designed to protect a mother's "title" to the children. That would explain why the triggering event that would cause the father to lose everything was his introduction of a new mother (i.e., a stepmother) to the children.

From the minimal evidence that is available, it is not possible to know what would happen to the children if the father remained single. The law implies that he would be entitled to stay in his house in that case, but it is not clear whether he would also have the right to keep the children. It is possible that the children were expected to go with the mother in all cases as a matter of course, the only legal question being whether the father would get to stay in his house and keep all of his property or not.

The only valid conclusion that can be drawn from what evidence we have of the earliest known custody law is that it reflected neither an absolute paternal rights principle nor an absolute maternal preference rule. Instead, it was grounded in the concept of marital fault.

The Code of Lipit-Ishtar

A tradition of solicitousness toward women in the law of domestic relations can be found in the other of the earliest legal codes to address the subject of child custody. The Code of Lipit-Ishtar, ca. 1924 B.C., imposed an obligation on husbands to support their wives and their children, including any children born out of wedlock; but there was no

[11] LAWS OF ESHNUNNA 59 (n.d.); *see* REUVEN YARON, THE LAWS OF ESHNUNNA (1988)

corresponding obligation on the part of women to support husbands and children.[12] Women had support rights; men did not. It seems reasonable to infer from this that this society allocated the child-raising role (custody) to mothers, while allocating the wage-earner role (support-payer) to fathers. [13]

Assyria

In contrast to the Laws of Eshnunna and the Code of Lipit-Ishtar, ancient Assyrian laws were not solicitous toward women at all. They apparently authorized husbands to abuse their wives with impunity. While that does not necessarily mean that husbands prevailed over wives in custody disputes, it does suggest the possibility that in ancient Assyria a husband's commission of domestic violence might not have barred an award of custody to him.

The Code of Hammurabi

The Code of the sixth Babylonian king, Hammurabi, ca. 1780 B.C., is probably the best preserved of the ancient Mesopotamian legal codes, and the most famous. Section 137 deals with child custody:

> If a man [leaves a woman or a] wife who has granted him children, to that woman he shall return her marriage portion and shall give her the usufruct of field, garden, and goods, and she shall bring up her children. From the time that her children are grown up, from whatever is given to her children they shall give her a share like that of one son, and she shall marry the husband of her choice.[14]

The Code described a married couple's children as "hers," not "his." Evidently, ancient Babylonians viewed children as the property of their mothers, not their fathers. Further, the Hammurabi Code, unlike the Laws of Eshnunna, did not impose any limitations linked to the father's

---

[12] Lipit-Ishtar was the fifth ruler of the first dynasty of Isin.

[13] *Cf.* Francis R. Steele, *The Code of Lipit-Ishtar*, 52 AM. J. ARCHAEOLOGY 425 (July-September 1948).

[14] HAMMURABI, CODE OF LAWS, *reprinted in* THE OLDEST CODE OF LAWS IN THE WORLD: THE CODE OF LAWS PROMULGATED BY HAMMURABI, KING OF BABYLON, 2285-2242 B.C. (C.H.W. Johns trans., 1903)

remarriage to someone else. Section 137 secured the right of sole custody to every mother, whether the ex-husband became remarried or not.

Other provisions of the Hammurabi Code gave the father paramount rights over children while he and the mother were still married and living together. He could use the children as collateral for debts and sell them into slavery for up to three years.[15] It appears that upon divorce or separation, though, the mother's rights became paramount. This suggests that coverture may have been part of ancient Babylonian culture and law. Under the doctrine of coverture, a woman's rights are suspended, or at least subordinated, while she is married and living together with her husband, but are revived if the marriage is dissolved. That seems to be the system that is reflected in the Hammurabi Code. In any event, it is clear that the wife's right to custody upon divorce or separation was regarded as superior to the husband's right to custody, notwithstanding the superior position the father held in an intact family unit.

The Babylonian mother's right to sole custody of the couple's children was not absolute, however. It was defeasible upon proof that she had plunged the family into debt, tried to ruin her house and neglected her husband.[16] In other words, Babylonian law applied a maternal custody presumption that was rebuttable by proof of marital fault.

The Hittites

The Hittites, ca. 1650-1100 B.C., are said to have adopted a "liberal and pragmatic approach to the institution of marriage."[17] Apparently, a Hittite woman could initiate a divorce proceeding as easily as a man could,

---

[15] *See* A.R. COLÓN & P.A. COLÓN, A HISTORY OF CHILDREN: A SOCIO-CULTURAL SURVEY ACROSS MILLENNIA 18-19 (2001)

[16] CODE OF HAMMURABI § 141, *reprinted in* 2 G.R. DRIVER & J.C. MILES, THE BABYLONIAN LAWS 55 (1968.) A divorced man would forfeit all of his property and children if he remarried after the divorce, but it is unclear what would happen to a divorced mother if she were to remarry before the children had grown up. It is possible that she, like the divorced man, would then forfeit her custody and property rights and be "driven from the house," too, but it is also possible the law would simply have regarded the divorced mother's purported second marriage as void.

[17] TREVOR BRYCE, LIFE AND SOCIETY IN THE HITTITE WORLD 119 (2002)

and divorces were not uncommon.[18] If both the mother and the father were members of the free class, then custody of all but one of their children went to the mother upon divorce. On the other hand, if the father was a member of the free class and the mother was a member of the slave class, then custody of one child went to the mother and the rest went to the father.[19]

---

[18] *Id.*

[19] BILLIE JEAN COLLINS, THE HITTITES AND THEIR WORLD 24 (2007).

TIMELINE OF ANCIENT LAW CODES

ca. 2380-2360 B.C.   Code of Urukagina of Lagash
ca. 2050 B.C.   Code of Ur-Nammu
ca. 1930 B.C.   Laws of Eshnunna
ca. 1870 B.C.   Code of Lipit-Ishtar
ca. 1790 B.C. Code of Hammurabi (Babylonia)
ca. 1650-1500 B.C.   Code of the Nesilim (Hittites)
ca. 1250 B.C.   42 Laws of Maat (Egypt)
ca. 1075 B.C.   Code of the Assura (Assyria)
11th century B.C.   Kang Gao (Zhou Dynasty, China)
7th century B.C.   Draconian constitution (Greece)
ca. 600-400 B.C.   Torah/Law of Moses (Hebraic)
ca. 600-200 B.C.   Laws of Manu/Dharmasastra (India)
5th century B.C.   Gortyn Law Code (Greece)
451 B.C.   The Twelve Tables (Rome)
429-439 A.D.   Codex Theodosianus (Rome)
529 A.D.   Justinian Code (Rome)
570 A.D.   Shari'a (Islamic)
668-689 A.D.   Omi Code/Asuka Kiyomihara Code

3. EGYPT

Some primitive human social groups thought of children as inchoate human beings. A person's status as a human being was conditional upon the passage of time and the performance of a ritual. Until a child earned his status as a human being, his parents generally had the same rights and powers over him as they had over any other kinds of property. They could keep and raise him; or they could trade, sell, abandon or kill him.[20]

Egypt did not follow the primitive model.

Much of the recorded history of ancient Egypt was lost when the Library of Alexandria burned down, but what evidence there is suggests that the people of ancient Egypt not only viewed children as human beings and not as property, but they also held children in extraordinarily high regard.

---

[20] SANDER J. BREINER, SLAUGHTER OF THE INNOCENTS: CHILD ABUSE THROUGH THE AGES AND TODAY (1990); Emile Eyben, *Family Planning in Greco-Roman Antiquity*, 11/12 ANCIENT SOC'Y 5-82 (1980-1981). Population control was not the only reason for the practice of infanticide in ancient civilizations. The Sabeans, for example, boiled, deboned and ate male children as part of a religious festival. COLÓN & COLÓN, *supra* note 15.

Evidence that ancient Egyptians regarded children as people, not property, may be found in their rules against infanticide. Abhorrence of infanticide was so strong that a parent who killed a child would be punished by being made to carry the dead child on his or her person for three days.[21]

Concern for children extended to the unborn, too. Because an unborn child was regarded as a distinct human being, a pregnant woman could not be executed, inasmuch as doing so would involve the execution of an innocent person, the fetus.[22]

By the time of the Fifth Dynasty of the Old Kingdom (ca. 2400 BC), women and men were relatively equal before the law in Egypt.[23] Women could own property, obtain employment, run businesses, and so on. With respect to the custody of children, however, men and women were not equals. Upon divorce, only the mother had a right to custody of the children, and this was true whether the divorce was initiated by the husband or by the wife.[24] The maternal preference in child custody cases was in full force in Egypt more than 4,000 years ago.

---

[21] BREINER, *supra* note 20 at 15-16. On the other hand, Egyptian law authorized killing the children of captured fugitives. *Id.* at 27.

[22] WILL DURANT, THE STORY OF CIVILIZATION, PT. I (1954).

[23] *See* BREINER, *supra* note 20 at 14, 27.

[24] CHRISTOPHER D. HEANAN, ANCIENT EGYPT (retrieved on July 23, 2011), www.scribd.com/doc/49116704/Ancient-Egypt

4. GREECE

Children did not fare as well in ancient Greece as they did in Egypt. Except in Thebes and Epheseus, the parental right to kill one's child upon birth was absolute. In fact, parents were legally required to kill defective children.[25] Ritual sacrifices of children to appease the gods were not uncommon. In Arcadia, they continued well into the second century A.D.[26] By the time of the Roman Conquest, infanticide was so widespread that most families either had only one child or they had no children at all.[27] "Surplus" children (that is, more children than the family could support) were abandoned in the wilderness to die.[28] Children born out of wedlock were aborted, killed

---

[25] Valerie French, *Children in Antiquity*, *in* CHILDREN IN HISTORICAL AND COMPARATIVE PERSPECTIVE: AN INTERNATIONAL HANDBOOK AND RESEARCH GUIDE 21 (Joseph M. Hawes and N. Ray Hiner eds., 1991). The parental right to kill or abandon a child terminated, however, ten days after the birth of the child. If the child had been accepted into the family and had not been killed, then the parental right of infanticide was forfeited. BREINER, *supra* note 20 at 50.

[26] BREINER, *supra* note 20 at 59.

[27] *Id.* at 50.

[28] THE HISTORY OF CHILDHOOD 1 (Lloyd de Mause ed., 1975); WILLIAM B. RYAN, INFANTICIDE: ITS LAW, PREVALENCE, PREVENTION AND HISTORY (London, J. Churchill 1862); Laila Williamson, *Infanticide: An Anthropological Analysis*, *in* INFANTICIDE AND THE VALUE OF LIFE (Marvin Kohl ed., 1971)

or sold into slavery.[29] In general, the first-born child, whether male or female, would be kept and raised, provided it was healthy. If the second child born was a boy, then he might be killed. Any additional children after that usually were killed, for fear that more heirs would divide the inherited land.[30] Even when Solon freed slaves and enacted laws limiting parental authority in the sixth century B.C., infanticide still was not prohibited.[31]

In all cities except Athens, a father in ancient Greece had the right to sell his children into slavery at any time during their childhood.[32]

Ancient Greece was predominantly a warrior society. Nowhere was this clearer than in Sparta. Spartans practiced a primitive form of eugenics to build the military strength of the country. Parents there would throw their children off cliffs if they appeared to be unhealthy or defective in some way. Babies with birth defects were exposed (left in the wilderness to die.)[33] Male infants with no discernible birth defects were tested by being left in the wilderness to fend for themselves. This was how they were expected to prove themselves healthy enough to earn the right to live and secure a place in the family. The state required parents to kill any male baby that did not pass inspection.[34]

Spartan boys left the family at the age of seven to be raised by the state in something like a military academy. There, they were subjected to severe forms of corporal punishment. Every year at the altar of Orthia, young boys would be whipped to bleeding in a perverse game in which the first one to cry was the loser. At the altar of Artemesia, children were flogged to death. Male children seem to have been born, bred, raised and educated for the sole purpose of becoming warriors.[35] Those who did not appear likely to serve that purpose well were regarded as having no value at all, and destroyed.

---

[29] BREINER, *supra* note 20 at 46.

[30] *Id.* at 49.

[31] *Id.* at 55.

[32] *Id.* at 50; Lloyd de Mause, *The Evolution of Childhood*, 1 HIST. OF CHILDHOOD Q.: J. OF PSYCHOHISTORY 503-75 (1974)

[33] *See* PLUTARCH, LIFE OF LYCURGUS (n.d.) *and* XENOPHON, CONSTITUTION OF THE LACEDAEMONIANS (n.d.); *see also* ARISTOTLE AND XENOPHON ON DEMOCRACY AND OLIGARCHY 75-79 (J.M. Moore trans., 1975)

[34] COLÓN & COLÓN, *supra* note 15 at 68

[35] *See* BREINER, *supra* note 20 at 51-52, 59

Sexual abuse of male children was a commonplace in ancient Greece. Older men expected young boys to engage sexually with them, and most did.[36] It was rare for a boy to pass into adulthood without having been sodomized. Boy brothels and boy prostitutes could be found in every city.[37] Young boys were sold at public auctions to the highest bidder, to be used for sexual purposes, and then sold as slaves.

Sex roles in ancient Greece were very rigidly defined. Men worked and participated in civic activities outside the home, while women stayed home and raised children.[38] The ancient Greek writer Xenophon described the division of labor between the sexes as follows:

> God from the first adapted the woman's nature, I think, to the indoor and man's to the outdoor tasks and cares. For he made the man's body and mind more capable of enduring cold and heat, and journeys and campaigns; and therefore imposed on him the outdoor tasks. To the woman, since he has made her body less capable of such endurance, I take it that God has assigned the indoor tasks. And knowing that he had created in the woman and had imposed on her the nourishment of the infants, he meted out to her a larger portion of affection for new-born babes than to the man.[39]

For this reason, Xenophon concluded, "to the woman it is more honourable to stay indoors than to abide in the fields, but to the man it is unseemly rather to stay indoors than to attend to the work outside."[40]

---

[36] G. Devereus, *Greek Pseudo-Homosexuality and the Greek Miracle*, 42 SYMBOLAE OSLOENSES 69-92 (1967); L.E. Shiner, *The Darker Side of Hellas: Sexuality and Violence in Ancient Greece*, 9 PSYCHOHISTORY REV. 111-35 (1980)

[37] BREINER, *supra* note 20 at 48-49.

[38] GEORGE THOMSON, STUDIES IN ANCIENT GREEK SOCIETY (1st Amer. ed. 1965); *see also* FAMILIES IN GLOBAL AND MULTICULTURAL PERSPECTIVE 45 (B. Ingoldsby & S. Smith eds., 2d ed. 2006) (describing ancient Greece as "the nadir for female status in family and general relations.")

[39] XENOPHON, OECONOMICUS 30, *reprinted in* XENOPHON: MEMORABILIA, OECONOMICUS, SYMPOSIUM, APOLOGY (E.C. Marchant trans., 1923).

[40] *Id.*

Unlike Egypt and other ancient civilizations, the custody of children in ancient Greece went to the father in the event of a divorce. If a woman bore a child shortly after the divorce, then the former husband had a right of first refusal to custody of the child. If he declined, then the mother could either raise the child herself or kill him.[41]

---

[41] GORTYN LAW CODE, INSCRIPTIONES CRETICAE 4.72, cols. iii.45 – iv.54 (M. Guarducci ed., 1935-1950); D. SCHAPS, ECONOMIC RIGHTS OF WOMEN IN ANCIENT GREECE 48-88 (1979).

5. ROME

Children did not fare much better in early ancient Rome than they did in ancient Greece.[42] Parents were governed by the state for acts committed in public, but within their own homes they had absolute authority over their children. The head of the household had the right, upon the birth of a child into the household, to either accept the child or kill him; and parents were permitted to beat and kill their children with impunity. The only condition was that they were required to raise at least one daughter to adulthood.[43]

Acceptance of a male child was never final. The head of the household could banish a son from the home at any time if he misbehaved. Starvation of children was common. As in Greece, children could be sold into slavery.[44]

Laws enacted in the eighth century B.C. banned infanticide. An exception was recognized, though, for disabled and genetically deformed

---

[42] For a comparison of the seemingly contradictory attitudes of ancient Greco-Romans toward children (harsh and abusive vs. "interest and delight"), see French, *supra* note 25 at 13-29.

[43] BREINER, *supra* note 20 at 104-06; *see also* W. HUNTER, INTRODUCTION TO ROMAN LAW 30 (9th ed. 1934); COLÓN & COLÓN, *supra* note 15 at 90.

[44] DIONYSIUS HARLICARNASSENSUS, ROMAN ANTIQUITIES (Edward Spelman trans., London, Booksellers of London and Westminster 1758)

children. Parents continued to have the right to kill those children, provided at least five neighbors agreed with the decision.[45]

Physical and sexual abuse of male children reached the same extraordinary levels in ancient Rome that they did in ancient Greece. Male children were often sold into concubinage or to brothels, and young male slaves were commonly kept for sexual purposes. There were boy brothels in every city. In addition, Plutarch referenced many instances of teachers sexually abusing male students eleven years of age and younger. Male children were sometimes castrated as babies so they could be sold to brothels or to men who enjoyed sodomizing them. It was believed that producing children who could be used sexually or as court eunuchs would help advance a parent's political ambitions.

Horace's *Epodas* describes a young boy's liver being removed and used to make a love potion. There was also a market for boys' testicles as an ingredient in medical potions.[46]

The Law of the Twelve Tables

The Law of the Twelve Tables, ca. 450 B.C., sets out a summary of Roman law that was in effect at that time. A provision giving recognition to common law marriages appears in Table VI, which is titled, "concerning ownership and possession." Some historians cite this as evidence that Roman law classified women as property.[47] As explained by the Roman jurist Gaius in the second century A.D., however, a wife was regarded, for purposes of the Twelve Tables, as a lawful heir to property.[48] Also, wives had dowry rights.[49] Property does not have rights, and property does not inherit property. It seems irrational, therefore, to interpret the title of Table VI as evidence that Roman law treated women as property. A more logical explanation is that Table VI was simply intended to describe the

---

[45] BREINER, *supra* note 20 at 106-07; French, *supra* note 25 at 21; *see generally* Valerie French, *Birth Control, Childbirth and Early Childhood, in* 3 CIVILIZATION OF THE ANCIENT MEDITERRANEAN 1362 (Michael Grant and Rachel Kitzinger eds., 1988).

[46] Legislation prohibiting the castration of babies for this purpose was enacted during the latter part of the first century. BREINER, *supra* note 20 at 112-15.

[47] *See* S.P. SCOTT, THE CIVIL LAW 68 (1932)

[48] Gaius, *Third Commentary, in* SCOTT, *supra* note 47.

[49] M. Corbier, *Divorce and Adoption as Familial Strategies, in* MARRIAGE, DIVORCE, AND CHILDREN IN ANCIENT ROME 47, 52 (B. Rawson ed., 1991)

circumstances in which an unmarried woman would have the same property rights as a married woman.

Of course, there is no question that the early laws of ancient Rome gave some men much more power than women, children and slaves. The Twelve Tables conferred on married fathers the privilege of *patria potestas*, a right of life and death over male children born to his wife during the marriage.

A father did not possess this authority over either daughters or children born out of wedlock. Also, a father who was still subject to the authority of another ascendant did not acquire *patria potestas* power, because his child, in that case, would still be subject to the same authority as the father was.

The Tables imposed upon fathers a duty to kill any sons who were born with a deformity or abnormality. Additionally, sons could be sold into slavery.[50]

Devolution and reform

Roman law was not static. The period between 150 B.C. and 1 A.D. was the culmination of what was probably the lowest point in the recorded history of children. Romans generally seemed to have lost interest in raising children during this time. At one point, the senate decreed that no male children at all should be raised. If a male child was born to a couple, his parents were required to kill him. Infanticide and abortion were rampant.[51] The divorce rate was very high. Cannibalism – parents literally eating their young – was not uncommon. Young boys were regularly sacrificed to the gods. Adults tortured and killed children for entertainment. One such "entertainment" involved dangling a young child from a pole and watching hyenas pull him down and eat him alive. These atrocities eventually led to significant legal reforms in the first few centuries A.D.[52]

---

[50] WILLIAM BLACKSTONE, COMMENTARIES ON THE LAWS OF ENGLAND 372-73 (19th ed., London, John Murray 1857); SCOTT, *supra* note 47.

[51] SUETONIUS, THE LIVES OF THE TWELVE CAESARS (Joseph Gavorse ed., 1965)

[52] BREINER, *supra* note 20 at 118-20; French, *supra* note 25 at 21.

Justinian

Modern legal historians assert that Roman law treated children as the property of their fathers, and that concern for the interests and well-being of children would not emerge in Western law until nearly two millennia later, in twentieth century America.[53] Justinian's *Digest* (a compendium of Roman judicial rulings), however, shows that Roman courts were treating children's interests as superior to parents' rights at least as early as the second century A.D., and that concern for the well-being of children continued throughout what is sometimes called the Golden Age of the early Byzantine period of ancient Rome.[54]

During this period, fathers had no absolute right to the custody of their children. In fact, mothers had the sole and exclusive right to custody of children born to them out of wedlock, while fathers generally had a right to custody of their children only during an intact marriage.[55]

Married fathers had some rights, but they were far from absolute. Gnaeus Domitius Annius Ulpianus, ca. 170 to 223 A.D., summarized second century Roman custody law as follows:

> If…it is the mother of the child who retains it in her possession, and it appears to be better that it should remain under her care than to be placed under that of its father, that is to say, if the reason is perfectly

---

[53] *See, e.g.,* Joan B. Kelly, *The Determination of Child Custody in the USA*, 4 FUTURE OF CHILDREN 121, 122 (Spring 1994); Ramsay Laing Klaff, *The Tender Years Doctrine: A Defense*, 70 CAL. L. REV. 335, 337 (1982) (declaring that "[t]he doctrine originated in the nineteenth century as a child-protective reform intended to elevate the interest of children above fathers' common law proprietary rights in children."); Lynne Marie Kohm, *Tracing the Foundations of the Best Interests of the Child Standard in American Jurisprudence*, 10 J.L & FAM. STUD. 347 (2008) ("The standard of the best interests of the child may generally be described as a principle deriving from Anglo-American family law")

[54] Emperor Justinian (525-65 A.D.) codified Roman law in the *Corpus Juris Civilis*, of which his *Digest* is part.

[55] *See* THE RULES OF ULPIAN, tit. V, *reprinted in* SCOTT, *supra* note 47; *see also* JAMES SCHOULER, A TREATISE ON THE LAW OF THE DOMESTIC RELATIONS 416 (4th ed., Boston, Little Brown & Co. 1889) ("The doctrine that a natural tie connects the illegitimate child peculiarly with his mother was recognized at the civil law…under the ordinance of Justinian.")

just, the Divine Pius decided, and it was stated in a Rescript by Marcus Severus, that relief should be granted to the mother by means of an exception.[56]

As this passage shows, Roman law recognized an exception to the paternal custody rule in the case of children who were already in the care of their mothers, such as where a married woman separated from her husband and took the children with her. In such cases, if a judge determined that it would be better for the children to remain with her than to go with the father, then the court would order that the children were to remain in the custody of their mother. Proof of the father's fault or bad character was sufficient to establish that it would be better for the children to remain with the mother.[57]

Under Roman law, then, a mother had -- in addition to an absolute right to custody of her children born out of wedlock -- a right to custody of children born to her during her marriage to the father if she and the children were living separately from the father and if it appeared to be in the children's best interests to remain with her.[58]

The passage quoted above dealt with situations in which the husband and wife were still married but living separate and apart from each other. A different legal question is presented when a married couple seeks a dissolution of the marriage. According to Justinian's Code, in the event of a

---

[56] ULPIANUS, ON THE EDICT, Bk. LXXI, *reprinted in* SCOTT, *supra* note 47; *see also* DIONYSIUS GODEFROY, CORPUS JURIS CIVILIS, PANDECTIS AD FLORENTINUM ARCHETYPUM EXPRESSIS, INSTITUTIONIBUS (Amsterdam, Elzevirs 1663); A. KRIEGEL AND E. OSENBRÜGGEN, CORPUS IURIS CIUILIS, (Lipsiae, sumtibus Baumgaertneri 1872); R. POTHIER, PANDECTÆ JUSTINIANEÆ IN NOVUM ORDINEM DIGESTÆ (Paris, F. I. Fournier 1818); *cf.* JUSTINIAN CODE, Bk. V, tit. 24, *reprinted in* SCOTT, *supra* note 47 ("[T]he proper judge, nevertheless, will decide whether, in case of divorce, the children should live with and be supported by the father or the mother")

[57] THE RULES OF ULPIAN, tit. V, *reprinted in* SCOTT, *supra* note 47.

[58] F. BLUME, ANNOTATED JUSTINIAN CODE (2d ed. 2009) https://uwacadweb.uwyo.edu/blume&justinian/. Ancient Roman writings also evidence some concern for the well-being of children. *See, e.g.,* CICERO, DE OFFICIIS I.iv (44 B.C.)("Nature produces a special love of offspring") *as translated in* C.S. LEWIS, ABOLITION OF MAN 101 app. (Simon & Schuster 1996) (1944); JUVENAL, SATIRE XIV 47 (n.d.) ("Great reverence is owed to a child.")

divorce, custody of legitimate children was never to be decided solely on the basis of the sex of a parent. When a married couple divorced, the court could award custody of children to either the mother or the father. As a general principle, at least, neither a divorcing mother nor a divorcing father had a superior claim. As stated in the Justinian Code: "[I]t is not provided by any constitution of ours or of our divine parents that the division of children among the parents should be made according to sex."[59]

> A constitution of Diocletian and Maximian left it to the judge to determine in his discretion to which of the parents the children should go....If a wife divorced her husband for good cause, and she remained unmarried, the children went to be in her custody, but to be maintained by the father; but if the mother was in fault, the father obtained the custody. If he was unable, from want of means, to support them, but she was able to do so, she was obliged to take them and support them.[60]

It appears, then, that Roman law actually favored mothers. In the case of children born out of wedlock, mothers had an absolute right to sole custody. In the case of married parents living separately, the *patria potestas* rule that appeared to give fathers absolute rights and powers over children born to them during a marriage to the children's mother was severely limited by the rule that custody would be awarded to the mother if the children were already living with her and it appeared to be in their best interests to remain in her care. In the case of a divorcing couple, the law awarded custody to the mother unless the father could prove both that he had the ability to support the children financially and that the mother was at fault for the breakup of the marriage.

---

[59] Bk. V, tit. 24, *quoted in* BLUME, *supra* note 58.
[60] H. Chisholm, *Divorce, in* ENCYCLOPEDIA BRITANNICA 336 (11th ed. 1910)

6. CHINA

Ancient Chinese civilization evolved along a different path than either Greece or Rome. In China, the law imposed reciprocal obligations on parents and children, protecting children from harmful parents while at the same time protecting parents from disrespectful children. For example, Chinese law punished criminally any son who failed to properly mourn for a deceased parent or grandparent. Elder abuse (striking one's parent or grandparent) was punishable by death.[61]

Although infanticide was practiced in earlier primitive periods, it was illegal for at least 2,000 years of China's history.[62] Other laws for the protection of children included a ban on selling lost or abandoned children into slavery; criminal punishments for severely beating one's child; laws defining sexual intercourse with a girl under twelve years of age, and incest with any female child, as rape; and laws imposing the death penalty for the rape of a boy under the age of twelve, or for the rape of a female child of any age.[63]

---

[61] TA TSING LEU LEE (George T. Staunton trans., London, Strahan and Preston 1810)

[62] BREINER, *supra* note 20 at 172.

[63] TA TSING LEU LEE, *supra* note 61. Prior to 600 B.C., a parent could legally sell

In early Chinese civilizations, caring for children was the exclusive province of mothers.[64]

This is still the case among the Mosuo in the Xiaoliangshan Mountains of Yunnan province, where women continue to have an exclusive right to custody of children. The Mosuo are a truly matriarchal culture. Property passes matrilineally, women are in charge of making all major decisions, and children belong to their mother and her extended family. Fathers are regarded as procreation instruments only, although they do enjoy rights of visitation.

The rest of China evolved differently. When China transitioned from a matrifocal family system to a clan system, it became the norm for fathers to assume responsibility for the care of older male children.

The clan system was in place at least as early as the Zhou Dynasty (1045 to 256 B.C.) It was originally limited to nobility. There is some controversy over when it became widespread among commoners, but the generally accepted theory is that clans emerged among common people in the southern and eastern regions of China during the Song Dynasty (960 to 1267) and spread to northern and western regions during the Ming and Quing Dynasties (1368 to 1911.) [65]

Under the clan system, women were expected to be the primary caretakers of children until the age of seven, at which time boys were placed in their fathers' care, while girls remained with their mothers. This arrangement apparently did not have anything to do with a legislative or judicial determination of what was in children's best interests. Rather, it

---

his child into slavery. The practice was outlawed in 600 B.C. BREINER, *supra* note 20 at 183; *cf.* ILLUSTRATIONS OF THE TAO, ANCIENT CHINESE, ANALECTS ix 22, *quoted in* C.S. LEWIS, ABOLITION OF MAN 101 app. (Simon & Schuster 1996) (1944) ("Respect the young.")

[64] BREINER, *supra* note 20 at 162; Stefan Anitei, *Mosuo, One of the Last Matriarchal Societies,*" *available at* http://news.softpedia.com/news/Mosuo-One-of-the-Last-Matriarchal-Societies-36321.shtml (September 23, 2006).

[65] ERKANG FENG ET AL., THE HISTORY OF CHINA'S PATRIARCHAL CLAN SYSTEM (ZHONG GUO ZONG ZU SHI) (Shanghai, Shanghai Renmin Press: 2009); *see generally* Jianhua Chang, *Review of Theories on Patriarchal Clan Systems Since Song and Ming Dynasties (Song Ming Yi Lai Zong Zu Zhi Xing Cheng Li Lun Bian Xi),* 1 ANHUI HISTORICAL STUDY 75-87 (2007)

simply reflected the division of labor between the sexes. Males worked and lived in the fields away from home for half of the year. They had little contact with young children until the male children became old enough to start working, which in ancient China was around the age of seven.

Later developments

It has been said that before the formation of the People's Republic of China in 1949, the country had no established legal traditions, at least not in the way that law is understood in Western cultures.[66] Confucianism was the predominant code of conduct in pre-Revolutionary China, and it placed a higher value on internalized virtue than obedience to law.[67] Clan elders instructed members of the clan on Confucian morality and traditions.

Confucius (551-479 B.C.) broached a philosophy of "filial piety" which taught that the young must be obedient to their elders; citizens must be obedient to their rulers; and women must be obedient to men.[68] For many centuries, women held a social and political position subordinate to men. Abuses have included such things as the sale and purchase of wives, enforced servility, and infanticide and foot-binding of female children.

Movement toward more egalitarian treatment of women began in the late nineteenth and early twentieth centuries. Foot-binding was outlawed in 1902, and during the May Fourth movement of the 1910's and 1920's, revolutionaries advocated for equality for women.[69] This movement, however, only involved and effected changes benefitting urban, elite women. The social position of the vast majority of women was not changed.

The Communist Revolution that resulted in the formation of the People's Republic of China in 1949 yielded major changes in family relations that affected all women and men in China, not just the urban elite.

---

[66] Marasinghe, M.L., *An Empiricist's View of the Chinese Legal System*, 15 VAL. L. REV. 283, 285 (1981)
[67] STANLEY B. LUBMAN, BIRD IN A CAGE: LEGAL REFORM IN CHINA AFTER MAO 13 (1999); JAMES M. ZIMMERMAN, CHINA LAW DESKBOOK 32 (2005).
[68] Li, Yuhui, *Women's Movement and Change of Women's Status in China*, 1 J. INT'L WOMEN'S STUD. 30-40 (2000), available at http://vc.bridgew.edu/jiws/vol1/iss1/3
[69] JUDITH STACEY, PATRIARCHY AND SOCIALIST REVOLUTION IN CHINA. Berkeley: University of California Press.

Declaring that "women hold up half the sky," Mao Tse-tung (also known as Mao Zedong) initiated reforms aimed at equalizing the sexes immediately upon the formation of the People's Republic. Article 6 of the basic law declared: "The People's Republic of China shall abolish the feudal system which holds women in bondage. Women shall enjoy equal rights with men in political, economic, cultural, educational and social life. Freedom of marriage for men and women shall be put into effect."[70] This was implemented by the Marriage Law of 1950, which banned many traditional practices such as arranged marriages, child betrothal, concubinage, and prostitution; required equal treatment of women and men in family law; and enabled women, for the first time, to obtain divorces.

The Marriage Law, as amended in 1980, includes a provision which, while allowing a wife to divorce her husband, prohibits a husband from divorcing his wife while she is pregnant or within a year after the birth of a child. It also requires courts to award custody of breast-fed children to their mothers. Courts are required to give preferential treatment to women with respect to the division of property in a divorce, but there is no explicit maternal preference with respect to the custody of weaned children. Instead, custody of these children is to be allocated in accordance with the parents' agreement. If they fail to agree, then a court will decide the issue for them. In such cases, "the best interests of the child" is the applicable legal standard, and the specific rules for determining what is in a child's best interests are similar to those that are applied in the United States.[71]

---

[70] COMMON PROGRAM OF THE CHINESE PEOPLE'S POLITICAL CONSULTATIVE CONFERENCE art. 6 (1949)

[71] MARRIAGE LAW OF THE PEOPLE'S REPUBLIC OF CHINA art. 34, 36, 39 (1980); Peter Zhu, *How China Court Decides Child Custody*, available at http://www.chinalawblog.org/law-topics/divorce/224-child-custody (April 11, 2012)

7. HEBRAIC LAW

Ancient Hebraic law generally was protective of children. The Talmud conferred upon children a right to be cared for and educated by a parent, and provided for the imposition of penalties on parents who violated those rights. Child sexual abuse was punished severely. Pederasts were subject to stoning.

Examples of references to the importance of protecting and caring for children in the Old Testament include *Deuteronomy* 30:19 ("[C]hoose life, that you and your children may live"); *Malachi* 4:6 ("And he shall turn the heart of the fathers to the children, and the heart of the children to their fathers"); *Isaiah* 54:13 (protection of descendants). The New Testament, although not part of Jewish law, contains numerous references to the high value that Jesus Christ placed on children and the obligation to protect and care for them. *See, e.g., Matthew* 18:6 ("[I]f anyone causes one of these little ones who believe in me to sin, it would be better for him to have a large millstone hung around his neck and to be drowned in the depths of the sea"); *Colossians* 3:21 ("Fathers, provoke not your children to anger, lest they be discouraged"); *2 Corinthians* 12:14 ("[F]or the children ought not to lay up for the parents, but the parents for the children"); *Ephesians* 6:4 ("And, ye fathers, provoke not your children to wrath: but bring them up in the nurture and admonition of the Lord"); *1 John* 5:1 ("Whosoever believeth that Jesus is the Christ is born of God: and every one that loveth him that begat loveth him also that is begotten of him"); *Matthew* 7:11 ("[K]now how to give good gifts unto your children"); *Matthew* 18:3 ("[U]nless you...become like little children, you will never enter the kingdom of heaven"); *Matthew* 18:4 ("[The] child is the greatest in the kingdom of heaven.")[72]

The law was especially solicitous toward female children. A father owed a higher moral responsibility to a daughter than to a son.[73]

Although child abuse apparently was comparatively rare, early Hebrews did practice forms of ritual child sacrifice and genital mutilation.[74] In addition, the *Torah* called for the execution of stubborn or rebellious sons.[75] This provision, however, apparently was not often enforced, if at all. Infanticide waned over time, and by 55 A.D. it had become a criminal offense.[76]

Because women were believed to be inherently moral, only fathers could be punished for the abuse or neglect of a child.[77]

Children born out of wedlock were not treated differently in the law, so long as the father was known. Fathers owed the same duties of support to them as they owed to children born to them during a valid marriage.[78]

Both parents shared responsibility for the care of their children. Legally, the child belonged to the father at the age of three, but Hebraic law gave women and children special consideration in other respects.[79]

---

[72] TRACTATE NIDDAH (Isidore Epstein ed., 1989); *see generally* John T. Carroll, *Children in the Bible*, 55 INTERPRETATION 121, 122 (April 2001) ("The biblical tradition prizes children as a blessing given by a gracious God.")

[73] TRACTATE KETHUBOTH (Isidore Epstein ed., 1989)

[74] BREINER, *supra* note 20 at 75; W. FELDMAN, THE JEWISH CHILD (1918)

[75] *Deuteronomy* 21:18-21

[76] BREINER, *supra* note 20 at 77, 98.

[77] *Id.* at 77; SOLOMON GANZFRIED, CODE OF JEWISH LAW (1928)

[78] BREINER, *supra* note 20 at 78.

[79] *Id.* at 74, 77; GANZFRIED, *supra* note 77.

As in ancient China under the clan system, ancient Hebrew children remained in their mother's care until they reached a specified age (usually six) at which time the father assumed responsibility for the care of male children, while female children remained in their mother's care. According to the Babylonian Talmud, if the parents divorced, daughters were to remain with the mother. Later Jewish law, which seems to have been influenced by the Roman law, held that custody of a daughter was not necessarily to be awarded to the mother in all cases, but was to be determined according to the best interests of the child.[80]

Explanation of the sources of Jewish law

The three main sources of Jewish law are the *Torah*, the *Mishnah* and the *Gemara* ("Talmud.")

Torah

The term *Torah* has three meanings. First, it may be used to refer to the first five books of the Bible: *Genesis*, *Exodus*, *Leviticus*, *Numbers*, and *Deuteronomy*. Collectively, these are called the *Pentateuch*. They are said to have been given to Moses by God on Mount Sinai over 3,000 years ago.

The term is also used, at times, to refer to the entire Hebrew Bible (*Tanakh*), including not only the Pentateuch but also the Prophetical Books and the Hagiographa. Together, these comprise what Christians call the Old Testament.

Finally, *Torah* is sometimes used to refer to all Jewish law, as given and as authoritatively interpreted over the centuries.

Mishnah

In addition to the written scriptures, Jewish law also encompasses an oral tradition explaining what they mean and how to apply them. This was compiled into written form around 200 A.D. in a document called the *Mishnah*.

---

[80] I. Singer, *Entry for "daughter in jewish law," in* THE JEWISH ENCYCLOPEDIA (1901); *see also* JOSEPH KARO, SHULḤAN 'ARUK (S. I. Levin & Edward A. Boyden trans., New York, Hermon Press 1965) (1565)

The Mishnah is divided into six sections called *sedarim*. Each seder contains at least one division. These divisions are called *tractates*. Nashim is the seder dealing with marriage, divorce, and contracts. The two tractates most relevant to custody law are the Kethuboth and the Gittin. The *Tractate Kethuboth* addresses the obligations of husbands and wives toward each other. The *Tractate Gittin* deals with divorce.

Gemarah (Talmud)

Over the next three centuries, more commentaries explaining or elaborating on the *Mishnah* were written down. These were compiled and written down around 500 A.D. in a document called the *Gemarah*, which is also known as the *Talmud*.

There are actually two Talmuds: the Jerusalem Talmud and the Babylonian Talmud. Of the two, the Babylonian is the more comprehensive.

Additional sources of law

The foregoing are the primary sources of Jewish law. In addition to these, there are *midrashim*. These are stories that are derived from the Bible and used to teach Jewish law or moral lessons.

Responsa are answers to specific questions about Jewish law posed to, and answered by a renowned rabbi. These began being prepared in the Middle Ages, and they continue to be prepared by rabbis today.

Codifications of Jewish law have also been attempted, beginning in the Middle Ages. The most respected of these are Rambam's *Mishneh Torah* and Joseph Cato's *Shulchan Arukh*.

Finally, there is the somewhat more controversial mystical tradition known as the *Kabbalah*. The *Zohar* is the primary work in this tradition.

8. ISLAMIC LAW (*Shari'a*)

Shari'a, the Arabic term for Islamic law, is a body of rules on a variety of subjects including but not limited to divorce and child custody. It comes from four sources: the Quran, the Sunnah, *ijma*, and *qiyas*. The principal source is the Quran. Next is the Sunnah, describing the practice and conduct of the Prophet Mohammed.[81] *Ijma* refers to the consensus of Islamic scholars on particular points of law. It is the basis for a decision on questions that are not explicitly addressed in either the Quran or the Sunna. If there is no established consensus, then resort is had to *qiyas*, i.e., reasoning by analogy to established principles.[82]

Under Shari'a, guardianship (in this instance meaning child support and management of the child's property) is the exclusive responsibility of fathers.[83] The child's paternal grandfather is the natural guardian if the

---

[81] Fatima Akaddaf, *Application of the United Nations Convention on Contracts for the International Sale of Goods (CISG) to Arab Islamic Countries: Is the CISG Compatible with Islamic Law Principles?* 13 PACE INT'L L. REV. 16, 17 (2001).

[82] *Id.* at 18.

[83] *See, e.g.,* NAWAWI, MINHAJ ET TALIBIN (E. Howard trans., 1977); 7 WAHBAH ZUHAILI, FIQH AL ISLAMI WA ADILLATUHU (1984). On the exclusively male nature of the child support obligation, see 2 AMEER ALI, TREATISE ON THE MUHAMMADAN LAW 587 (3d ed. n.d.), *quoted in* A. Ibrahim, *Custody of Muslim*

father is not available.[84] The mother, on the other hand, has the right to physical custody until the child reaches a specified age.

> When the child does not reach the age of discretion, the mother has the greater right to his upbringing inasmuch as this is of the question of the child, not the question of the degree of love, attachment and affection of the parents.[85]

In other words, there is a maternal preference founded on a belief that a child's interests are better served by maternal care than by paternal care. That belief, in turn, is founded on an assumption that mothers know best how to nurture and educate children. As authority, legal scholars usually cite the following *hadith* (ca. 610 A.D.):

> A woman complained to the Prophet stating that, "my womb was a resting place of this son of mine, my breasts a drinking place for him and my lap a soothing place for him, but his father divorced me and wishes to snatch him away from me." The Prophet replied, "You have a better right to take him till you marry someone else."[86]

This passage has been interpreted to mean that in the event of a divorce, the mother has the first right to physical custody of the children, at least those that are young males, or female.[87]

Infants, 4 J. OF MALAY. & COMPAR. L. 19-94 (1977)

[84] JAMAL J. NASIR, THE ISLAMIC LAW OF PERSONAL STATUS 206 (2d ed. 1990).

[85] AL SHAFI'I, 8 KITAB AL UMM 235 (n.d.).

[86] 2 SUNAN ABU DAWUD, KITAB AL TALAQ 6 (A. Hasan trans., 2000.) The maternal custody presumption does not appear to apply during periods of time in which the mother has become remarried to another man. A mother who marries another man after divorce may still be awarded custody of the children; she simply loses the benefit of the preferential presumption and will stand on an equal footing with others who may be seeking custody of the child. *In re* Omar b. Sheik Salleh, M.L.J. 186 (1948).

[87] *See, e.g.,* AL-MISRI, AHMAD IBN NAQIB, RELIANCE OF THE TRAVELER 552-53 (Nuh Ha Mim Keller ed. & trans., 1994); IBN QUDAMAH, AL MUGHNI 133 (n.d.); *see also* NASIR, *supra* note 84 at 173-74

Those familiar with American law will recognize this as a version of the "tender years" doctrine, according to which motherly nurturing is deemed superior to that of any other person, including the father.

In some Islamic countries, female nurturing skills are considered so far superior that if a child's mother cannot assume custody for some reason, then the child will be placed in the custody of a female relative, such as an aunt or the child's maternal grandmother, in preference to the father.[88] It has been reported that the maternal preference is so strong, in fact, that in some countries even imprisoned mothers retain custody of their children while they are incarcerated, at least such of their children as are under seven years of age.[89]

A mother may voluntarily consent to relinquish custody of a child to the father in a divorce, but she may revoke her consent and reclaim custody at any time, irrespective of any attachment the child may have formed with the father in the meantime.[90]

Islamic jurists differ as to the effect of the child's age, sex and preferences on these rules. The Hanbali and Shafii schools hold that a female should have custody of children who are under seven years of age, but that upon attaining the age of seven the child may choose his custodian.[91] The Malikis hold that a female should have custody of male children until the age of puberty, and of female children until they become married.[92] The Hanafi school holds that a female should have custody of a male child until the boy is able to care for himself, which normally occurs at the age of either seven or nine. There is a split of opinion among Hanafi jurists as to when female custody of female children ends, some setting it at the age of

---

[88] *See* 2 SUNAN ABU DAWUD, KITAB AL TALAQ 617 (A. Hasan trans., 2000)

[89] Kristine Uhlman, (2004), *Overview of Shari'a and Prevalent Customs in Islamic Societies – Divorce and Child Custody*, prepared for the California State Bar 2004 Winter Section Education Institute / International Law / Family Law Workshop on International Custody Abduction: Non-Hague, Islamic Countries (2004), retrieved from http://www.expertlaw.com/library/family_law/islamic_custody.html on August 28, 2013

[90] Mohamad Salleh v. Azizah, 4 J.H. 212 (1984). The rules concerning the expression of preference by an older child still apply in that event, however.

[91] Uhlman, *supra* note 89.

[92] NASIR, *supra* note 84 at 187.

puberty, i.e., nine or eleven years of age; others holding that it lasts until the girl reaches the age of majority.[93]

Because Islamic law is concerned with protecting the best interests of the child, custodial rights are not absolute. A parent may be denied custody of a child if he or she is not fit for parenting. Grounds for a finding of parental unfitness include insanity; nonage; inability to provide proper care for the child; and inability to protect and advance the child's physical and moral interests.[94]

Some juristic schools construe Islamic law as prohibiting a mother from retaining custody if she marries another man while the father is still living and eligible for custody.[95] Others maintain that the prohibition applies only to marriages to people who are not related to the child, or who are related to the child in certain ways.[96] The Shafii and Shia schools apply the maternal preference if the mother and father are both Muslims, and in cases where the child of a Jewish or Christian mother shares the mother's religion; and the Hanfi school regards apostasy (denouncement of Islam) grounds for denying a mother custody.[97] Other Sunni schools generally only require the mother to raise the child in the Islamic faith.[98]

It is sometimes said that noncustodial parents have no visitation rights under Shari'a law. This is not strictly true. A custodial parent cannot be compelled to permit overnight visits in the home of the noncustodial parent, but she is not permitted to conceal a child from the other parent. The custodial parent must bring the child to a place where the noncustodial parent can see him.[99]

That Islamic law for many centuries has applied a maternal preference on the basis of a belief that custody is "of the question of the child, not the question of the degree of love, attachment and affection of the parents"[100]

---

[93] *Id.* at 188.

[94] *Id.* at 178.

[95] *Id.* at 173.

[96] *Id.* at 172.

[97] The Shia and Shafii schools, however, allow a Jewish or Christian mother to have physical custody of a child if the child shares her religion. *Id.* at 180

[98] *Id.*

[99] *Id.* at 185

[100] *See supra* note 85 and accompanying text.

belies the Western conceit that the notion of deciding custody on the basis of what is in children's best interests is a modern American innovation.[101] And it calls into question the validity of the proposition that the development of women's custody rights, as reflected in the maternal preference doctrine, correlates positively with the elevation of women's political and social status to a position of equality with men.[102]

The extent to which women in Muslim societies possess legal, social and political status equal to men is a matter of considerable controversy. If reports commissioned by the United States government are believed, "empirical studies document the persistence in Muslim societies of features of what many social scientists call the patriarchal gender system."[103] On the other hand, the current political climate is such that American reports on Muslim countries and cultures cannot necessarily be trusted to be the most accurate and objective. In any event, the fact that the maternal preference

---

[101] *See, e.g.*, CLAIRE BREEN, THE STANDARD OF THE BEST INTERESTS OF THE CHILD: A WESTERN TRADITION IN INTERNATIONAL AND COMPARATIVE LAW 44 (2002) ("The standard of the best interests of the child may generally be described as a principle deriving from Anglo-American family law"); MASON, *supra* note 1 at *xi* and 61 (describing the idea of mother as nurturer as a "fairly modern notion"); R. Behrman and L. Quinn, *Children and Divorce: Overview and Analysis*, 4 FUTURE OF CHILDREN (Spring/Summer 1994) (asserting that "the idea of basing custody decisions on the child's needs and interests is a relatively new one that emerged about 20 years ago"); Podell et al., *supra* note 2 at 51-52 (1972) (crediting American jurists David Brewer and Benjamin Cardozo, sitting as state court judges in cases decided in 1888 and 1925, respectively, as the originators of the idea that custody should be decided on the basis of what is in the best interests of children.)

[102] *See e.g.*, MASON, *supra* note 1 at *xvi* (describing "the interdependency of the status of women and the custody rules regarding children" as "the single most important factor in explaining the wide swings in custody law.")

[103] P. OFFENHAUER, U.S. LIBRARY OF CONGRESS, WOMEN IN ISLAMIC SOCIETIES: A SELECTED REVIEW OF SOCIAL SCIENTIFIC LITERATURE 10 (2005). For examples of writings critical of the treatment of women in Muslim countries, *see, e.g.*, JOHN LAFFIN, THE DAGGER OF ISLAM (1979); MUSAWAH, AN INITIATIVE OF SISTERS OF ISLAM, CEDAW AND MUSLIM FAMILY LAWS (2011); V. Moghadam, *Global Feminism and Women's Citizenship in the Muslim World: The Cases of Iran, Algeria and Afghanistan*, paper prepared for the Conference on Citizenship, Borders, and Gender: Mobility and Immobility, Yale University, May 8-10, 2003 (contending that "Muslim ... family laws {and} Sharia law ... codify women's subordination.") *See also* M. RAFIQUL-HAQQ & P. NEWTON, THE PLACE OF WOMEN IN PURE ISLAM (1996) (noting that verse 4:34 of the Quran requires wives to be obedient to their husbands.)

doctrine existed in Islamic law for many centuries prior to the women's rights movements of nineteenth and twentieth century America suggests that it most likely has more to do with sex role stereotyping than with movements to establish equal rights for women.

PART II. EUROPE

9. THE MEDIEVAL PERIOD
(5th to 11th Centuries)

Custody of children, as between divorcing or separating parents, was rarely an issue in the Middle Ages. The Roman Catholic Church regarded marriage as a sanctified, indissoluble covenant, that is to say, a life-long commitment, so divorces were quite rare. They were not impossible to obtain during the first few centuries of the Middle Ages, but the circumstances under which they would be granted were limited.[104] Consequently, custody law generally became relevant only upon the death of a parent. Disputes typically involved widows and widowers wrangling with relatives and other third parties over the custody of a deceased parent's children, not husbands and wives competing against each other for their own children.

The prevailing view, for many years, has been that medieval courts analyzed child custody issues in terms of the father's financial interests, without any regard at all for what was in a child's best interests, the idea being that courts viewed children as the property of their fathers. The theory has been that the concept of childhood as a distinct period of human development did not come into existence until modern times; that medieval

---

[104] SUSAN ATKINS & BRENDA HOGGETT, WOMEN AND THE LAW (1984)

parents simply thought of their children as miniature adults.[105] Consistent with this theory, historians assumed that people had no concern at all about the interests of children as such. Indeed, one historian has gone so far as to theorize that childhood in the Middle Ages was never more than "a nightmare of abuse and murder."[106]

Medievalists today are challenging this idea. They cite evidence of "tenderness toward infants and small children, interest in the stages of their development, awareness of their need for love."[107] According to historian David Nicholas, "[t]here can be little doubt that most parents in the Middle Ages valued their children and cherished them, even if the parents' means of disciplining their children seem unenlightened to modern eyes."[108]

At least one historian suggests that by the end of the twelfth century, the notion of children as mere items of property, if any such notion ever existed, "had also been joined by more favorable conceptions, by a sense of the child as a being in its own right, as a nature of 'potential greatness,' and by a sense of childhood as a distinctive and formative state of life."[109] Works of art from the period certainly suggest that at least some adults must have felt affection and sympathy for children, and must have abhorred violence against them.[110] References to kindness toward children can be

---

[105] *See, e.g.,* PHILIPPE ARIÈS, L'ENFANT ET LA VIE FAMILIALE SOUS L'ANCIEN RÉGIME (1960); IVY PINCHBECK & MARGARET HEWITT, CHILDREN IN ENGLISH SOCIETY (1969.)

[106] HISTORY OF CHILDHOOD, *supra* note 28 at 1; *see also* EDWARD SHORTER, THE MAKING OF THE MODERN FAMILY (1975); LAWRENCE STONE, THE FAMILY, SEX AND MARRIAGE IN ENGLAND 1500-1800 (1977)

[107] Mary McLaughlin, *Survivors and surrogates: children and parents from the ninth to the thirteenth centuries, in* HISTORY OF CHILDHOOD, *supra* note 28 at 117-18; *see also* BARBARA A. HANAWALT, THE TIES THAT BOUND: PEASANT FAMILIES IN MEDIEVAL ENGLAND 187 (1986) ("[C]hildhood was a recognized separate period of life" and parents were aware of, and attended to, children's needs); David Nicholas, *Childhood in Medieval Europe, in* CHILDREN IN HISTORICAL AND COMPARATIVE PERSPECTIVE: AN INTERNATIONAL HANDBOOK AND RESEARCH GUIDE 31 (Joseph M. Hawes and N. Ray Hiner eds., 1991).

[108] Nicholas, *supra* note 107 at 35.

[109] McLaughlin, *supra* note 107 at 140.

[110] Ilene H. Forseth, *Children in Early Medieval Art: Ninth Through Twelfth Centuries, in* 4 J. OF PSYCHOHISTORY 31-70 (1976); *see also* S. CRAWFORD, CHILDHOOD IN ANGLO-SAXON ENGLAND (1999); NICHOLAS ORME, MEDIEVAL CHILDREN 2-5 (2001); SHULASMITH SHAHAR, CHILDHOOD IN THE MIDDLE AGES (1990).

found in eleventh century literature, too.[111] Germanic law codes clearly distinguished between children and adults.[112] And in 1376 the city of York enacted an ordinance prohibiting citizens from letting their horses run loose, the stated purpose being to protect children while they were playing in the streets.[113] This kind of ordinance suggests a view of children as developing human beings whose desire to play must be protected. It is not consistent with a view of children as either property or miniature adults

Also contradicting the traditional account of the history of custody law is the fact that the patriarchal laws of early ancient Rome were not, in fact, carried over into England in the Middle Ages. As we have seen, those early Roman laws were supplanted by a maternal preference doctrine during the first few centuries A.D.

In the first part of the Middle Ages (sometimes called the Anglo-Saxon period, ca. 550 to 1066 A.D.), it appears that women's social positions and roles were neither rigidly defined nor inferior to men's. Women were not limited to child care and homemaking functions. Married women had independent status and women in general contributed to production as men did.

Although children in the Middle Ages were in the guardianship of their fathers until they reached the age of majority or left home, fathers did not have a superior right to physical custody. To the contrary, women were free to divorce their husbands if grounds existed; and upon separation and widowhood, a mother had the right to custody of the children and one-half of the marital estate, in addition to a right to receive financial support from her former husband.[114] A mother who did not take custody of the children, however, could not be assured of receiving half of the marital estate.

---

[111] Nicholas, *supra* note 107 at 33.

[112] David Herlihy, *Medieval Children, in* ESSAYS ON MEDIEVAL CIVILIZATION: THE WALTER PRESCOTT WEBB MEMORIAL LECTURES 115-16 (1978); Nicholas, *supra* note 107 at 32.

[113] *See* Lorraine C. Attreed, *From Pearl Maiden to Tower Princes: Towards a New History of Medieval Childhood,* 9 J. MEDIEVAL HIST. 47 (1983).

[114] ATKINS & HOGGETT, *supra* note 104 at 9-10; J. PERKIN, WOMEN AND MARRIAGE IN NINETEENTH CENTURY ENGLAND 1 (1989); DORIS M. P. STENTON, THE ENGLISH WOMAN IN HISTORY (1957); Dooms of Aethelobert, Nos. 79-81, *cited in* Henry Foster and Doris Freed, *Life with Father,* 11 FAM. L.Q. 321, n.2 (1978).

Custody of children also went to the mother upon the death of the children's father. The law did not allow a father to appoint someone other than the mother as a testamentary guardian for the children.[115]

---

[115] CHRISTINE FELL ET AL., WOMEN IN ANGLO-SAXON ENGLAND 79-80 (1984); *see also* FRANCES GIES & JOSEPH GIES, MARRIAGE AND THE FAMILY IN THE MIDDLE AGES 111 (1987).

10. FEUDAL ENGLAND
(1066 to the 14th Century)

Following the Norman Conquest in 1066, and with the advent of feudalism and the increased influence of ecclesiastical law near the end of the Middle Ages, women lost many of the legal advantages they had possessed during the first few centuries of the Middle Ages. The doctrines of coverture (suspending a woman's rights during a marriage) and the unity of husband and wife (the legal fiction that a married couple is a single unit, with the husband being the legal representative of the unit) divested married women of equal rights during marriage. At the same time, the Church made marriage indissoluble except by death. A married couple could get a divorce *a mensa et thoro*, giving each spouse the right to live separate and apart from the other while still being married to each other (what today would be called a legal separation, or a "divorce from bed and board") but a divorce *a vinculo matrimonii* (an absolute divorce, i.e., one that actually terminated the marriage) required an Act of Parliament.[116] Only the wealthiest couples could afford that. Taken together, coverture, the indissolubility of marriage, and the legal fiction of marital unity, seemed to leave married women with few legal entitlements other than rights of support and maintenance.

---

[116] Blake W. Odgers, *Changes In The Common Law And In The Law Of Persons, In The Legal Profession, And In Legal Education*, *in* A CENTURY OF LAW REFORM 14 (1902).

It is tempting to assume, based on these developments, that fathers possessed an absolute right to the custody of their children. That, however, was not the case.

Third-party custody disputes

Since divorces were rare, most custody disputes involved contests between a parent and a third party (or between two non-parents, if both parents were dead.) This was most likely to occur when a father died leaving a will in which he named a third party to take care of the children. In such cases, the law recognized the father's legal right to designate a testamentary guardian for his child other than the child's mother.[117] But courts recognized a distinction between legal and equitable rights.[118] Fathers possessed legal rights, but a mother could possess equitable rights. And equitable rights overrode legal rights.

There were different kinds of courts in feudal England, each applying different sets of rules and laws. Law courts strictly enforced a father's legal rights, but chancery courts, exercising *parens patriae* power as courts of equity, could and sometimes did ignore the father's legal rights, instead recognizing and enforcing the mother's equitable right to custody of the children. Because equitable rights overrode legal rights, a court of equity could award custody to the children's mother notwithstanding a legally valid testamentary appointment of a third-party custodian in the father's will.[119]

The manorial courts applied a different set of laws, collectively referred to as "customary law." Customary law directed that children should be placed in the custody of their mother upon the death of the father. The common law (applied in law courts) specified that upon the death of a father intestate, the guardian of the child should be the person with the nearest blood relationship to the child who could not inherit the father's land. In most cases, that person would be the mother. This was congruent with the law of socage guardianship applied in the royal courts, according to which mothers were granted physical custody of children upon the death of

---

[117] SUSAN MAIDMENT, CHILD CUSTODY AND DIVORCE 111 (1984).

[118] Legal rights are set out in statutes and case law. Equitable rights are not as precisely defined; they derive from a judge's sense of fairness and justice.

[119] P.H. Petit, *Parental Control and Guardianship*, *in* A CENTURY OF FAMILY LAW 1857-1957, at 56 (R.H. Graveson & F.R. Crane eds., 1957)

the father and were often appointed guardians of their property, too, since they were not in a position to inherit from the heir. A *socage tenure* was a feudal interest in land requiring the performance of a service (e.g., farming) or the payment of rent, rather than knight service. A *guardianship in socage* was one that arose when lands in socage tenure came to a child by descent. A guardian in socage was entitled to custody of the child and possession of the child's lands. The guardian in socage was the child's next of kin, but excluded anyone who could possibly inherit the estate.[120]

Yet another set of rules applied in the case of lands held in military tenure (knight service.) In those cases, land reverted to the overlord upon the death of the tenant pursuant to the feudal doctrine of wardship. When the tenant died, the heir would immediately be taken from his or her family and placed in the overlord's home.[121] The mother could then regain guardianship only by repurchasing the child out of her dower estate, or by prevailing upon the overlord for a voluntary relinquishment of the child. Such requests usually were granted if the child was still very young, but might not be granted in the case of older children.[122]

Wardships eventually fell into disuse; were "more often honored in the breach than in the following;" and by 1500 had become virtually defunct.[123] They resurfaced briefly in the sixteenth century. In 1540, a court of wards and liveries was established to resolve issues involving them.[124]

---

[120] *See* 1 F. POLLOCK. & F.W. MAITLAND, THE HISTORY OF ENGLISH LAW BEFORE THE TIME OF EDWARD I 321 (2d ed., Cambridge, University Press 1898); 2 HENRY DE BRACTON, ON THE LAWS AND CUSTOMS OF ENGLAND 250-55 (Samuel E. Thorne trans., 1968); E. Clark, *The Custody of Children in English Manor Courts*, 3 L. & HIST. REV. 337 (1985); 21 CYCLOPEDIA OF LAW AND PROCEDURE 13 (William Mack ed., 1906)

[121] PINCHBECK & HEWITT, *supra* note 105 at 58-74; Sue S. Walker, *Widow and Ward: The Feudal Law of Child Custody in Medieval England*, 3 FEMINIST STUD. 104, 110 (Spring-Summer 1976); *see also* HENRY E. BELL, AN INTRODUCTION TO THE HISTORY AND RECORDS OF THE COURT OF WARDS AND LIVERIES (1953); JOEL HURSTFIELD, THE QUEEN'S WARDS: WARDSHIP AND MARRIAGE UNDER ELIZABETH I (1958). This was called "guardianship by chivalry."

[122] Walker, *supra* note 121; *see also* BELL, *supra* note 121; HURSTFIELD, *supra* note 121.

[123] Wright, *supra* note 1 at 247.

[124] BELL *supra* note 121 at 2.

The Abolition of Military Tenures Act of 1646 finally abolished the feudal tenures of wardship, as well as the court of wards and liveries.

The law of wardship was always the exception, never the general rule.[125] Apart from the category of cases involving lands held in military tenure, minor children normally remained with their mothers when the father died or the marriage ended.[126]

Custody disputes between spouses

Canon law applied in divorce and separation proceedings. It embraced early versions of the maternal preference and tender years doctrines. In every case, the mother had an absolute right to custody of children up to the age of three, and a preferential claim as to other children. The father, for his part, owed a duty of child support to the mother.[127] The community as well as courts believed mothers to be the ones most naturally suited for nurturing children. For that reason, children normally would not be removed from their mothers except when the mother was obviously incapable of caring for them.[128]

---

[125] Wright, *supra* note 1; *see also* PETER LASLETT, FAMILY LIFE AND ILLICIT LOVE IN EARLIER GENERATIONS 160-73 (1977).

[126] JAMES A. BRUNDAGE, LAW, SEX, AND CHRISTIAN SOCIETY IN MEDIEVAL EUROPE 480 (1987).

[127] BERNARDUS PARMENSUS, GLOSSA ORDINARIA, X. 4.7.5 *s.v. secundum facultates* (n.p., 1472); *see also* BRIAN ABEL-SMITH & ROBERT STEVENS, LAWYERS AND THE COURTS: A SOCIOLOGICAL STUDY OF THE ENGLISH LEGAL SYSTEM, 1750-1965, at 10 (1967); BRUNDAGE, *supra* note 126; 2 DE BRACTON, *supra* note 120 at 254-55; RANULF DE GLANVILL, THE TREATISE ON THE LAWS AND CUSTOMS OF THE REALM OF ENGLAND COMMONLY CALLED GLANVILL vii, 11 (G. D. G. Hall ed. & trans., 1983); H.R. Helmholz, *Support Orders, Church Courts, and the Rule of Filius Nullius: A Reassessment of the Common Law*, 63 VA. L. REV. 435 (1977).

[128] Clark, *supra* note 120 at 343.

11. THE EARLY MODERN PERIOD
(15th & 16th Centuries)

The Protestant Reformation in the sixteenth century made divorces possible in many parts of Europe. Custody of children was not often an issue, though. Despite Protestant reforms, divorces and separations continued to be rare.

Because the Roman Catholic Church continued to ban divorces, England continued to prohibit divorces notwithstanding the Protestant Reformation.

When custody issues did arise, it appears the courts generally adhered to the maternal preference and tender years doctrines, preferring to place children in the care of mothers, and imposing support obligations on fathers. "[T]he policy of promoting maternal interests in physical custody of children was consistent in the ecclesiastical courts, the manorial courts, and the royal courts for all nonmilitary tenures from the Conquest to the eighteenth century."[129]

It is not clear whether this pattern originated from a concern for the welfare of children, or simply reflected the sex-based division of labor of

---

[129] Wright, *supra* note 1 at 247.

the time. Philippe Ariès has suggested that neither early modern Europeans nor their medieval predecessors had a concept of childhood. According to Ariès, children were treated like miniature adults, and they occupied the lowest rung on the social ordering of human beings, with a legal status barely above that of chattel.[130] If this is true, then the maternal preference would have been an outgrowth of the sexual division of labor, not something that was based on considerations about what is best for children.

There is some evidence of concern for children in early modern Europe, however.[131] Infanticide, for example, was a serious crime, punishable by death.[132] Child abusers were punished severely.[133] Excessive discipline of a child was a crime. "Moderate corporal punishment was a regular and encouraged part of discipline both at home and at school in Reformation Europe….Both children and adults, however, viewed harsh and arbitrary discipline as exceptional and condemned it, while outright brutality brought firings and fines and even deep personal remorse."[134]

After reviewing over 400 diaries and autobiographies dating from the sixteenth to the early twentieth century, Professor Linda A. Pollock concluded that early modern Europeans did, in fact, have a concept of childhood. According to Pollock, children were not subjected to any greater brutality during that period than in later periods.[135] Another historian, reviewing infant death records between 1400 and 1750, concluded that "it seems likely that in most places the great majority of children were cherished and as well cared for as the age's primitive understanding of hygiene and disease and the economic pressures upon families permitted."[136]

---

[130] ARIÈS, *supra* note 105.

[131] *See* LINDA A. POLLOCK, FORGOTTEN CHILDREN: PARENT-CHILD RELATIONS FROM 1500 TO 1900 (1983.)

[132] ROBERT MUCHEMBLED, POPULAR CULTURE AND ELITE CULTURE IN FRANCE 1400-1750, at 194 (L. Cochrane trans., 1985) (recounting the story of a father and his two daughters who, in 1530, were executed for committing infanticide.)

[133] POLLOCK, *supra* note 131 at 126.

[134] STEVEN OZMENT, WHEN FATHERS RULED: FAMILY LIFE IN REFORMATION EUROPE 149 (1983)

[135] POLLOCK, *supra* note 131 at 261-71; *accord*: RALPH A. HOULBROOKE, THE ENGLISH FAMILY, 1450-1700, at 134-38 (1984).

[136] HOULBROOKE, *supra* note 135 at 136-40.

As noted, mothers were not favored for custody in the case of military tenures. Historians Frederick Pollock and Frederic William Maitland outlined the concerns behind this aversion in the following way:

> A fatherless heir must be in ward to some one. Who shall be his guardian? His mother? No. Why not? She will take another husband and have sons by him, and they, greedy of the heritage, will slay their first-born brother, or the step-father will slay his step-son. Who then shall be the guardian? The child's blood relations? No. Why not? Lest, thirsting for his heritage, they destroy him. For the prevention of such faithless cruelty, it is establishing that the boy be in ward to one who was bound by his father by the tie of homage. And who is such a one? The lord of the land who never can inherit that land in desmesne....[137]

"[T]o commit the care of a child to the custody of his expectant heir," they theorized, "was to set the wolf to guard the lamb."[138] If Pollock and Maitland are correct, then it appears that custody law was indeed rooted in a desire to protect children and to do what was in children's best interests, at least insofar as the wardship involved in military tenures was concerned.

As in feudal times, courts in the early modern period deemed a mother's guardianship to be the most appropriate in all nonmilitary tenures, especially in the case of young children.[139] Some historians have attributed this to the fact that these mothers could not inherit from their heirs. On the other hand, for most people in the nonmilitary categories, there was not usually a lot, if anything, at stake in terms of inheritance. Socage guardianships generally were not profitable.[140]

Elaine Clark has suggested a better explanation, namely, that "mothers were thought the most capable of nurturing the young."[141] As evidence of

---

[137] FREDERICK POLLOCK AND FREDERIC WILLIAM MAITLAND, THE HISTORY OF ENGLISH LAW BEFORE THE TIME OF EDWARD I 1 307 (Boston: Little, Brown & Co. 1895)

[138] *Id.* at 308.

[139] SARA M. BUTLER, DIVORCE IN MEDIEVAL ENGLAND: FROM ONE TO TWO PERSONS IN LAW 113

[140] *Id.* at 114.

[141] Clark, Elaine, *City Orphans and Custody Laws in Medieval England*, 34 AM. J.L. HIST. 168, 176 (1990)

this, she cites the fact that borough custumals and mayors never advocated removing young children from the care of a mother without her consent.[142] According to Clark, "[m]unicipal officials recognized the needs of mothers as did urban courts.... Many fathers, too, expected mothers to 'guide and govern' the young and, when possible, to become the guardians of orphans at law."[143]

Of course, these facts, standing alone, do not establish that courts were inclined to consider children's interests when making custody decisions. They do, however, suggest a strong probability that courts concerned themselves with children's best interests in the early modern period, and entertained a belief that maternal care was superior to paternal care, at least in the case of young children.

Whether concern for the welfare of children was the rationale for applying a maternal preference doctrine is not possible to determine with absolute certainly, of course. It is equally possible that the practice of awarding custody of children to mothers simply followed the division of labor in society -- women birthing and tending to children in the home; men earning money outside of the home to support their families. Historian Sara Butler has garnered some evidence that in the event of a divorce, women were enthusiastic for custody and men were not. She persuasively argues that for this reason it was more likely that courts awarded custody to mothers than to fathers in the event of a divorce.[144] Moreover, like Xenophon, Europeans may simply have assumed that maternal care was superior to paternal care because the sexual division of labor was believed to have been divinely preordained.

---

[142] *Id.*

[143] *Id.*

[144] BUTLER, *supra* note 139 at 116-17.

12. 17th & 18th CENTURY ENGLAND

In the seventeenth and eighteenth centuries, England had three principal sets of courts, each applying three different sets of laws – canon law, common law and equity.[145] Law courts had jurisdiction over property and debts, as well as legal actions for the recovery of money damages. They applied common law. Chancery courts had jurisdiction over trusts and alimony, and they applied rules of equity. Chancery also exercised wardship over orphans. Ecclesiastical courts applied canon law, which was summarized in the Canons of 1604. Among other things, cannon law governed the rules of marriage. Ecclesiastical courts in seventeenth and eighteenth century England, however, did not exercise jurisdiction over child custody.[146] Decision of custody issues fell to the law and equity courts.

Despite the Reformation, and although English governance did eventually diverge from the Roman Catholic Church, English law continued to prohibit divorce well into the nineteenth century. In fact, England did

---

[145] There were also admiralty and university courts. The jurisdiction of these courts, though, did not extend to marital disputes or child custody proceedings.

[146] 2 BISHOP, COMMENTARIES ON THE LAW OF MARRIAGE AND DIVORCE, OF SEPARATION WITHOUT DIVORCE, AND THE EVIDENCE OF MARRIAGE IN ALL ISSUES § 526 (Boston: Little, Brown 1864)

not enact its first divorce law until 1857.[147] Before then, the only judicial remedies available to an English married couple desiring to uncouple were annulment and legal separation (then called *divortium a mensa et thoro*, or divorce from bed and board without right of remarriage.) The two grounds for a divorce *a mensa et thoro* were adultery and extreme physical cruelty. An absolute divorce (*divortium a vinculo*, or divorce with right to remarry) required an Act of Parliament, that is, the enactment of a special law making an exception to the general legal prohibition against divorce. Although Parliament occasionally granted a woman a divorce on the grounds of her husband's adultery, many Members of Parliament treated adultery on the part of the wife as the only permissible grounds for a divorce.[148]

The paternal right of guardianship

The general rule applied in seventeenth and eighteenth century English law courts was that children were in the natural guardianship of their fathers. Therefore, in any custody contest between a father and a non-parent third party, the father had a superior claim to his children, unless he had entered into a deed of separation (separation agreement) placing the children in the mother's custody.

Although it is frequently asserted that the paternal right arose out of a view of children as the property of their fathers, it was actually an early application of the "best interests of the child" standard. The Chancery court, in its role as *parens patriae* role (protector of children) deemed paternal care better for children than third-party custody, because parents normally are naturally inclined to protect, care for, and support their children.[149]

---

[147] "England in the early modern period was neither a separating nor a divorcing society: death was virtually the sole agent for dissolving marriage." LAWRENCE STONE, ROAD TO DIVORCE: ENGLAND 1530-1987, at 2 (1990).

[148] *See, e.g.*, 43 H.L. JOUR. 55, 75-8, 101-4, 190, 219, 220, 290, 319, 333; 5 JOHN CAMPBELL, LIVES OF THE LORDS CHANCELLORS 473-76 (Philadelphia, Blanchard & Lea 1846); JOHN F. MACQUEEN, A PRACTICAL TREATISE ON THE APPELLATE JURISDICTION OF THE HOUSE OF LORDS AND THE PRIVY COUNCIL, TOGETHER WITH THE PRACTICE OF PARLIAMENTARY DIVORCE 475-78, 504-08, 518 (London, A. Maxwell & Son 1842); STONE, *supra* note 147 at 360-62.

[149] Kohm, *supra* note 53 at 346; *see also* LYNN D. WARDLE & LAURENCE C. NOLAN, FUNDAMENTAL PRINCIPLES OF FAMILY LAW 858 (2002)

The father is entitled to the custody of his own children during their infancy, not only as guardian by nurture, but by nature....If he can in any way gain them, he is at liberty to do so, provided no breach of the peace be made in such an attempt.[150]

This was the rule of law that applied as between a father and a third party. The rule was not extended to disputes between mothers and fathers until the nineteenth century, in the infamous *De Manneville v. De Manneville*[151] decision.

The four guardianships

The common law of England recognized four types of guardianship.[152]

The first of these was the *medieval wardship* discussed earlier (*guardianship in chivalry.*) For lands held in military tenure, it linked custody of an heir to ownership of the estate.

The second one was *guardianship by nature*, so named to reflect the natural bond existing between a person and his heir. A propertied, older male child's father normally was his guardian by nature. Upon the father's death, the mother was the guardian by nature. Fathers were not guardians by nature of their daughters or of their younger or non-propertied sons, inasmuch as these children could not inherit from them, and therefore were not heirs.

The third type of guardianship was the *guardian in socage*. A guardian in socage had custody of the child's lands as well as his person. The guardian in socage was the child's nearest next of kin to whom the child's inheritance could not possibly descend. If the father was deceased, the guardian in socage typically would be the mother, unless her circumstances were such that she could not guarantee productivity, or she could not guarantee that the heir would not become a burden on the community.

---

[150] *Ex parte* Hopkins, 24 Eng. Rep. 1009, 1010 (1732).

[151] 32 Eng. Rep. 763 (1804), discussed *infra.*

[152] *See generally* 14 CHARLES VINER, A GENERAL ABRIDGEMENT OF LAW AND EQUITY 160-205 (2nd ed., London, G.G.J. & J. Robinson 1791)

The fourth kind of guardianship was the *guardian by nurture*. Status as a guardian by nurture was unrelated to the child's property-holding or inheritance rights. All children, whether male or female, younger or older, propertied or non-propertied, heirs or not, could have a guardian by nurture. The guardian by nurture could be either the mother or the father, and had the right to the governance of the child. When one parent died, the other parent became the guardian by nurture. Guardianship by nurture terminated altogether if both parents died. Only natural parents could be guardians by nurture.

A guardian's powers varied depending on how the guardianship arose and by whom she was appointed. Under the 1646 statute, a father could appoint a guardian in his will (testamentary guardian) and courts generally would give effect to such provisions even if he named someone other than the mother to serve as the guardian.[153] Courts interpreted their power to control testamentary guardians quite expansively, though. As Lord Cottenham put it: "[M]others…have no right, as such, to interfere with testamentary guardians [but] if…I think it proper now to leave the child in the custody of the mother…it is in consequence of that power which the court has of controlling the power of testamentary guardians."[154] Courts could and did place children in the custody of their mothers despite the fact that the father's will named a different guardian. And if the father did not appoint a guardian in his will, the equity courts could and often did appoint the mother guardian.[155]

The 1646 statute greatly altered the four guardianships. It abolished altogether the military tenures wardship (or *guardianship in chivalry.*) The guardian in socage could be, and often was, replaced by a testamentary guardian. The father's guardianship by nature was extended to include not just older male heirs, but also daughters and young children. And a father's appointment of a testamentary guardian overrode a mother's guardianship by nurture.

---

[153] 12 Car. 2, c. 24 § 8 (1646); *Ex parte* Edwards, 3 Atk. 519, 26 Eng. Rep. 1099 (1747); Bedell v. Constable, Vaugh. 177, 180, 124 Eng. Rep. 1026 (1680).

[154] Talbot v. Earl of Shrewsbury, 4 Myl. & Cr. 672, 683, 41 Eng. Rep. 259(1840).

[155] *See, e.g.*, Villareal v. Mellish, 2 Swanst. 536, 36 Eng. Rep. 719 (1737); Eyre v. Countess of Shaftsbury, 2 P. Wms. 103, 24 Eng. Rep. 659 (1722); Dormer v. Dormer, Weedon, & Webb, Finch. Chanc. Rep. 432 (1679).

Meanwhile, the manorial courts, which had applied a maternal preference as a matter of customary law, had become obsolete by the end of the eighteenth century. Canon law, which was applied in the ecclesiastical courts, also had expressed a preference for mothers, but law courts had jurisdiction over custody in the eighteenth century. The law courts, for their part, tended to regard a father's protection and support to be of paramount importance to children.

The net effect of these developments was that the maternal preference waned considerably. Indeed, eighteenth century English custody law has been likened to the *patria potestas* of early ancient Rome.[156]

In the case of an absolute divorce (i.e., one actually terminating the marriage), marital fault, not the sex of the parent, was the applicable standard for deciding custody. The commission of adultery rendered a parent unfit to have custody of children as a matter of law.[157] Since adultery was the only recognized grounds for an absolute divorce, martial fault – specifically, adultery -- was the basis of decision in custody disputes between divorcing parents.

The rule with respect to children born out of wedlock, however, continued to be that the mother's right to custody was exclusive and absolute; the father had no rights.[158]

Deeds of separation

Although no-fault divorce was not available in seventeenth and eighteenth century England, married couples sometimes separated from each other. To establish enforceable rights and obligations while living

---

[156] JOHN H. BAKER, AN INTRODUCTION TO ENGLISH LEGAL HISTORY 33-34, 201 (2002); 2 HENRY DE BRACTON, ON THE LAWS AND CUSTOMS OF ENGLAND 34-37 (Samuel E. Thorne trans., 1968); THE INSTITUTES OF JUSTINIAN bk. 1, tit. 9 (Thomas C. Sandars trans., London, J.W. Parker & Son 1853) (describing paternal power as the basis of the paterfamilias and of family and guardianship law); C. Donahue, *Ius Commune, Canon Law, and Common Law in England*, 66 TUL. L. REV. 1745, 1758-60 (1992)

[157] De Manneville v. De Manneville, 102 Eng. Rep. 1055 (1804); LEONARD SHELFORD, A PRACTICAL TREATISE OF THE LAW OF MARRIAGE AND DIVORCE 678-90 (Philadelphia, J.S. Littell 1841); STONE, *supra* note 147 at 171-72.

[158] Rex v. Moseley, 5 East 224, 102 Eng. Rep. 1055 (1798); Rex v. Soper, 5 T.R. 278, 101 Eng. Rep. 156 (1793)

separate and apart, a husband and wife could enter into a *deed of separation*. This was simply a private agreement addressing such matters as division of property, child support, spousal maintenance, and custody of children.[159]

Due to the legal fiction of the unity of husband and wife, a wife had no legal personality separate from her husband, so a contract between a husband and wife established no legally enforceable rights. To be enforceable, it was necessary to secure the cooperation of a person who had an identity separate from the husband to act as trustee for the wife. The contract would then be between the husband and the wife's trustee, which made it enforceable. Any man, even the wife's new lover, could serve as the wife's trustee. In this way, a married woman could "assume the appearance of a *feme sole* and [was] to all intents and purposes capacitated to act as such."[160]

Legal separations were very popular with couples for whom divorce was not an option either because they could not prove that adultery had occurred, or because they did not want the fact publicly known.

---

[159] STONE, *supra* note 147. During this period, some husbands attempted to terminate their marital obligations by executing a deed of sale of their wives to other people. Such deeds (popularly called "wife-sales" today) were illegal and invalid. *See, e.g.*, Rex v. Delaval, 97 Eng. Rep. 915, 1283-84 (1763) (describing such purported sales as "notoriously and grossly against public decency"); Coot v. Berty, 88 Eng. Rep. 1283-84 (1699) (holding that wife-sales are not valid, and therefore cannot be used as a defense to an action for dower); SAMUEL P. MENEFEE, WIVES FOR SALE 233 (1981) (attempting a wife-sale was "punished with laudable severity"); JOHN J.S. WHARTON, AN EXPOSITION OF THE LAWS RELATING TO THE WOMEN OF ENGLAND 312 (London, Longman, Brown, Green, and Longmans 1853) ("It is a vulgar error that a husband can get rid of his wife by selling her…Such an act on his part would be severely punished by the local magistrate.")

[160] Corbett v. Poelnitz, 99 Eng. Rep. 943 (1785); *see also* Rodney v. Chambers, 102 Eng. Rep. 380-82 (1802) ("Courts will give effect to contracts for separate maintenance.") A court would decline to enforce such an agreement if it purported to free the parties to engage in illegal acts such as adultery, cohabitation or bigamy. Vane v. Vane, 27 Eng. Rep. 586 (1740). Deeds of separation contingent upon a future separation were void. Durant v. Titley 146 Eng. Rep. 1067, 1070-71 (1819); WHARTON, *supra* note 159 at 394. Moreover, Chancery refused to enforce a marital separation, but would enforce certain provisions of a separation agreement, such as the provisions imposing an obligation on the husband to pay maintenance to the wife. Elsworthy v. Bird, 57 Eng. Rep. 390 (1825); Legard v. Johnson, 30 Eng. Rep. 1052-53 (1797); 2 JOHN E. BRIGHT, A TREATISE ON THE LAW OF HUSBAND AND WIFE AS RESPECTS PROPERTY 327-79 (London, W. Benning & Co. 1849).

It was customary for these separation agreements to provide for the wife to have custody of the children and the husband to pay for their support, at least as concerned boys up to the age of seven, and girls of any age.[161]

It has been suggested that fathers may have been persuaded to forego custody claims by the "rising tide of sentiment about maternal love and nurturing that mothers made the best custodians of young children."[162] It is also possible that during negotiations some fathers may have been persuaded to concede custody rights in exchange for a larger share of property and/or a reduction in spousal support. And it is also possible that some of these fathers simply accepted unquestioningly the sex-based division of labor that apparently had been a feature of western civilization since the days of ancient Greece.

Although separation agreements typically gave the mother custody of the children, some of them called for the parents to share joint custody of the children, in order to "give both parents a fair intercourse with them" and to instill in children "affectionate regard for the character and person of both" parents.[163]

Deeds of separation generally were enforceable unless and until one of the parties committed an act creating grounds for either a limited divorce (*a mensa et thoro*) or an absolute divorce (one granted by an Act of Parliament.) This meant that the separation agreement was enforceable until one or the other spouse became guilty of either adultery or extreme physical cruelty. In that case, the innocent party could proceed with a divorce and obtain custody of the children notwithstanding the existence of the separation agreement.[164]

Although English courts had upheld the validity of these agreements throughout the eighteenth century, they came under attack in the early nineteenth century. In a case decided in 1820, King's Bench jurist Lord

---

[161] STONE, *supra* note 147 at 151-53, 172, 177.

[162] *Id.* at 174.

[163] JOHN F. MACQUEEN, THE RIGHTS AND LIABILITIES OF HUSBAND AND WIFE 352 (London, S. Sweet 1849); *see also* STONE, *supra* note 147 at 177.

[164] Lewis v. Lewis, GLRO, DL/C/179 (1782); *see also* Guth v. Guth, 29 Eng. Rep. 729-33 (1792).

Eldon refused to enforce a writ of habeas corpus that had been issued to specifically enforce a separation agreement in which the couple had agreed that the mother was to have custody of the children. In the course of so ruling, Lord Eldon declared that a father could not sign away his parental rights and responsibilities by means of a private agreement with a third party (the wife's trustee.)[165] This holding was reiterated by the Chancery Court of Appeals in 1858, which declared that it would be "contrary to public policy to allow a husband, though guilty of adultery and cruelty, to transfer to his wife his rights and duties with reference to his children."[166] The English doctrine of the inalienability of parental rights was reaffirmed yet again in 1897.[167]

Limitations on the paternal right to custody

Throughout the eighteenth century, English courts tended to recognize paternal custody rights more in the breach than in the observance. The circumstances under which a father could lose custody, even to a third party, were numerous, and were much broader than what would be required to remove a child from a parent under modern American law.

First, and reasonably enough, the early English courts would not grant custody to a father who had physically or sexually abused his children, or who had allowed another person to do so.[168]

Wife-beating (then called "cruelty to wife") was also grounds for denial of custody to a father. The objection to paternal custody under such circumstances seemed to have had more to do with the perceived immorality of such conduct than with concern for the safety or psychological well-being of children. The rule was applied irrespective of any evidence concerning the impact of the abuse on the child.[169]

---

[165] MACQUEEN, *supra* note 163 at 351; STONE, *supra* note 147 at 172.

[166] Vansittart v. Vansittart, 4 K. & J. 61, 70 Eng. Rep. 26 (1858); *see generally* JOHN F. MACQUEEN, A PRACTICAL TREATISE ON THE LAW OF MARRIAGE, DIVORCE AND LEGITIMACY 166, 277 (London, W. Maxwell 1860)

[167] *See* J. ROBERTS, DIVORCE BILLS IN THE IMPERIAL PARLIAMENT 93 (1906).

[168] Whitfield v. Hales, 12 Ves. 492 (1806); Rex v. DeLavel, 1 S.W. Black 410, 97 Eng. Rep. 913 (K.B. 1763).

[169] *Ex parte* Warner, 4 Bro. C.C. 102, Y.B. 33 Geo. 3, fol. 19b (1792); *see also* Potts v. Norton, 2 P. Wms. 110*n*, 24 Eng. Rep. 666*n* (1792).

Another way a father could lose custody was by engaging in an immoral act, which could include but was not limited to adultery.[170]

Low income fathers did not have a right to custody. In 1601, Parliament enacted the Poor Law, authorizing the government to separate children from pauper parents and to place poor children in apprenticeships until the age of majority. Courts, for their part, held that a father's nonsupport of a child, like his failure to provide a child with a proper education, was grounds for denial of custody to him.[171] This was true even if the inability to provide financial support was due to circumstances beyond the father's control. Courts sometimes would appoint guardians for children whose fathers were not financially able to provide for them.[172]

The fact that a father's financial circumstances were such that he needed to reside abroad was also grounds for denying him custody.[173]

Another way a father could lose custody of his children was by equitable estoppel. If a father allowed another person to assume responsibility for the care of his child, or if he encouraged his children's expectations by allowing them to reside with someone else, a court might hold that he was estopped from making a claim to custody of them.[174] Similarly, if a father accepted benefits under a will that appointed a guardian for the children other than the father, then he forfeited his right to challenge the guardian so appointed.[175] And even though the courts articulated the rule that fathers had the right to custody of their children, they refused to allow the writ of habeas corpus to be used to order a person to return a child to his father. The writ could be used to order the release of a child from a person's custody, but it could not be used to order the return of a child into a father's custody. In other words, a court could declare a

---

[170] Wellesley v. Wellesley, 2 Bligh (N.S.) 124, 4 Eng. Rep. 1078 (H. L. 1828); Wellesley v. Duke of Beaufort, 2 Russ. 1, 38 Eng. Rep. 236 (Ch. 1827).

[171] Blisset's Case, Lofft. 748, 749, 98 Eng. Rep. 897 (1774).

[172] Wilcox v. Drake, 2 Dick 631 (1784).

[173] Creuze v. Hunter, 2 Bro. C.C. 500, 30 Eng. Rep. 113 (1790).

[174] *Ex parte* Warner, 4 Bro. C. C. 101, 102, Y.B. 33 Geo. 3, fol. 19b (1792); Creuze v. Hunter, 3 Cox 242, 30 Eng. Rep. 113 (1790); *Ex parte* Hopkins, 3 P. Wms. 152, 24 Eng. Rep. 1009 (1732). The doctrine does not appear to have been applied in situations where the children were residing with the mother pursuant to a deed of separation. Westmeath v. Westmeath, 1 Jac. 125 (1821).

[175] Blake v. Leigh, Ambl. 306 (1756).

father's right to custody, but it would then be entirely up to the father to employ some sort of self-help means of securing the child's return. Thus, while articulating a "paternal rights" doctrine in theory, the courts effectively nullified it in practice.[176]

Although fathers possessed the legal right to appoint someone other than the mother as a testamentary guardian for the children upon their deaths, this right, too, was recognized more in the breach than in the observance. In these kinds of cases, courts were inclined to speak of children's "natural right to the care of their mother," and to place children in their mother's care following the death of the father anyway.[177]

Best interest of the child

By the end of the eighteenth century, English courts were applying a "best interest of the child" standard in custody cases, notwithstanding the lip service they paid to a father's supposed "right" to custody of his children. "[B]y the end of the century judges spent less time trying to justify their power to interfere and more time analyzing the healthiness of the child-rearing environment."[178] Courts "would not allow the colour of parental authority to work the ruin of his child."[179] The approach was justified as an exercise of the Crown's *parens patriae* jurisdiction over those of its citizens (in this case, children) who were unable to care for themselves. The state's *parens patriae* power was seen as overriding parental rights.[180]

---

[176] Rex v. DeLaval, 97 Eng. Rep. 913, 914 (K.B. 1763); Rex v. Smith, 2 Stra. 982 (1735) (refusing to order the child's aunt to return the child to the father's custody.)

[177] Mellish v. De Costa, 2 Atk. 14, 26 Eng. Rep. 405 (1737) (removing children of deceased father from the care of their grandparent and placing them with the mother.) Courts were somewhat less inclined to do this, however, if the mother had deserted the family prior to the father's death.

[178] Wright, *supra* note 1; *see also* WALTER C. TIFFANY, HANDBOOK ON THE LAW OF PERSONS AND DOMESTIC RELATIONS 268 (2d ed. 1909) ("Long prior to [the Talfourd Act of 1839] the Court of Chancery in England had … refused to recognize any right in the father to demand the custody of his child, regardless of the child's interests, and had interfered to protect the welfare of the child…"); 2 JOSEPH STORY, COMMENTARIES ON EQUITY JURISPRUDENCE § 1341 (Boston: Hilliard, Gray & Co. 1836)

[179] Powel v. Cleaver, 2 Bro. C.C. 499, 29 Eng. Rep. 274, 283 (Ch. 1789).

[180] *See* Blisset's Case, Lofft. 748, 749, 98 Eng. Rep. 897, 899 (K.B. 1774) ("[T]he power of a father over a child, however despotic the law allowed it to be in other

In short, English courts, by the end of the eighteenth century, were not deciding custody cases on the basis of a view of children as the property of their fathers. Rather, they were awarding custody on the basis of a consideration of what was in the best interests of the child. In *Blisset's Case*,[181] for example, the court rejected the argument that fathers have a paramount right to the custody of their children, and instead proceeded to grant custody to the mother. The explicit basis for the decision was that "the court will do what shall appear best for the child."[182]

Sometimes the application of the "best interest of the child" standard resulted in an award of custody to the mother; sometimes to the father, and sometimes to a third party.[183]

Children born out of wedlock

Out-of-wedlock births were scandalous and rare in seventeenth century England, not exceeding three percent of all births. Mothers had custody of their illegitimate children for the first few years. When they reached the age of seven, though, the father, if known, could claim a right to custody of them if he wished. Unless the mother was financially able to support them herself (and she typically was not), children born out of wedlock were "bound out" (apprenticed) to others, the parish sometimes requiring the father to pay a sum of money to the master in exchange for his assumption of responsibility for the child.

A court could order the parents to reimburse the parish for the cost of caring for the child. If the father refused to acknowledge his paternity, the mother could be required to appear in court and make a statement under oath declaring the identity of the child's father. On that basis, the court would then issue a support order against the man so named. Women who could not or would not identify the father could be imprisoned until they

---

respects as to the child, itself, was yet subordinate to the power and constitution of the state.")

[181] *Id.*

[182] *Id.*

[183] *Id.; see also* Rex v. Delavel, 3 Burr. 1434, 97 Eng. Rep. 913 (K.B. 1763) (denying custody to father); Rex v. Smith, 2 Strange 982, 93 Eng. Rep. 983 (1735) (denying father's claim of a right to custody, and allowing aunt to retain custody, on the grounds that it was in the child's best interests to allow the child to choose whether to reside with his father or with his aunt, and he had chosen his aunt)

agreed to identify someone as the father.

A law enacted in 1609 made both the mother and the father punishable criminally, the potential sentence including imprisonment for up to a year. The severity of the sentence impelled a number of women to try to hide their pregnancies, anonymously abandon their babies on other people's doorsteps, or commit infanticide. Partly for this reason, the focus of the penal law in this area subsequently shifted from retribution to fiscal concerns. A mother could avoid imprisonment by naming the father of the child so that the state could seek reimbursement of support from him. Under the Bastardy Act of 1733, the man the mother identified as the father could secure his release from prison by either giving security to indemnify the parish or agreeing to marry the woman.

13. NINETEENTH CENTURY ENGLAND

Near the end of the eighteenth century, reports of the decisions of the courts of chancery increasingly referenced arguments about a special kind of bond existing between mothers and their children, and the supposed natural superiority of maternal care for children. Traditional accounts of history cite this as evidence that mothers were coming to view their children as children rather than as "miniature adults," that is to say, they were coming to have an interest in the welfare of their children (or became more interested in their children than they had been before) during this period.

It has been suggested that increased maternal concern was occasioned by the rise in the practice of maternal breastfeeding in preference to the use of wet-nurses.[184] There is not a lot of scientific evidence to support the idea that parental affection for a child either correlates with or is caused by breastfeeding, though. One can find plenty of examples of children whose mothers neglected, abandoned or abused them despite having breastfed them as infants. Attachment disorders arise in both breastfed and bottle-fed babies. Moreover, adoptive parents and their children often form strong

---

[184] STONE, *supra* note 147 at 170.

mutual attachments despite the lack of a connection through breastfeeding. It is possible that using one's body to provide for the emotional needs of a child (e.g., holding and comforting a baby) may have as much or more to do with the formation of the parent-child attachment as using one's body to provide for a child's physical needs does. Nevertheless, the idea that mothers somehow acquired a heightened interest in parenting during this period remains a very popular one.

> [I]n the period after 1780, motherhood increasingly came to be considered by women as an end in itself, and no longer as merely a biological device for the production of...heirs to property. In consequence the mother-child bond became even closer and more intimate, especially in families where marital relations were strained.[185]

It seems unlikely, however, that a maternal instinct or a mother's capacity to love her children suddenly and spontaneously sprang into existence where women previously had lacked it. It also seems a little insulting to women (and, as we have seen, contrary to the historical record) to suggest that women at one time had thought of their children as nothing more than "biological devices" for the inheritance of property.

A more plausible explanation for the fact that mothers (and their attorneys) began to advance a "natural rights" argument for maternal custody in the chancery courts in the late eighteenth and early nineteenth centuries is that English mothers, by that time, had lost the advantage of the maternal preference that the manorial and ecclesiastical courts had afforded them. By the end of the eighteenth century, neither of these courts continued to have jurisdiction over child custody matters. Faced with law courts applying legal doctrines favorable to fathers, and with no maternal preference presumption upon which to rest their cases anymore, mothers and their advocates increasingly were forced to turn to the courts of equity for favor. Only the chancery courts had the power and the authority to override a father's legal rights.

---

[185] *Id.*, *citing* JUDITH S. LEWIS, IN THE FAMILY WAY: CHILD-BEARING IN THE BRITISH ARISTOCRACY, 1760-1860, at 55-56 (1986).

The kind of argument that was needed to win in a court of equity was not one that appealed to principles of law. In courts of equity, appeal was to be made to a judge's sense of fairness, and to his concern for the welfare of children. An argument about the propriety of an exercise of the chancery court's *parens patriae* power to protect a vulnerable child from an allegedly harsh or cruel father could carry the day there. Eloquent expressions of the high order of the mother-child bond, and invocations of stereotypes about a mother's gentler, more nurturing nature relative to a father's, might have little effect on the minds of judges who applied legal principles strictly, logically and rationally. They could and did have tremendous effect, though, on the hearts of the chancery court judges, whose decisions were to be guided more by conscience and a desire to protect the vulnerable than by formulaic laws.

It was most likely for this reason that late eighteenth and early nineteenth century English lawyers frequently were making arguments in the chancery courts that mothers were naturally more gentle, nurturing and protective of children than fathers were, and that mothers therefore were the most suitable custodians for children. Sometimes they stated the argument more narrowly, asserting that girls should always be placed in their mother's custody, and that young boys should be placed in their mother's custody until they attained seven years of age. Judges sometimes saw a father's influence in preparing a boy for a trade, profession, military service, self-sacrifice and other attributes and responsibilities of manhood as an important consideration in cases involving older male children.

De Manneville v. De Manneville

One of the early nineteenth century attempts to persuade British courts to re-establish an explicit preference for mothers occurred in 1804. It was not successful. Neither the law courts nor the chancery courts could be persuaded to accept the argument that children of tender years should never be separated from their mothers. The cases were *Rex v. De Manneville*[186] and *De Manneville v. De Manneville*.[187]

---

[186] 5 East 221, 102 Eng. Rep. 1054 (K.B. 1804)
[187] 10 Ves. 52, 32 Eng. Rep. 762 (Ch. 1804)

The material facts in these cases were not really in dispute. Although not initiating a divorce or a legal separation proceeding, Mrs. Margaret De Manneville alleged that her husband was such an unpleasant man that she moved out of the family home, taking the couple's then-eight-month-old daughter with her. Mr. De Manneville then came to her home and took the child back with him. Mrs. De Manneville applied to the King's Bench for a writ of habeas corpus to require the father to release the child to her. Lord Ellenborough denied the writ, holding that a married father is entitled to custody of his children while he is still married to their mother, even if the children are very young.[188] She then turned to the chancery court for equitable relief. The chancery court, however, also refused to intervene. Explaining his refusal, Lord Eldon stated that unless a child was in danger of being harmed, "the law is clear that the custody of a child, of whatever age, belongs to the father."[189] The ruling touched off a wave of outrage both in England and abroad, the ripples of which continue to be felt to this day.

Lord Eldon's declaration was not a correct statement of English law. It was not true that custody of a child always belonged to the father. To begin with, unmarried mothers possessed a sole and exclusive right to custody of their children. Only married fathers could claim a right to custody of their children; unmarried fathers could not. More to the point, Lord Eldon ignored earlier chancery court decisions that had held that the chancery court's paramount concern was with what was in a child's best interests, and that the state's interest in advancing a child's best interests outweighed a father's legal rights. If maternal custody served a child's interests better than paternal custody did, then a court of equity would award custody to the mother irrespective of any claim of legal right the father might assert. Those earlier rulings were consistent with established principles of equity jurisprudence. Lord Eldon's ruling was not.

The sweep of Lord Eldon's dictum in *De Manneville* was very broad. Unfortunately, he was not the only English jurist who overstated fathers' rights under English common law. The venerable Sir William Blackstone

---

[188] Rex v. De Manneville, 5 East 221, 102 Eng. Rep. 1054 (K.B. 1804); *see also* CAROLINE NORTON, THE SEPARATION OF THE MOTHER AND CHILD BY THE LAW OF "CUSTODY OF INFANTS" CONSIDERED 33-37 (London, Roake & Varty 1838).

[189] De Manneville v. De Manneville, 10 Ves. 52, 63, 32 Eng. Rep. 762 (Ch. 1804)

also incorrectly asserted that under English law "a mother, as such, is entitled to no power, but only to reverence and respect."[190] This is one of the most frequently-cited quotations in Anglo-American jurisprudence. It has led to an enormous amount of misunderstanding.

Despite Blackstone's broad statement to the contrary, neither *De Manneville* nor any other decision altered the common law doctrine that fathers could acquire custody rights only through marriage to the mother, or that unmarried mothers had an exclusive right to custody of all children born to them out of wedlock.

The decision did, however, hinder the ability of a married mother to move away from her husband and take the children with her, unless grounds for a divorce or a legal separation (both of which were called "divorces" at that time) were proven. The ruling in *De Manneville* meant that a married woman had no legally enforceable right to move away from her husband and take the couple's children with her unless her husband had been guilty of adultery or physical cruelty, or the children were at risk of being harmed.

Coverture

Lord Eldon explained the rationale for his ruling in terms of the legal doctrine of coverture. Under that doctrine, the law treated a husband and wife as one person. The woman's status as a separate juridical person was said to be "suspended during the marriage, or at least is incorporated and consolidated into that of the husband."[191] The husband possessed both his own and his wife's rights, just as he was responsible for his own and his wife's debts, obligations, torts and crimes. An unmarried woman (*feme sole*), by contrast, possessed all of her own rights and responsibilities, including the right to sole custody of her children. According to Lord Eldon,

---

[190] 1 WILLIAM BLACKSTONE, COMMENTARIES ON THE LAWS OF ENGLAND 452-53 (Oxford, Clarendon Press 1765-69); *cf. Ex parte* Knee, 1 Bos. & P.N.R. 148, 127 Eng. Rep. 416 (1804) (observing that at common law, the mother of a child born out of wedlock has the right of custody to the exclusion of the father.)

[191] 1 BLACKSTONE, *supra* note 190 at 442. The coverture doctrine also helps explain why courts came to view separation agreements as unenforceable. Because a husband and wife were regarded in law as a single entity, "a man cannot grant any thing to his wife, or enter into covenant with her...." *Id.*

coverture had the effect of suspending all of a married woman's rights, even her right to custody of children.

After Lord Eldon's edict in *De Manneville*, English law allotted presently-existing parental rights, including custody, only to unmarried women and married men. Married women and unmarried men had no presently-existing right to custody of their children.

The doctrine of coverture had some surprising consequences. For example, on the authority of *De Manneville*, English courts held that a married or separated woman could not use the writ of habeas corpus to obtain custody of a child unless the child was in the care of a person other than the father.[192] Yet women who bore children without the benefit of marriage were able to use the writ to secure custody of their children from anybody, even the father. With respect to custody rights, then (though certainly not in other ways), the law seemed to give women who fornicated an important legal advantage that it denied to women who took the moral high road by "saving themselves for marriage."

The natural rights of parents

De Manneville is often cited for the proposition that English common law treated child custody as the natural right of fathers, but not mothers. In fact, however, English common law treated child custody as a natural right of mothers, not of fathers.

A *natural right* is one that does not require the enactment of a statute, the initiation of a court proceeding, or the formation of a contract; it arises naturally. *Legal rights*, by contrast, have their origin in positive law, i.e., man-made laws, contracts and declarations. Since a woman's right of custody arose from the fact of giving birth, irrespective of whether or not she had performed the additional step of entering into a marriage contract, and irrespective of any legal enactment giving her the right of custody, it came within the meaning of a natural right. A father, by contrast, did not have a right to custody merely by virtue of fathering a child. Rather, a father's right came into existence if and only if he had undertaken the additional legal step of entering into a valid contract of marriage with the mother. It was

---

[192] *Ex parte* Skinner, 9 Moore 278, 279, 27 Rev. Rep. 710 (1824).

only through coverture, as an incident of the contract of marriage to the mother, that a father could acquire custody rights to his child. That is to say, an English father did not have a natural right to custody of his children, but he might acquire a legal right to custody of his children by entering into a legally valid marriage prior to their birth. So long as a woman remained unmarried, she retained her natural right to custody of her children. If she became married, then her husband acquired a legal right to custody of any children born to the couple during the marriage, and the mother's natural rights were suspended for the duration of the couple's marriage.

Lord Eldon's ruling did not alter these principles. It reaffirmed them.

Limitations on the scope of De Manneville

A more fundamental misinterpretation of the *De Manneville* decision – and one that is now almost universal – is that it gave fathers an "absolute right to custody."[193] As we have seen, this is clearly false with respect to fathers of children born out of wedlock. They had no custody rights. Only married fathers did.

A married father's rights were not absolute; nor were they superior to the mother's rights in every circumstance. The doctrine of coverture applied only so long as a married couple remained married. It had no application to the determination of child custody in a divorce proceeding. Whether the

---

[193] *See, e.g.*, Young v. Young, 4 S.C.R. 3 (1993) (Can.) (*citing De Manneville* for the proposition that "[a]t common law, the right to custody of children was originally incontestable and reposed with the father to the exclusion of any claims of the mother"); ANN M. HARALAMBIE, HANDLING CHILD CUSTODY, ABUSE AND ADOPTION CASES 2 (1993) (describing fathers' rights as "nearly absolute"); Christopher L. Blakesley, *Child Custody and Parental Authority in France, Louisiana and Other States of the United States: A Comparative Analysis*, 4 B.C. INT'L & COMP. L. REV. 283, 292 (1981) ("nearly absolute"); Kenneth Brown, *Customary rules and the welfare principle: Post-independence custody cases in Solomon Islands and Vanuatu*, 21 J. PAC. STUD. 83-101 (1997) ("absolute right"); Cynthia Lee Starnes, *Swords in the Hands of Babes: Rethinking Custody Interviews after Troxel*, 2003 WIS. L. REV. 115, 119 (2003) (*citing De Manneville* in support of a claim that England adopted the "Roman law" that "fathers had an absolute right to custody of their children"); Yuri Joakimidis, Back to the Best Interests of the Child: Towards a Rebuttable Presumption of Joint Residence 15 (Joint Parenting Association Policy Monograph, 2nd ed. n.d.) (describing father's right to custody as "almost irrefutable"); *cf.* BLACKSTONE, *supra* note 50 at 372-73

kind of divorce sought was an absolute or a limited one, custody of children generally went to the innocent party, and that person could be either the mother or the father.

In early nineteenth century England, a divorce could be granted only if the spouse from whom the divorce was sought was guilty of wrongdoing. Adultery was grounds for either kind of divorce, absolute or limited. A limited divorce could also be granted on the basis of physical cruelty. Conduct of either kind was regarded as so highly immoral as to render a person unfit to parent. Accordingly, in the event of a divorce, custody of the children generally would be awarded to the party who was not at fault for the divorce, i.e., the innocent party. Depending on the circumstances, that could be either the father or the mother.

Those were not the only possible bases upon which a court of chancery might award custody to the mother instead of the father. As Lord Eldon acknowledged in *De Manneville*, the chancery court had the power to award custody to the mother whether or not grounds for divorce existed, if doing so would protect a child from harm.[194] Even after *De Manneville*, chancery courts recognized that harm to a child could be either moral or physical. If a married woman wished to separate from her husband and take the children with her, but she could not prove that he had committed adultery or that he had been physically cruel to her, she might nevertheless prevail by demonstrating that he had engaged in behavior, or had adhered to beliefs, that could be a bad influence on the children's moral development.

Paternal misconduct

In 1827, the chancery court had occasion to decide whether marital fault (adultery), standing alone, sufficed as grounds for an award of custody to the mother in a case in which neither party sought a divorce. Reasoning that marital misconduct renders a person morally unfit to parent, the court ruled that adultery could indeed furnish grounds for removing a child from his father if the child was aware of the affair.[195] If the father brought his paramour along with him on trips with his children, then he would be

---

[194] *See* note 189, *supra*, and accompanying text.
[195] Ball v. Ball, 2 Sim. 25, 36-37 (1827).

deemed unfit to parent. In so doing, he forfeited all claim of entitlement to the custody of children.[196]

Early English law, both before and after *De Manneville*, also recognized certain other kinds of conduct or circumstances, in addition to adultery, that rendered a father unfit to parent, and that would work a forfeiture of his custody rights. A father who was guilty of child abuse ("ill-treatment and cruelty") thereby forfeited his right to custody of them.[197] A father who permitted a daughter to engage in prostitution forfeited his right to custody of the daughter.[198] Abandonment vitiated a father's right to custody, as did neglect of a child's financial, physical or educational needs.[199]

Courts treated a father's insolvency as the legal equivalent of abandonment, even if his poor financial condition was due to circumstances beyond his control.[200] Thus, a father's financial inability to support his children was grounds for denying him custody of his children.

Atheism, blasphemy, or a lack of religious convictions would also work a forfeiture of a father's custodial rights, as the famous atheist poet Percy Bysshe Shelley learned in 1817.[201]

Equitable estoppel

Another way a father could lose custody rights was by equitable estoppel. This could occur where a father had allowed a child to be raised by another person, particularly if the father accepted benefits from the person, or if the child stood to receive an inheritance from the person.[202]

Ecclesiastical courts

The ecclesiastical courts were tribunals of the Church of England that had jurisdiction over all proceedings related to marriage. Although these

---

[196] Wellesley v. Duke of Beaufort, 2 Russ 1, 38 Eng. Rep. 236 (1827)

[197] Whitfield v. Hales, 12 Ves. Jr. 492, 33 Eng. Rep. 186 (1806).

[198] Rex v. DeLaval, 2 Burr. 1434, 97 Eng. Rep. 913 (1763).

[199] Blisset's Case, Lofft. 748, 749, 98 Eng. Rep. 897 (1767).

[200] *Id.*

[201] Shelley v. Westbrook, Jac. 266, 37 Eng. Rep. 850 (Ch. 1817)

[202] Colston v. Morris, Jac. 257, 22 Rev. Rep. 246 (1821); Lyons v. Blenkin, 1 Jac. 245, 37 Eng. Rep. 842 (Ch. 1821)

courts did not have jurisdiction over custody, they did have jurisdiction to order spousal support (alimony.) They used that power to coerce fathers into ceding custody to mothers, penalizing them with higher alimony obligations if they refused to do so:

> [B]y the 1820's they were openly using this authority to manipulate child custody on behalf of the mother. The court defended this delicate financial blackmail on the increasingly familiar grounds that: 'the welfare of the child would probably best be served under her maternal care.'[203]

Chancery

Chancery courts, which did have jurisdiction over custody, were very receptive to maternal custody. Though chancery judges (*chancellors*) sometimes felt constrained by the English common law rule that married fathers have the right to custody of their children, this did not prevent them from making statements like, "I know of no act more harsh or cruel than depriving the mother of proper intercourse with her child."[204] In 1827, Lord Eldon awarded the custody of a daughter and two sons to their mother and not their father, on the grounds that the father was engaged in ongoing "scandalous" adultery and was therefore unfit to parent.[205] This ruling was consistent with his statement in *De Manneville* that chancery courts may award custody to a mother notwithstanding the father's legal rights, where doing so will protect a child from harm. As one commentator observed:

> [T]he court of chancery will interfere to disturb the paternal rights only in cases of a father's gross misconduct; such misconduct seeming, however, to be regarded with reference rather to the interests of the child than the moral delinquency of the parent. If the father has so conducted himself that it will not be for the benefit of the infants that

---

[203] STONE, *supra* note 147 at 177 (quoting Kempe v. Kempe, 162 Eng. Rep. 669 (1828).)

[204] Ball v. Ball, 57 Eng. Rep. 703, 704 (1827)

[205] Wellesley v. Duke of Beaufort, 2 Russ 1, 38 Eng. Rep. 236 (1827); ANN. REG. 293-313 (Ch. 1827).

they should be delivered to him, or if their being with him will injuriously affect their happiness, or if they cannot associate with him without moral contamination, or if, because they associate with him, other persons will share their society, the court will award the custody to another. [206]

Four years later, in *Mytton v. Mytton*,[207] the Chancery court declared that the children in that case were to remain with their mother, apparently because it deemed maternal custody to be in their best interests.

By 1848, the Chancery court had firmly re-established as a principle of English equity jurisprudence that courts were to award custody of children neither on the basis of the father's legal rights, nor solely on the basis of marital fault or the sex of the parents. Rather, courts were to structure custody and access in a way that best advanced the interests of children.[208] Beliefs about the impact of marital fault and a parent's sex on child development continued to be operative, but they were employed only as a means of determining what was in a child's best interests. The best interest of the child was the overarching consideration.

The Custody of Infants Act of 1839 (Talfourd Act)

The *De Manneville* decision was very unpopular. In the ensuing years, momentum grew for legislation to overturn it. The circumstances and writings of Caroline Norton ultimately provided the needed impetus.

---

[206] SCHOULER, *supra* note 55 at 360, *citing, inter alia,* Anonymous, 11 E. L. & Eq. 281, 61 Eng. Rep. 260 (Ch. 1851) (awarding custody to mother on basis of father's immorality) *and* Warde v. Warde, 2 Phil. 786 (1849) (holding that court of equity has "an absolute control over [children under seven] without regard to the peculiar common-law right of the father to the custody of all his children" and may award custody of older children to the mother if it is in the children's best interests.)
[207] 162 Eng. Rep. 1298 (1831),
[208] MACQUEEN, *supra* note 163 at 351-54; MACQUEEN, *supra* note 166 at 174-75; SCHOULER, *supra* note 55 at 359 ("[T]he courts of chancery, in assuming a liberal jurisdiction over the persons and estates of infants, soon made the claims of justice override all considerations of parental or rather paternal dominion, at the common law"); 2 JOSEPH STORY, EQUITY JURISPRUDENCE § 1341 (6th ed., Boston, Little Brown & Co. 1853); *see also* Barnardo v. McHugh, A.C. 388, 61 L.J. & Q.B. 721 (Eng. 1891) (observing that although the English law courts may not have enforced mothers' rights, "in equity regard was always had to the mother....")

Mrs. Norton was an English socialite and author. She was married to a Member of Parliament and was well connected to others. In 1836 she separated from her husband. While they were separated, her husband accused her of having an affair with Lord Melbourne, who was then the Whig prime minister, and he filed a lawsuit against Lord Melbourne for criminal conversation. The lawsuit garnered a great deal of media attention. It ultimately was dismissed, and Mr. Norton did not pursue a divorce. Mrs. Norton, meanwhile, was unable to divorce him. As a result, the couple lived separate and apart from each other without the benefit of a divorce or other court order addressing custody of the children. Through it all, Mr. Norton kept the children concealed from her, even after his lawsuit was dismissed. Based on the precedent set in the *De Manneville* case, Mrs. Norton felt powerless to obtain any help from the courts.

Caroline Norton wrote very powerfully and eloquently about the suffering she experienced as a mother unable to see her children. The combination of her eloquent exaltations of motherhood and of her own suffering as a parent alienated from her children, together with the notoriety of the lawsuit and the strength of her connections with Members of Parliament, impelled the passage of what is sometimes described as the first piece of feminist legislation in history, the Custody of Infants Act.

The English Parliament enacted this law in 1839.[209] Sometimes called the Talfourd Act, after its author Sir Thomas Talfourd, it specifically authorized English courts to award custody of young children (defined in the statute as children under the age of seven) to their mothers.

The Talfourd Act sometimes is erroneously identified as the source of the tender years doctrine.[210] The tender years doctrine expresses a preference for awarding the custody of young children to their mothers. The Talfourd Act did not establish any preference. It merely authorized courts to make custody awards of young children to their mothers. Courts retained discretion to award custody of young children to either the mother or the father, as the court saw fit. It is true that by overruling *De Manneville*,

---

[209] An Act to Amend the Law Relating to the Custody of Infants, 2 & 3 Vict. Stat., c. 54 (1839)

[210] *See, e.g.*, Kohm, *supra* note 53 at 347 (describing the Talfourd Act as "the British law that brought the Tender Years doctrine to common law.")

Parliament thereby enabled the courts to develop and apply a preference for mothers in custody cases, but the Act itself did not mandate such a preference.

In any event, the notion that mothers should have custody of very young children had been around for many years – indeed, centuries -- before the Talfourd Act. The *De Manneville* judges had strayed from it. The Talfourd Act reined them in, letting them know in no uncertain terms that courts do have the power to award custody of young children to their mothers even in the absence of a divorce, so long as she is not guilty of adultery.

Although courts had granted visitation rights to noncustodial mothers even prior to the Talfourd Act, the Act expressly confirmed their authority to do so.[211] It did not address the visitation rights of fathers[212]

The Matrimonial Causes Act of 1857

In 1857, the English Parliament enacted the Matrimonial Causes Act.[213] This law authorized courts to grant divorces. Previously, a court could only grant a divorce *a mensa et thoro,* which today would be called a legal separation (or a "divorce from bed and board.") A divorce *a mensa et thoro* was not a true divorce inasmuch as the couple remained married to each other afterwards. An absolute divorce, i.e., one that actually terminated the marriage so that the former spouses were free to marry other people afterwards, was called a divorce *a vinculo matrimonii.* A special Act of Parliament had been required for that kind of divorce. The Matrimonial Causes Act eliminated that requirement. It allowed a couple to obtain either

---

[211] *See, e.g.,* De Manneville v. De Manneville, 10 Ves. Jr. 52, 32 Eng. Rep. 762 (Ch. 1804) (reserving custody to father, but granting mother the right of "intercourse," i.e., contact and visitation, with the child.); Clout v. Clout, 2 Swabey & T. 391, 164 Eng. Rep. 1047 (Eng. 1861).

[212] At least one English court interpreted the omission of a grant of visitation rights of fathers in the Talfourd Act as indicative of a legislative intention to impose no restrictions on a court's apparently inherent power to award visitation rights to fathers. Thus, in Boynton v. Boynton, 2 Swabey & T. 275, 164 Eng. Rep. 1001 (Eng. 1861), a grant of visitation rights to an adulterous father was upheld, on the basis that the Talfourd Act only prevented courts from granting visitation rights to adulterous mothers, not to adulterous fathers.

[213] 20 & 21 Vict., c. 85 (1857)

kind of divorce from the courts without having to lobby Parliament for special legislation.

The Matrimonial Causes Act also created a secular divorce court and moved jurisdiction over matrimonial litigation from the ecclesiastical courts to the newly created divorce court. The divorce court had jurisdiction over child custody, as well.

The maternal preference and marital fault in the new divorce court

By the time Parliament enacted the Matrimonial Causes Act of 1857, it had become the rule in the Court of Chancery that custody of children would be awarded to the innocent party in divorce cases.[214] The new divorce court continued to apply that rule, but now expressed a preference for granting custody of children under the age of fourteen to the mother, provided she was the innocent party.[215] The court would not award either custody or visitation rights to a mother who was guilty of adultery. This rule, which had been codified in the Custody of Infants Act of 1839, derived as much from a concern for the protection of public morality as from a desire to promote the best interests of the child: "It will probably have a salutary effect on the interests of public morality that it should be known that a woman, if guilty of adultery, will forfeit, as far as this court is concerned, all right to the custody of or access to her children."[216]

The Custody of Infants Act of 1873

The Custody of Infants Act of 1873[217] authorized courts to award mothers custody and visitation of children up to the age of sixteen, and removed the prohibition against awards of custody or visitation to adulterous mothers.[218]

---

[214] 3 HANSARD 147: 1268-69, 1750 (1857).

[215] Clout v. Clout and Hollebone, Eng. Rep. (Divorce, 1047) (1861); Ryder v. Ryder, 164 Eng. Rep. 981 (1861); Thompson v. Thompson and Sturnfells, Eng. Rep. (Divorce, 1052) (1861); Boyd v. Boyd and Collins, Eng. Rep. 861 (1859); WILLIAM E. BROWNING, THE PRACTICE AND PROCEDURE OF THE COURT FOR DIVORCE AND MATRIMONIAL CAUSES 91-94 (London, Butterworths 1862).

[216] Seddon v. Seddon and Doyle, 2 Sw. & Tr. 640, 164 Eng. Rep. 1147(1862)

[217] 36 & 37 Vict., c. 12

[218] Handley v. Handley, P. 124 (Eng. 1891)

The Act further declared that separation agreements transferring a father's right of custody to the mother may be enforced, provided the transfer was in the child's best interests. Courts were authorized to refuse to enforce such an agreement if they determined that enforcement was contrary to the child's best interests in a particular case.

With the enactment of this law, the focus of English courts in the late nineteenth century was squarely on what were believed to be children's temporal needs, irrespective of the mother's marital fault. Judges assumed that children's primary temporal need was for maternal care, fathers being necessary only for financial support. Thus, England entered the twentieth century with child custody laws expressing a very strong maternal preference.

Children born out of wedlock

The foregoing developments in the law related to the custody of the children of married parents, not children born out of wedlock. Put another way, the changes in custody law that took place in nineteenth century England affected the rights of married parents, not unmarried ones. The rights and obligations of unwed mothers and putative fathers remained the same as they had been at common law.

At common law, children born out of wedlock were regarded as *nullius filius* (the child of no one.)[219] This meant that they had no rights of inheritance.

It is sometimes inferred from the use of the term *nullius filius* that common law courts regarded children as literally having no mother or father; that their legal status was identical to that of orphans. This is a misconception. English courts used the *nullius filius* doctrine as a basis for denying inheritances to children born out of wedlock, and for denying parental rights to fathers. They did, however, recognize the parental rights of mothers. Specifically, they recognized both the customary right and the natural right of unwed mothers to raise their children, with children born out of wedlock taking their settlements in the parishes of their mothers.[220]

---

[219] Norma Adams, *Nullius Filius: A Study of the Exception of Bastardy in the Law Courts of Medieval England*, 6 U. TORONTO L.J. 361 (1946).

If a mother was unable to properly care for a child, whether due to lack of adequate financial resources or some other reason, then the state could exercise its *parens patriae* power to protect the child. This was accomplished, first, by apprehending the father and compelling financial support from him. If that could not be done (because the father was not known, could not be found, or was destitute), then it fell upon the parish to support the child. In many cases, this resulted in relegating the mother and child, or in some cases the child alone, to a workhouse, from which the child could be bound out as an apprentice or servant to other people.[221]

For custody purposes, children born out of wedlock were not *nullius filius*. They were the children of their mothers. And for child support purposes only, they were the children of their fathers. A father's failure to support his child born out of wedlock was a criminal offense.

Early English common law had imposed support obligations on the fathers of children born out of wedlock. This rule was abolished in the sixteenth century. The Act of 1576[222] restored it, decreeing that children born out of wedlock should be supported by their putative fathers. Courts ordered them to do so. The Bastardy Act of 1733 gave courts the specific power to imprison a putative father until he either provided financial support for his children or agreed to marry the mother.[223] On the other hand, he had no right to custody or visitation with his children. "To say that in consequence of an … adjudication which imposes on him the duty of supporting a child proved to be his, the putative father acquires rights…is altogether illogical and opposed to all authority."[224]

---

[220] Barnardo v. McHugh, A.C. 388, 61 L.J. & Q.B. 721 (Eng. 1891) (noting that although an unwed mother's right to custody of her child may not have been enforceable in the law courts of England, "in equity [the Chancery courts] regard was always had to the mother.")

[221] GILES JACOB, THE COMPLEAT PARISH OFFICER (London, E. & R. Nutt & R. Gosling, 1723); *see also* 32 Westminster City Archives F5037, *St Martin in the Fields, Bastardy and Settlement Examination Books, 1745-1749* (1746); *see generally* ILLEGITIMACY IN BRITAIN, 1700 – 1920 (Alysa Levene et al. eds. 2005); PAUL SLACK, THE ENGLISH POOR LAW, 1531 – 1782 (1990)

[222] 18 Eliz. C. 3

[223] Hard's Case, 2 Salk. 427, 91 Eng. Rep. 371 (1696); Anthony Camp, *Records of illegitimate children*, 17 FAM. TREE MAG. (UK) 7-9 (May 2001).

[224] *In re* Bates, 39 Vict. 178, 185 (1875)

Numerous cases held that as between the putative father and the mother of a child born out of wedlock, the mother's right to custody was superior; and the father's right, "if any such right existed," was secondary.[225]

The mother of a child born out of wedlock was entitled to custody even if placement with the father was shown to be in the child's best interest in a particular case.[226]

Throughout the nineteenth century and into the twentieth, mothers of children born out of wedlock possessed the sole and exclusive right to custody, although courts of equity sometimes placed a child in the custody of someone other than the mother when placement with the mother would put the child in harm's way.[227]

---

[225] *See, e.g.*, Rex v. Mosely, 10 Vesey 52 (1844); *In re* Lloyd, 3 Mann. & G. 547, 133 Eng. Rep. 1259 (1841); Rex v. Hopkins, 7 East 579, 103 Eng. Rep. 224 (1806); *Ex parte* Knee, 1 Bos. & P.N.R. 148, 127 Eng. Rep. 416 (1804)

[226] *Ex parte* Knee, 1 Bos. & P.N.R. 148, 127 Eng. Rep. 416 (1804); *see also* Strangeways v. Robinson and Another, 4 Taunt. 498 (1812) ("[T]he father has no right to the custody of the child.")

[227] SCHOULER, *supra* note 55 at 417; *cf. In re* Ullee, 53 L.T.N.S. 711 (Eng. 1885) (court of equity may consider the child's best interests if the child is older than seven years of age.)

PART III. EARLY AMERICA

14. COLONIAL AMERICA

Divorce in colonial America

Custody disputes between parents were a rarity in colonial America. To begin with, many children came to America as indentured servants, so they did not have parents to fight over them. The majority of the people who came to the colonies south of New England were indentured servants; and most of them were children.[228]

Children who came to America with parents, or who were born to parents in colonial America, usually did not stay in the homes of their parents for very long. It was customary for parents to apprentice their children, i.e., send them out to live with and work for another family, at or around the age of ten.[229] Children born out of wedlock frequently were "bound out" to a master shortly after weaning.

Also, mortality rates were much higher in colonial times than they are today. In the South, most children lost at least one parent before attaining

---

[228] RICHARD MORRIS, GOVERNMENT AND LABOR IN EARLY AMERICA 391 (1946)
[229] R.W. Beale, *The Child in Seventeenth-Century America, in* AMERICAN CHILDHOOD: A RESEARCH GUIDE AND HISTORICAL HANDBOOK 15-57 (Joseph M. Hawes and N. Ray Hiner eds., 1985); MASON, *supra* note 1 at 2.

the age of fourteen. Throughout the rest of colonial America, nearly half of all children under twenty-one lost at least one parent. It was not uncommon at all for one or both parents to die while their children were still young.[230]

Another significant reason for the rarity of custody disputes between parents in colonial America is that divorces were extremely rare. Only six divorces were granted during the entire seventy-two years of Plymouth Colony's existence. That is an average of one divorce every twelve years. In the sixty-two years from 1636 to 1698, there were only two petitions in New Hampshire (an average of one every thirty-one years); twelve in Rhode Island (an average of one every five years); forty in Connecticut; and forty-four in Massachusetts (less than one per year in each.)[231]

It is sometimes suggested that divorces were rare in colonial America because women did not have the right to divorce their husbands.[232] This is not true. In fact, in colonial Massachusetts and Connecticut, most divorces were filed by women, not men.[233] Indeed, the first divorce ever granted in America was initiated by a woman, not a man. It occurred in the Massachusetts Bay Colony in 1639, when James Luxford's wife requested a divorce from him on the grounds of bigamy. The magistrate granted her a divorce, awarded her all of her husband's property, ordered him placed in stocks, fined him and banished him to England.[234]

---

[230] MASON, *supra* note 1; STEPHANIE COONTZ, MARRIAGE: A HISTORY 10 (2005); V. FOX & M. QUIT, LOVING, PARENTING, AND DYING: THE FAMILY CYCLE IN ENGLAND AND AMERICA, PAST AND PRESENT 401 (1980)

[231] RODERICK PHILLIPS, PUTTING ASUNDER: A HISTORY OF DIVORCE IN WESTERN SOCIETY 138 (1988). The number of divorces actually granted was significantly lower than the number of divorces requested. In Massachusetts, for example, only 27 divorces were actually granted between 1639 and 1692. MASON, *supra* note 1 at 16.

[232] *See, e.g.,* Chandler-Gilbert Community College, *Overview of 1600's/1700's, in* WOMEN LEADERS AND ACTIVISTS: EXPERIENCES OF WOMEN LEADERS AND ACTIVISTS AS TOLD BY CGCC STUDENTS IN PARTNERSHIP WITH CHANDLER MUSEUM'S COMMUNITY HISTORY PROGRAM, (retrieved on August 22, 2011), http://www.cgc.maricopa.edu/Library/communityHistory/Women Activists/index-2.2.shtml.html ("In the 1600-1700's…women could not get a divorce"); *see also* MASON, *supra* note 1.

[233] MASON, *supra* note 1 at 16.

[234] GLENDA RILEY, DIVORCE: AN AMERICAN TRADITION 12 (1991).

The second divorce in colonial America occurred five years later, in 1643. This one, too, was initiated by a woman. In this case, a woman named Anne Clarke divorced her husband on the grounds that he had committed adultery and had abandoned her and their children.[235]

A more plausible explanation for the rarity of divorce in the colonies has to do with the religious beliefs of the people who settled there. The traditional Roman Catholic view of marriage then, as now, was that marriage is an indissoluble holy sacrament. Consistent with that view, Catholic countries in western Europe had enacted laws forbidding divorce. Despite the Protestant Reformation making divorce permissible at least in the case of adultery, the Church of England had continued the Catholic prohibition against divorce. Because of the unity of church and state in sixteenth and seventeenth century England, a private divorce literally required an Act of Parliament. That is to say, the only way that one could obtain a divorce was by convincing Parliament to pass a bill granting the divorce. This effectively limited divorces to only the wealthiest citizens. Court-issued divorces were not authorized in England until much later.[236]

Colonial charters authorized the American colonies to make only such laws as were not repugnant to the laws of England. The middle and southern colonies complied by adopting the English prohibition against divorce. Some southern colonies continued to prohibit divorces even after the American Revolution. South Carolina, for instance, did not authorize divorces until 1868.[237] New England colonists, however, were more independent. Established and settled by Puritans, Independents and Separatists fleeing persecution for rebelling against the Church of England, these colonies followed the Protestant view that divorce should be permitted under some circumstances, particularly in cases in which a spouse had committed adultery. The fact that a more liberal attitude toward divorce prevailed in those colonies did not mean that divorce was condoned or encouraged there, though. Religious beliefs about the sanctity of marriage were prevalent and legally enforced in these colonies, too.

---

[235] *Id.* at 13.

[236] RODERICK PHILLIPS, UNTYING THE KNOT: A SHORT HISTORY OF DIVORCE 37 (1991)

[237] DOROTHY A. MAYS, WOMEN IN EARLY AMERICA: STRUGGLE, SURVIVAL AND FREEDOM IN A NEW WORLD 111 (2004)

New England colonies were theocratic. There was no wall of separation between church and state. In Massachusetts Bay Colony, for example, voting rights were conditioned upon church membership. As in other New England colonies, laws regulating interpersonal relations were based on Biblical precepts. It was common for these laws to be accompanied by a scripture from the Old Testament.[238] The Bible treats marriage as a lifelong commitment.[239] Adultery (or more precisely, sexual immorality) appears to be the only grounds for divorce that the Bible permits.[240] Consistent with *Leviticus* 20:10, the penalty for adultery in the New England colonies was death.[241] A person in colonial America, then, would need to accuse his or her spouse of a crime punishable by death in order to get a divorce. In light of the consequences, the incentive either to refrain from adultery or to conceal it was strong.

The Duke of York's Laws, enacted in 1664 to govern the American colonies that would eventually become the states of New York, New Jersey and Pennsylvania, limited the right to remarry to situations in which one's spouse either had died or could be presumed dead due to lengthy absence. This meant that while a married person could obtain what today would be called a legal separation, the only recognized basis for an absolute divorce was the death of one's spouse.

The British government prohibited colonial laws that authorized divorce on grounds of adultery or other sexual offenses because they were contrary to the English legal prohibition against divorce. Although the New England colonies demonstrated some willingness to defy English law, they were reticent (initially, at least) about doing it too freely. While not strictly obeying the English prohibition against divorce, they nevertheless made

---

[238] M. Reggio, *History of the Death Penalty, in* SOCIETY'S FINAL SOLUTION: A HISTORY AND DISCUSSION OF THE DEATH PENALTY (L. Randa ed., 1997.)

[239] *See, e.g., Matthew* 19:6 ("[W]hat God has joined together, let man not separate"); *see also Malachi* 2:16 (declaring that a man who divorces his wife "covers his garment with violence.")

[240] *Matthew* 19:9 ("[W]hoever divorces his wife, except for sexual immorality, and marries another, commits adultery.")

[241] *See, e.g.,* the Duke of York's CAPITALL LAWES (1664) *reproduced in* CHARLES LINCOLN, THE COLONIAL LAWS OF NEW YORK FROM THE YEAR 1664 TO THE REVOLUTION 20 (2006); *see also* Capital Law 9 in the 1641 Massachusetts Body of Liberties, *reproduced in* 7 OLD SOUTH LEAFLETS 261, 274 (Boston: Directors of the Old South Work, n.d. [c. 1900]).

divorces very difficult to obtain, such as by requiring a person seeking a divorce to secure the approval of the governor.

It is for these reasons that even in the liberal Massachusetts Bay Colony, where divorce for reasons of "adultery, desertion…and the cruel usage of the husband"[242] had been authorized in 1629, it was still exceedingly rare. The first divorce under the Massachusetts Bay Colony law was not granted until ten years after its enactment.[243]

Custody of children upon divorce

The rarity of divorce, the common practice of binding out the children of unmarried couples to third parties, and the absence of good records leave us with very little information about how custody disputes between parents were actually decided in colonial America.

It is known that English colonists brought the concept of coverture with them when they settled America. Under the law of coverture, married women's rights and obligations were subsumed within those of their husbands during the marriage. More precisely, in the absence of an agreement otherwise, a married woman had no legal right to own property or to enter into contracts independent of her husband. Coverture did not prohibit married women from possessing and exercising contract and property rights. A prenuptial agreement (then known as a "marriage settlement") could give legally enforceable rights to a married woman.[244] In the absence of such an agreement, though, the law treated a married couple as a unity, with the husband being the manager of the unity. Pursuant to this doctrine, the husband had the right to make decisions about the family's residence, religion and the upbringing of the couple's children. The

---

[242] PHILLIPS, *supra* note 236 at 137.

[243] Connecticut's law was the most liberal, allowing divorce for "adultery, fraudulent contract, or willful desertion for three years with total neglect of duty, or seven year's providential absence being not heard of after due enquiry made and certified." Connecticut Records 2:328, discussed in EDMUND S. MORGAN, THE PURITAN FAMILY 37 (1980). The "duty" mentioned in the Connecticut law appears to refer to the husband's duty to support his wife financially. *Id.*

[244] M. BEARD, WOMAN AS A FORCE IN HISTORY: A STUDY IN TRADITIONS AND REALITIES (1962); RICHARD MORRIS, STUDIES IN THE HISTORY OF AMERICAN LAW, WITH SPECIAL REFERENCE TO THE SEVENTEENTH AND EIGHTEENTH CENTURIES 126-55 (1930).

claims of third parties to custody of a married couple's children were inferior to that of the father.

The fact that the father had a paramount right to custody of his children in disputes with outsiders to the marital unity does not necessarily mean that he had a paramount right to custody as against the mother when the marital unity was severed, though. Divorced and widowed women possessed many legal rights, including the rights to enter into contracts, sue in court in their own names, and own property in their own names. Since women regained their legal personhood and rights upon divorce, the fact that the English system of coverture was instituted in America cannot be taken to mean that women had no right to custody of their children upon divorce.

Compounding the uncertainty about how custody of children as between parents was decided is the fact that records of colonial American divorces typically did not contain child custody provisions. Children are mentioned in these records only in the context of explaining how the conduct of the party at fault (i.e., the adulterous, cruel, non-supporting or deserting parent) had harmed them. Child custody was not addressed.[245]

It has been suggested that the reason child custody provisions did not appear in colonial divorce records is that the father's right to custody was so well established that colonial women did not even bother trying to get custody of children.[246] The argument in support of this theory goes like this: American colonists carried English law over with them. English law gave fathers a paramount right to custody of their children, a rule that was established in the English case of *Rex v. De Manneville*.[247] In that case, an English court refused to order a father to give a child of tender years to the mother. Since American colonies followed English law, the argument goes, they must have followed the *De Manneville* rule that fathers have a paramount right to custody of their children.

---

[245] Nancy F. Cott, *Eighteenth Century Family and Social Life Revealed in Massachusetts Divorce Records*, 10 J. SOC. HIST. 29-30 (Autumn 1976).

[246] *See, e.g.*, LINDA KERBER, WOMEN OF THE REPUBLIC: INTELLECT AND IDEOLOGY IN REVOLUTIONARY AMERICA 183 (1980); MASON, *supra* note 1 at 17.

[247] 5 East 221, 102 Eng. Rep. 1054 (K.B. 1804)

A major flaw in this argument is that the *De Manneville* case was decided in 1804, long after the colonial period in America had ended. The paternal custody rule the case established could not have been "carried over" by the colonists, because it did not exist yet. If the colonists brought English law with them, it would have been seventeenth century English law, not nineteenth century English law. It would have consisted of a conglomeration of pre-*De Manneville* customary law (the law applied in the manorial courts), canon law (the law applied in ecclesiastical courts), common law (applied in the law courts) and rules of equity (applied in chancery courts.)

The common law of England moved toward a paternal preference in the seventeenth century. As we have seen, though, sixteenth and seventeenth century manorial and ecclesiastical courts applying customary law and canon law, respectively, favored maternal custody.

Moreover, with the exception of the concept of coverture, it is not at all clear that American colonies were particularly disposed to follow English common law anyway. To begin with, not all colonies were English. The French had colonies in America, too, most notably New France (now the country of Canada) and Louisiana. There were also Dutch settlements along the eastern seaboard. Unlike the English, neither Dutch nor French law embraced the concept of coverture. Rather, the laws of these countries treated women as equal economic partners in a marriage.[248]

Even within the English colonies, an inclination to reject English laws was present almost from the beginning. Legal historian Lawrence Friedman aptly describes the relationship between English and American colonial law as follows:

> [T]he colonial condition was not like the relationship of a ward to a city, or a county to a state. Even as a matter of theory, it was not clear which acts of Parliament and which court decisions were binding on the colonies. Throughout the colonial period, the colonists borrowed as much English law as they wanted to take or were forced to take. Their appetite was determined by requirements of the moment, by

---

[248] Alan Taylor, American Colonies 372 (2001)

ignorance or knowledge of what was happening abroad, and by general obstinacy.... Legal cultures differed in different colonies. New England deviated from standard English law more than the Southern colonies did. The connection between the two sides of the Atlantic was ... never harmonious. The colonies quarreled with the mother country over law as well as politics and taxes.[249]

In the course of conducting an intensive study of the Massachusetts Bay Colony, law professor George L. Haskins compiled considerable evidence that the notion "that the law of the colonies was essentially the common law of England" is demonstrably false.[250] He concluded, to the contrary, that "[t]he conditions of settlement and of development within each colony meant that each evolved its own individual legal system... thirteen separate legal systems."[251]

It is known that Pennsylvania and every other New England colony except Rhode Island rejected many concepts central to English common law, such as the law of primogeniture.[252] And Virginia's criminal laws of 1611 (Dale's Laws) were substantially more severe than England's. The Capital Lawes enacted in colonial Massachusetts were expressly based, not on English law, but on Biblical law, as this example illustrates: "If any man or woman be a WITCH, that is, hath or consulteth with a familiar spirit, they shall be put to death. *Exod.* 22.18 *Levit.* 20.27 *Deut.* 18.10.11."[253] English law called for the death penalty in cases of theft; the Quaker laws of West New Jersey did not.[254] A 1700 Pennsylvania law gave magistrates the power to literally gag all persons who were "clamorous with their tongues," something that was not part of English law. (Five years later, the British disallowed this law.)[255] Nicholas Trott, compiling laws for South Carolina in

---

[249] LAWRENCE FRIEDMAN, A HISTORY OF AMERICAN LAW 16 (1973)
[250] GEORGE HASKINS, LAW AND AUTHORITY IN EARLY MASSACHUSETTS 4-6. (1960)
[251] *Id.* at 6.
[252] *See* THE LAWS AND LIBERTIES OF MASSACHUSETTS 53 (reprint 1929) (1648); *see generally* FRIEDMAN, *supra* note 249 at 57-58.
[253] GENERAL LAWS AND LIBERTIES OF THE MASSACHUSETTS COLONY 14 (photo. reprint 1887) (1672)
[254] FRIEDMAN, *supra* note 249 at 61.
[255] 2 STATUTES AT LARGE OF PENNSYLVANIA FROM 1682 to 1801, at 85 (James T.

1712, stated that many of the laws of England were either "altogether useless" in South Carolina or "impracticable" because of differences in institutions.[256]

In 1678, the Massachusetts legislature defiantly declared, "The lawes of England are bounded within the fower seas, and does not reach America."[257]

Those colonies that permitted divorces on any grounds other than presumed death due to prolonged absence were openly and knowingly defying the English legal prohibition against divorce. And New England Puritans took pains to oblige husbands to behave kindly and generously toward their wives, a concept foreign to English common law, under which husbands had considerably more power and authority over their wives. As historian Cornelia Dayton has put it, the Puritans' effort "to create the most God-fearing society" tended "to reduce the near-absolute power that English men by law wielded over their wives."[258] Under English common law, domestic violence was not grounds for divorce. An abused woman simply had to put up with her husband's cruelty, her only recourse being a legal separation, not a divorce.[259] In New England, by contrast, a husband's cruelty to his wife not only was grounds for divorce, but it was also grounds for criminal punishment of the husband. The *Massachusetts Body of Liberties* declared, "Everie marryed woeman shall be free from bodilie correction or stripes by her husband, unless it be in his owne defence upon her assalt." A wife's abuse of her husband, on the other hand, was not grounds for divorce; nor does it appear to have been a crime[260]

Mitchell and Harry Flanders ed., 1896)

[256] 2 STATUTES AT LARGE OF SOUTH CAROLINA 401 (Nicholas Trott ed., 1837)

[257] TAYLOR, *supra* note 248 at 276.

[258] *Id.* at 173; CORNELIA DAYTON, WOMEN BEFORE THE BAR: GENDER, LAW AND SOCIETY IN CONNECTICUT, 1639-1790 (1979)

[259] More precisely, a divorce *a mensa et thoro*. A divorce *a mensa et thoro* was a divorce from bed and board, meaning that it entitled a married couple to live separately from each other, while still remaining married to each other. Unlike an absolute divorce, a divorce *a mensa et thoro* did not give the parties the right to remarry. Hence, it was not really a divorce at all; rather, it was what we would call a *legal separation* today.

[260] 1641 Massachusetts Body of Liberties 80, *reproduced in* 7 OLD SOUTH LEAFLETS 261 (Boston: Directors of the Old South Work, n.d. [c. 1900])

Again, these New England colonies were religious societies founded by Puritans, Independents and Separatists. They viewed themselves as radically different from England, and they were intent on establishing a new nation with new laws that they believed would please God better than those that had evolved in the European countries from which they had fled. Some English laws were carried over, but many were rejected. "Designed to please God, Puritan New England was a selective distillation from the more complex and conflicted culture of seventeenth century England. The New English left behind many traditional customs and institutions that they believed offended God in England."[261] And some New England colonies went further than others in their rejection of English laws and traditions. Rhode Island and Connecticut, for example, espoused the separation of church and state; Massachusetts, originally, did not.

In contrast to the English, New England colonists viewed adultery not only as grounds for divorce, but also as a mortal sin so abominable as to warrant the death penalty. Even if not killed, those who committed adultery or any other act egregious enough to furnish grounds for a divorce, were deemed morally unfit, and for that reason, ostracized and punished severely. Therefore, the most likely explanation for the failure of courts to address custody of children in divorce cases is that it was a foregone conclusion that the person who had committed acts so morally reprehensible as to justify his or her spouse in getting divorced obviously could not be entrusted with the care of children.

This would be consistent with the Puritan attitude toward fornicators. According to Dorothy Mays, the Puritans believed that neither the father nor the mother of a child born out of wedlock was entitled to custody because they were both morally unfit to raise children, each of them having engaged in the sinful act of copulation without the benefit of marriage.[262] There is no logical reason why the same would not have held true with respect to a spouse who engaged in adultery, which at that time was regarded as being on the same order of sinfulness and immorality as fornication.

---

[261] TAYLOR, *supra* note 248 at 179.
[262] MAYS, *supra* note 237 at 71.

When the Massachusetts Bay Colony court determined in 1639 that James Luxford's adultery was so heinously immoral as to warrant placing him in stocks, fining him, banishing him, and stripping him of all his property, the idea of entrusting him with the care of children most likely would have seemed so absurd to the Puritan mind that it would have been ludicrous even to suggest it, much less address it in the divorce decree.

Legal historian Mary Mason asserts that the powerlessness of women with respect to custody of children during marriage applied to divorce, as well. The only reason she gives for this belief, however, is the fact that "existing studies give no indication that women attempted to challenge their husband's right to the custody of their children in divorce actions." That may be true, but existing studies also give no indication that men who were at fault for a divorce attempted to challenge a divorcing woman's right to the custody of their children in divorce actions. A fact is not established as true simply because no evidence of its falsity has been found yet. Mason goes on to concede that another possible explanation for the absence of custody disputes during the colonial period "is that mothers often got custody of the children without a fight," pointing out that "[w]omen were most often granted divorces in cases of adultery or desertion, and it is unlikely that the father deserted with children in tow."[263]

As we shall see, when early American courts first started addressing custody issues in divorce cases, marital fault, not the sex of the parent, was usually the determinative factor. This much the American colonists seemed to have shared in common with their English predecessors. A spouse obtaining a divorce in colonial America -- that is to say, the spouse who was not at fault, whether that was the husband or the wife -- took custody of the children as a matter of course. A divorce decree was treated in the law as a reward for the virtuous spouse, and its terms were expressly directed toward the punishment of the guilty spouse. It would hardly make sense to "reward" the virtuous spouse by taking his or her children away, or to "punish" the immoral one by placing children in his care.[264]

---

[263] MASON, *supra* note 1 at 15, 17.

[264] Some examples of early American cases awarding custody to the mother on the basis of her husband's marital misconduct include, *inter alia*, Codd v. Codd, 2 Johns. Ch. 141 (N.Y. 1816) (granting custody to wife, where husband was guilty of cruelty to wife); Prather v. Prather, 4 S.C. Eq. (4 Des.) 33 (S.C. 1809) (granting custody to

This conclusion is buttressed by cases decided close to the colonial period that include references to divorced mothers with custody of the children even though the divorce decree had not addressed the issue of custody. Early American courts construed divorce decrees that were silent as to custody as giving the party who obtained the divorce (i.e., the innocent spouse) the right to custody of the children.[265]

To an early American colonist, awarding custody based on marital fault would simply have been an application of the "best interest of the child" standard. Since parents are role models for their children, and since a high premium was placed on the moral upbringing of children, it would stand to reason that placement of a child with a parent who had committed a sin so serious as to justify a divorce -- and in some cases, the death penalty -- would be deemed contrary to a child's interests.

Children of separated parents

As in England, the fact that divorces were prohibited or difficult to obtain did not prevent married couples from separating from each other without the benefit of a divorce. Yet, the doctrine of coverture called for the suspension of a married woman's rights during the marriage. Accordingly, it would seem logical to think that a married man would have the right custody of the couple's children in cases of separation without divorce. As we have seen, this was how Lord Eldon interpreted the doctrine of coverture for the English courts. Unlike the English courts, though, American courts did not apply the doctrine of coverture to defeat the custody rights of mothers.

In *Nickols v. Giles*,[266] a married woman left her husband and went to live with the children's grandfather, taking the children with her. Her husband sued for the return of the children. The court refused to grant the husband's request, noting that he did not own a home and had little property, while the children's grandfather did own a home and property. The court concluded that the children were being well cared for; they were

---

wife where husband "drove" wife from home); *see also* Stanton v. Willson, 3 Day 37 (Conn. 1808) (granting custody to the wife.); *cf.* FRIEDMAN, *supra* note 249 at 184.
[265] *See, e.g.*, Pawling v. Willson, 13 Johns. 192 (N.Y. 1816); Lemunier v. McCearly, 37 La. Ann. 133 (1885) (stating rule.)
[266] 2 Root 461 (Conn. 1796)

not likely to be as well provided for by the father; and therefore they should remain in their mother's custody.

Unlike in England, mothers in America generally retained custody of children upon a couple's separation. "Separations, even separations without fault on the part of husbands, made mothers into the proper custodians of their children."[267] As *Nickols* illustrates, the best interest of the child, not the rights of the husband/father, was the determinative question.

Children born out of wedlock or in need of protection

England's 1601 Poor Law empowered the state to take custody of children whose parents lacked the financial ability to support them, and to place them in apprenticeships. The concept of the state as *parens patriae*, which the Poor Law reflected, was carried over to and greatly expanded upon in colonial America. In eighteenth century Virginia, for example, grounds for the state's removal of children from their parents included not only poverty, but also a parent's idleness, dissoluteness, incapability, unchristian beliefs or practices, failure to teach a child a trade, educational neglect and failure to provide "good breeding" to a child.[268] Religious values and a strong work ethic shaped the American colonists' definition of what was in a child's best interests.

The Massachusetts Bay Colony placed a high premium on education. In 1642, it enacted a law authorizing courts to remove children from parents who failed to educate them.[269]

Child abuse was also grounds for removing a child from the home.[270]

As in England, mothers possessed the sole right to custody of children born out of wedlock, and such children were placed out with another family if the mother was unable to provide for them herself. The placement

---

[267] HARTOG, *supra* note 1 at 38; *see also* SALLY ROESCH WAGNER, SISTERS IN SPIRIT: HAUDENOSAUNEE (IROQUOIS) INFLUENCE ON EARLY AMERICAN FEMINISTS (2001).

[268] Douglas R. Rendleman, *Parens Patriae: From Chancery to the Juvenile Court*, 23 S.C. L. REV. 205, 210 (1971)

[269] ANCIENT CHARTERS AND LAWS OF MASSACHUSETTS BAY, Ch. XXIL (1642)

[270] *See, e.g.* Clyde E. Buckingham, *Early American Orphanages: Ebenezer and Bethesda*, 26 SOC. FORCES 311, 311-21 (1948).

typically was made in exchange for the child's provision of services to the foster family. A town's poor law official was authorized to effect the placement of these children.

15. INDEPENDENCE

As colonists became increasingly emboldened in their defiance of English law during the years leading up to the declaration of independence from England, English divorce laws were among those most openly defied. In 1773, the British government sent official notice to the colonies advising them of the king's "expressed will and pleasure that you do not upon any pretense whatsoever give your assent to any Bill or Bills that may have been or shall hereafter have been passed ... for the divorce of persons joined together in holy marriage."[271] Massachusetts and Connecticut disobeyed this order, granting divorces anyway. In other states, private bills granting divorces to married couples were regularly passed, only to be overturned later by the British government. This helped fuel the growing disenchantment with British rule.

Religious dissent grew, as well, in Maryland, South Carolina and Virginia, where the Church of England had been established by law. Throughout the eighteenth century, the number of Quakers, Baptists and Presbyterians greatly increased in these colonies. By the time of the

---

[271] PHILLIPS, *supra* note 231 at 150.

Revolution, they comprised, by Thomas Jefferson's estimate, two-thirds of the population.[272]

After the Revolution, Americans not only disestablished the Church of England; they tore it down. Objects sacred to the Church of England were put to profane uses, even to the extent of using a baptismal font as a horse trough.[273]

By the time of the Revolution, Americans had discarded much of whatever aspects of English law they had carried over with them. They were in the mood for new and better laws.

The uneasy status of English common law

When the Revolutionary War ended, citizens of the newly formed country debated extensively the question whether to discard English law along with English governance. Many influential people argued that new democratic states needed new institutions, including new laws.[274] During the famous Shay's Rebellion in Massachusetts in 1786, mobs stormed the courthouses to prevent judgments enacted on the basis of British common law from being enforced. Thomas Paine, writing in 1805, argued that American courts should not "hobble along by the stilts and crutches of English and antiquated precedents," which he described as "tyrannical."[275] In the end, some English common law came to be incorporated into the laws of some states. Much of it, however, did not.

The newly formed federal government did not adopt the common law of England at all. States, for their part, were not uniform with respect to the question whether to adopt all, some or none of the English common law after the Revolution. A small number of states incorporated English common law *en toto*. For example, a 1776 Virginia law automatically made all of the common law of England and all acts of Parliament in aid of the common law that were enacted before the fourth year of the reign of King

---

[272] SYDNEY G. FISHER, MEN, WOMEN AND MANNERS IN COLONIAL TIMES 60 (2006).

[273] *Id.*

[274] FRIEDMAN, *supra* note 249 at 94

[275] THOMAS PAINE, 2 COMPLETE WRITINGS OF THOMAS PAINE 1003 (P. Foner ed., 1945).

James a part of the law of the State of Virginia.[276] To similar effect, Article 25 of the Delaware state constitution of 1776 stated: "The common law of England as well as so much of the statute law as has been heretofore adopted in practice in this State, shall remain in force," except to the extent "repugnant to the rights and privileges" set out in the constitution and declaration of rights. New York initially enacted a similar kind of law, but later, in 1828, it "specifically pronounced the British statutes dead."[277]

Most states adopted a more hostile attitude toward British common law. A 1799 New Jersey law, for example, provided, in part:

> [N]o adjudication, decision or opinion, made, had or given, in any court of law or equity in Great Britain...nor any printed or written report or statement thereof, nor any compilation, commentary, digest, lecture, treatise, or other explanation or exposition of the common law...shall be received or read in any court of law or equity in this state, as law or evidence of the law, or elucidation or explanation thereof.[278]

Kentucky's statute, enacted in 1807, declared that "reports and books containing adjudged cases in...Great Britain...since the 4th day of July, 1776, shall not be read or considered as authority in...the courts of this Commonwealth."[279]

Despite efforts to disestablish the common law of Great Britain, some lawyers continued to cite English precedents and treatises as authority in their arguments to the courts, in part because legal authority in the newly-founded country was sparse. American cases were not regularly reported at all until several years after the Revolution. To fill the gap, some lawyers cited reports of English cases, whether they were legally binding in the

---

[276] WILLIAM W. HENING, STATUTES AT LARGE, BEING A COLLECTION OF ALL THE LAWS OF VIRGINIA, FROM THE FIRST SESSION OF THE LEGISLATURE IN THE YEAR 1619 (Richmond, Samuel Pleasants 1821)

[277] FRIEDMAN, *supra* note 249 at 97.

[278] ELIZABETH G. BROWN, BRITISH STATUTES IN AMERICAN LAW, 1776-1836, at 82 (1964). The law was repealed in 1819.

[279] *Id.* at 132.

newly formed country or not.[280] In spite of the efforts of these lawyers, judges generally rejected the idea that the common law of England had become the common law of America.[281] Instead, they selected some aspects of English law to incorporate into American common law, and rejected others.

> Sweeping changes took place in American law, in the sixty-one years between 1776 and the death of James Kent. In that time, there developed a true republic of bees, whose flowers were the social and economic institutions that developed in their own way in the country. They, not Lord Ellenborough and Lord Kenyon, were the lawmakers who made American law a distinctive system: a separate language of law within the family founded in England.[282]

Just as states varied respecting the general question whether, and to what extent, English common law was to become part of American law, so states varied about whether and to what extent English law on the subject of child custody would be applied in the new country.

Divorce

Only South Carolina carried forward the English prohibition against divorce. Pennsylvania enacted a general divorce law in 1785; Massachusetts, in 1786; New York, in 1787; Vermont, in 1798. By 1800, every state except South Carolina had enacted a law authorizing divorces.

The grounds for divorce varied from state to state but they were all fault-based, requiring proof of some sort of misconduct on the part of the spouse from whom a divorce was sought. A divorce would not be granted unless it could be shown that one of the spouses had committed such a serious breach of the marital contract as to justify a finding that he or she was at fault for the breakdown of the marriage.

---

[280] FRIEDMAN, *supra* note 249 at 98.

[281] *See In re* Barry, 42 F. 113, 119 (C.C.S.D.N.Y. 1844) (observing that American decisions addressing the idea that the common law of England became the law of America "tend to repudiate the principle *in toto*.")

[282] FRIEDMAN, *supra* note 249 at 98.

At the same time, it was necessary for the spouse seeking the divorce to be innocent of wrongdoing herself. In many states, if both spouses were guilty of the same kind of marital misconduct, then neither could be granted a divorce.

As in colonial times, adultery was the principal grounds for divorce. In New York, it was the only grounds. In Vermont, adultery, desertion, long absence and intolerable severity were the grounds for divorce. Rhode Island's divorce law specified "gross misbehaviour and wickedness."[283] In New Hampshire, the fact that one's spouse had become a Shaker was grounds for a divorce.[284]

States recognized two kinds of divorce: *a vinculo* (absolute divorce) and *a mensa et thoro* (limited divorce, or "divorce from bed and board.") A divorce *a vinculo* severed the marital relationship; a divorce *a mensa et thoro* did not. In many states today, a divorce *a mensa et thoro* is called a legal separation rather than a divorce.

Coverture

The English doctrine of coverture was carried over to America, but American courts did not apply it to defeat a married woman's right to custody of her children upon divorce or separation.[285]

In cases involving actual conflict between husband and wife – in separation struggles over child custody, over the enforcement of

---

[283] NELSON BLAKE, THE ROAD TO RENO: A HISTORY OF DIVORCE IN THE UNITED STATES 50 (1962).

[284] Dyer v. Dyer, 5 N.H. 271 (1830). "Shakers" was the common name for members of the United Society of Believers in Christ's Second Appearing." Although not Quakers, the common name is generally believed to be an abbreviated form of "shaking Quaker." Like Quakers, Shakers believed in racial and gender equality. Unlike Quakers, though, Shakers took vows of celibacy and adhered to a form of millennial communalism.

[285] *See, e.g.*, Nickols v. Giles, 2 Root 461 (Conn. 1796); *see also* RICHARD N. GRESLEY, A TREATISE ON THE LAW OF EVIDENCE IN THE COURTS OF EQUITY 344 (2d ed., Harrisburg, Pa., I. G. McKinley & J. M. G. Lescure 1848); HARTOG, *supra* note 1 at 106-07 ("Marital unity pervaded early nineteenth century legal rhetoric [but] it was rarely determinative of legal results....Courts and treatises often rejected the fiction.")

separate maintenance agreements, over a husband's obligation to provide necessaries for his absent wife...wives were almost always recognized as separate legal persons...American women (and their children) were not subject to the exclusive custody of their husbands.[286]

The civil law of Louisiana was exceptional in this respect. It disadvantaged mothers with respect to temporary ("provisional") custody during the pendency of a divorce. Prior to attaining statehood in 1812, Louisiana territory was governed by French civil law, including the Projet du Gouvernement of 1800. Book 1, tit. vi, art. 32 thereof provided that custody of children was to remain with the husband during the pendency of a divorce. The Louisiana Civil Code contained a similar provision,[287] but the Code provision gave courts discretion to make an award of temporary custody to the wife during the pendency of the divorce if a reason for doing so existed. This provision was changed in 1888 to provide that custody was to remain with the wife during the pendency of a divorce unless "strong reason" for permitting the father to retain temporary custody was established. In any event, Louisiana courts were always free to award custody to either the mother or the father upon the conclusion of the divorce proceeding

In all other states, the coverture concept was applied, but it ceased to operate when the marital unity was severed in a divorce or separation proceeding.

American courts understood the doctrine of coverture as being intended for the protection of women, and therefore not something to be applied to their detriment. It gave married men exclusive decision-making authority during a marriage, but it also gave them exclusive responsibilities. "The obligation imposed on the husband to provide for [the] wants and protection [of the family] makes it necessary that he should exercise a control over all the members of his household."[288] Under coverture, married men were responsible for paying their wives' debts, including

---

[286] HARTOG, *supra* note 1 at 130-32.
[287] LA. CIV. CODE art. 146 (1870)
[288] *Ex parte* Hewitt, 11 Rich. 326, 329 (S.C. 1858); *see generally* TIFFANY, *supra* note 178 at 60.

premarital debts. Husbands, but not wives, were punished criminally for crimes committed by their spouses in their presence, and husbands were sued personally for torts committed by their wives. Husbands were legally responsible for the support of their wives and children, but wives were not legally responsible for the support of husbands and children. A married woman owed a duty of obedience to her husband, but she did not have a corresponding duty of support; nor was she responsible for her husband's debts, premarital or otherwise, his crimes or his torts. "Husbands were responsible for their wives' actions, but wives were considered separate people when the question of responsibility for the husband's actions was raised." A piece appearing in an early American legal periodical described it this way:

> If any ill the wife hath done,
> The man is fin'd – for they are one;
> If any crime the man doth do,
> Still he is fin'd for they are two[289]

These aspects of coverture -- protection from responsibility, and presumed incapability of fault – formed the basis for Blackstone's statement that the coverture doctrine was applied in America to make wives a "favourite" of the law.[290] Courts applied it when it advantaged a woman, and declined to apply it when it did not, such as when a wife sought custody of the couple's children in a divorce or legal separation. In those situations, courts often held that a wife could possess a right to custody and support notwithstanding her lack of other kinds of rights under the coverture doctrine.

---

[289] 3 N.Y. CITY-HALL RECORDER 56 (1818); Anonymous, *The State v. Henry Day*, 20 AM. JURIST 237, 240 (October 1838); TIFFANY, *supra* note 178 at 100; *see also* People v. Boyd, 3 N.Y. CITY-HALL RECORDER 134 (1818); People v. William Brown and Elizabeth, his wife, 3 N.Y. CITY-HALL RECORDER 56 (1818).

[290] 1 WILLIAM BLACKSTONE, COMMENTARIES ON THE LAWS OF ENGLAND 445 (William Jones, ed., San Francisco, Bancroft-Whitney, 1915)

Separations without legal justification

The coverture doctrine did not disadvantage married women with respect to custody of children in a divorce or legal separation ("divorce from bed and board") proceeding. Nor did the coverture doctrine work to the disadvantage of mothers who separated from their husbands and took the children with them, in those cases where the wife had good cause for leaving, such as the husband's adultery, cruelty or nonsupport of his wife or children. The one situation in which it worked to the disadvantage of a mother was when a married woman wished to separate from her husband even though the husband had not been guilty of any wrongdoing. Coverture gave the husband the right to choose the location of the family home. If his wife chose not to live with him there, the coverture doctrine did not give her a legal right to take the children and reside with them in a different home unless the husband either was unable to provide for them financially or had done something wrong.[291]

If a wife unjustifiably separated from her husband and took the children with her, then the husband might seek the assistance of a court to secure the return of the children. This was done by means of the writ of habeas corpus. A writ of habeas corpus (*habeas corpus ad subjiciendum*) is a court order directing a person or entity to bring another person into court. It was originally used to test the legality of a prisoner's detention. In both eighteenth century England and early America, however, courts permitted it to be used for the additional purpose of bringing children before the court so that the court could decide their disposition.[292]

The writ of habeas corpus was only a procedural device. It did not establish any new substantive rights. The only relief that could be granted pursuant to it was an order for the release of a person from an illegal

---

[291] *See, e.g.*, Commonwealth v. Briggs, 33 Mass. (16 Pick.) 203, 204 (1834) (reasoning that unless the husband is at fault for the separation, courts should not sanction unauthorized separations of husbands and wives by awarding custody to the spouse who leaves the family home without cause); Magee v. Holland, 27 N.J.L. 86, 88 (1858) (holding that a wife "has no right to leave [her husband] and take away the children, unless compelled to do so by ill usage"); State v. Barney, 14 R.I. 62 (1883) (holding that a wife does not have a right to forcibly remove children from the husband's home during the marriage without commencing a proceeding for divorce or legal separation.)

[292] *In re* Barry, 42 F. 113, 117 (C.C.S.D.N.Y. 1844)

restraint. If a court determined the detention of a child was unlawful, then it would declare the child free to leave the person who had been detaining him, but the writ neither authorized nor required a court to issue a custody order respecting the child.[293] In America, an exception was recognized in cases involving a child who was too young to exercise a sound discretion. In these cases, the court would exercise its discretion to determine which residence would serve the best interests of the child. The court would then order that custody arrangement on the child's behalf.[294]

Habeas corpus principles worked to the disadvantage of married men whose wives separated from them without justification and took the children with them, because such men could only secure an order declaring the wife's separation unjustified. The writ did not empower courts to order the mother to return children to the husband's custody.[295] Moreover, some states did not regard a mother's retention of children separately from her husband to be unlawful, so a father's writ of habeas corpus would be dismissed because there was no legal basis for it.[296]

Habeas corpus principles worked to the disadvantage of married women who separated from their spouses without justification. In the absence of a showing of a need to protect a child from harm a court lacked a substantive legal basis for determining the father's custody of the child to be unlawful. Parents have a natural right to the custody of their children. If a divorce or a legal separation proceeding were commenced, then a court might have a substantive legal basis for awarding custody to either the mother or the father, but in the absence of such a proceeding it did not, except in those cases where a wife or a child could be shown to be in need of protection from physical or moral harm; where the father was unable to

---

[293] *See, e.g., In re* Wollstonecraft, 4 Johns. Ch. 80 (N.Y. Ch. 1819) (awarding custody of thirteen-year-old daughter to mother, on father's writ of habeas corpus, on the basis that she had expressed a preference to remain with her mother.)

[294] *See, e.g., In re* Barry, 42 F. 113 (C.C.S.D.N.Y. 1844); State v. Paine, 23 Tenn. (4 Hum.) 523 (1843)

[295] *In re* Waldron, 13 Johns. 418, 420-21 (N.Y. 1816); Commonwealth v. Addicks, 5 Binn. 520 (Pa. 1813); *In re* Kottman, 2 Hill 363 (S.C. 1834) (refusing to order mother to return custody of child to father because "the only object of the writ of *habeas corpus* is to set at large those who are illegally restrained of their liberty....")

[296] *Id.* at 421 (denying writ to the father on the basis that the mother's possession of the children was not unlawful.)

support his wife and children financially; or where some other basis for blaming the husband for the wife's separation from him existed.[297]

Courts in different states came to different conclusions about the application of these principles in the case of children of tender years. Unlike the courts in England, most American courts ignored the coverture doctrine and the rules relating to writs of habeas corpus whenever they wished to keep young children together with their mothers.[298] These courts would dismiss a father's writ of habeas corpus even if the mother's separation from her husband was unjustified.[299] On the other hand, a few courts would deny a mother's writ, or would order the return of children to the father's home, if the court determined the mother was an unfit parent, or if the wife was clearly at fault for the separation and the husband was without fault.

---

[297] Commonwealth v. Briggs, 33 Mass. (16 Pick.) 203, 204-05 (1834); Magee v. Holland, 27 N.J.L. 86, 99 (1858); People *ex rel.* Olmstead v. Olmstead, 27 Barb. 9, 31 (N.Y. 1857) (holding that unless grounds for a divorce or legal separation exist, a court of equity may interfere with a father's custody of his children "only when he has been at fault in bringing about the separation"); People *ex rel.* Ordonaux v. Chegarey, 18 Wend. 637 (N.Y. 1836) (denying mother's writ of habeas corpus for custody of children whom her husband had enrolled in a boarding school, because a parent's enrollment of his children in a boarding school is not unlawful); *Ex parte* Hewitt, 11 Rich. 326 (S.C. 1858) (denying custody to wife who separated from her husband without justification and sought custody by means of a writ of habeas corpus, where there was no showing that the husband was immoral, cruel or unable to provide for his family financially.) If a legal separation proceeding was commenced, and no cause for the separation was found to exist, then the proceeding would be dismissed, with no award of custody to either party. Collins v. Collins, 2 Paige Ch. 9 (N.Y. Ch. 1829)

[298] *See, e.g.,* State v. Stigall, 22 N.J.L. 286 (1849); Commonwealth v. Addicks, 5 Binn. 520 (Pa. 1813); Prather v. Prather, 4 Des. 32 (S.C. 1809)

[299] *See, e.g.,* Commonwealth v. Addicks, 5 Binn. 520 (Pa. 1813) (refusing to order ten- and seven-year-old daughters into the custody of the father, although the cause of the separation was the wife's decision to move in with a man with whom she was having an adulterous relationship); *see also In re* Barry, 42 F. 113 (C.C.S.D.N.Y. 1844) (applying New York law, which the court found to be to the effect that fathers have no superior right to custody in the context of a habeas corpus proceeding in which the mother has separated from the father without justification and taken the children with her); McKim v. McKim, 12 R.I. 462 (1879) (holding that even if the father is a fit parent and the mother is at fault for the separation, a court must award custody of children of tender years, including young children, female children and unhealthy children, to the mother.)

It has never been dreamed that, when the mother has been at fault in the occurrences preceding the separation, she should be rewarded for her faults by the interposition of the court. If she breaks up the household, and departs from her husband's house, wrongfully ... she is not to be allowed to take with her the children of the union. [Any other rule would work to] the punishment of the innocent, and the solace of the guilty.[300]

A court might also deny the writ if it believed a reconciliation of the couple was still feasible.[301]

---

[300] People *ex rel.* Olmstead v. Olmstead, 27 Barb. 9, 31-32 (N.Y. 1857); *see also* People *ex rel.* Rhoades v. Humphreys, 24 Barb. 521 (N.Y. 1857) (reversing lower court's award of custody to wife, and holding husband is entitled to custody, on a writ of habeas corpus, where wife was violent, abusive and solely at fault for the separation, and husband was willing to take her back); *Ex parte* Hewitt, 11 Rich. 326 (S.C. 1858) (denying custody of seven-month-old child to wife who separated from her husband without justification and sought custody by means of a writ of habeas corpus, where there was no showing that the husband was immoral, cruel or unable to provide for his family financially); *but cf.* Commonwealth v. Addicks, 5 Binn. 520 (Pa. 1813) (dismissing husband's writ of habeas corpus despite wife's adulterous cohabitation with her paramour and the absence of any evidence of wrongdoing on the husband's part.)

[301] *See, e.g.,* Tarkington v. State, 1 Ind. 170, 172 (1848); People *ex rel.* Rhoades v. Humphrey, 24 Barb. 521 (N.Y. 1857)

16. 19th CENTURY CUSTODY STANDARDS

The best interests of the child

Early American courts decided the custody of children between divorcing and separating parents based on what they believed would serve the best interests of the child. In deciding what was in a child's best interests, they applied a general preference for the spouse who was not at fault for the breakdown of the marriage. In general, most courts did not apply a generalized preference for members of one sex relative to the other except in cases involving young children, as to whom most judges expressed a preference for maternal custody.[302]

The notion that early American law gave fathers something like an absolute property right to custody regardless of what was in the best interests of children has been repeated countless times in treatises, law review articles, and judicial opinions.[303] It seems almost heretical to point

---

[302] *See, e.g., In re* Waldron's Case, 13 Johns. 418 (N.Y. 1816) (awarding custody to a deceased mother's grandparent who possessed greater wealth than the father, on the basis that "[i]t is the benefit and welfare of the infant, to which the attention of the Court ought primarily to be directed.")

[303] *See, e.g.,* Hild v. Hild, 157 A.2d 442, 446 (Md. Ct. App. 1960) (asserting that "[a]t

out that it is not true. The idea may be attributable, in some part, to a

common law the father was generally entitled to the custody of his minor children, but ... modern courts invariably hold that the best interest and welfare of the child should be primarily considered in making an award of custody"); Stubblefield v. State, 106 S.W.2d 558, 560 (Tenn. 1937) (asserting that at common law fathers had "exclusive and legal right" to custody, even as against the mother of the child); WEST'S ENCYCLOPEDIA OF AMERICAN LAW (Jeffrey Lehmann and Shirelle Phelps eds., 2005) ("Before the late 1800s fathers had sole rights to custody"); *see also* AMERICAN BAR ASSOCIATION, GUIDE TO MARRIAGE, DIVORCE, & FAMILIES 172 (2006) ("From the early history of our country until the mid-1800's, fathers were favored for custody in the event of divorce. If a husband and wife divorced, the man usually received the property.... Since children were viewed as similar to property, he also received custody of the children"); DAVID BLANKENHORN, FATHERLESS AMERICA: CONFRONTING OUR MOST URGENT SOCIAL PROBLEM (1995) ("[I]t was established practice to award the custody of children to fathers"); DEBORAH L. FORMAN, EVERY PARENT'S GUIDE TO THE LAW 187 (1998) ("[U]ntil the beginning of the twentieth century, fathers had a nearly absolute right to retain custody of children after a divorce"); D. Beschle, *God Bless the Child: The Use of Religion as a Factor in Child Custody and Adoption Proceedings* 58 FORDHAM L, REV. 383 (1989) ("At common law, the father's rights as head of the household included recognition as the natural guardian of his child...[a woman was regarded] as the equivalent of an infant"); H. Hastings, *Custodial Rights in New Hampshire: History and Current Law*, 40 N.H. BAR J. (December 1999) ("No one disputes that mothers had no parental rights"); Joan B. Kelly, *The Determination of Child Custody in the USA*, 4 FUTURE OF CHILDREN 121-42 (Spring 1994) ("In divorce, until the mid-nineteenth century, fathers had a near absolute right to custody, regardless of circumstances"); Cynthia McNeely, *Lagging Behind the Times: Parenthood, Custody, and Gender Bias in the Family Court*, 25 FLA. ST. U. L. REV. 891, 897 (1998) ("The patriarchal American society mirrored the English practice of designating the father as the natural protector of children...thus, in the rare divorce case, fathers were awarded custody of children"); William C. Smith, *Dads Want Their Day: Fathers Charge Legal Bias Toward Moms Hamstrings Them as Full-Time Parents*, 89 A.B.A. J. 38 (February 2003) ("Through most of Anglo-American legal history, there was little custody litigation because there was nothing to fight over. Dad always got the kids. Under English and early American common law, children were regarded as paternal property"); G. CENGAGE, ENCYCLOPEDIA OF EVERYDAY LAW (2003), (retrieved on May 11, 2012), www.enotes.com/family-law-reference/child-support-custody ("Historically, fathers had sole rights to custody....[M]others had no such rights [until] the late nineteenth century"); J. WILDER, AMERICAN ACADEMY OF MATRIMONIAL LAWYERS, SOME CURRENT TRENDS IN CHILD CUSTODY LITIGATION IN THE UNITED STATES (retrieved on May 11, 2012), www.aaml.org/sites/default/files/some%20current%20trends%20in%20child-article.pdf ("At common law the father had an absolute right to custody of his children"); Jean Sternlight, A Brief History of Family Law in Florida and the United States: Insights Regarding an Attempt to Simplify Divorce Procedures 60 (1995), on file with C. McNeely, *quoted in* McNeely, *supra* at 896 (1998) (asserting that Americans imported English laws and practices giving fathers an "absolute right to

mistaken belief that American courts adopted and continued to apply English custody law.[304] Pertinacious as this idea may be, it is not true. As we have seen, American courts did not consider themselves constrained to follow English legal precedents, particularly with respect to child custody law. Nineteenth century American courts never regarded children as the property of their fathers.[305] And many courts expressly rejected the English rule that fathers have a paramount right to custody in disputes between parents.

Referring to the English rule that fathers have a superior right to custody, the South Carolina Supreme Court remarked, "It is a matter of congratulation that but little weight has been given to this class of cases by American Judges…. In this state we are committed to no such extreme doctrine…." And in 1849, the Illinois Supreme Court, referring to *De Manneville* and other English decisions giving fathers superior rights to custody, observed that an American "court of chancery has never been disgraced by such a decision." In an even earlier case, a Pennsylvania court, in rejecting a claim that fathers have a superior right to custody, observed that the claim is not supported by any case precedents, and that courts have "repeatedly denied" fathers' claims to custody and have "repeatedly …

---

custody"); *but cf.* 4 CHESTER G. VERNIER, AMERICAN FAMILY LAWS 17 (1936) ("This harsh English view [that fathers have the right to custody without regard to mothers' rights], later modified by statutes and decisions in Chancery, never prevailed in America.")

[304] *See, e.g.,* Thomas J. Walsh, *In the Interest of a Child: A Comparative Look at the Treatment of Children Under Wisconsin and Minnesota Custody Statutes*, 85 MARQ. L. REV. 929, 932 (2002) (asserting that a "common law preference for the father, adopted from England, continued in the United States until the late nineteenth or early twentieth century.")

[305] *See, e.g.,* Chapsky v. Wood, 26 Kan. 650, 652-53 (1881) ("a child is not in any sense like a horse or any other chattel…. [A] parent's right to the custody of a child is not like the right of property…."); Bennet v. Bennet, 13 N.J. Eq. (2 Beasl.) 114, 118 (1860) (holding that a statute requiring courts to award custody of young children to mothers only does not violate the Due Process Clause of the Fourteenth Amendment because children are not property); Thompson v. Thompson, 72 N.C. 32 (1875) (awarding custody to the mother and holding that a father may not give a third party custody of a child by contract); State v. Paine, 23 Tenn. (4 Hum.) 523, 533-35 (1843) (observing that while "uncivilized people" treated women and children as property of the father, civilized people treat women as having equal rights and give primary consideration to children's interests, not parents' rights, when deciding custody.)

supported" mothers' claims to custody.[306] Early nineteenth century American custody law differed considerably from early nineteenth century English custody law.

In 1840, a New York appellate court, referring to English custody law as it had been articulated in the *De Manneville* decision, observed that "this state has never been disgraced by laws so subversive of the welfare of infant children, of the rights of mothers, and of the morals of the people." The court then proceeded to award custody of the child to the mother, on the basis that "the mother is the most proper person to be entrusted with the custody of a child...." Concurring in the opinion, Justice Green C. Bronson noted, "we have never followed, and never intended to follow the [*De Manneville*] decision...."[307]

---

[306] *Ex parte* Schumpert, 6 Rich. 344, 347 (S.C. 1853); Miner v. Miner, 11 Ill. 43, 50 (1849); Commonwealth *ex rel.* d'Hauteville v. Sears 288 (Phila., Pa. Ct. of General Sessions 1840); *see also In re* Barry, 42 F. 113 (C.C.S.D.N.Y. 1844) (holding that "the judgment and discretion of the court is not to be controlled by any supposed legal right of the father in exclusion of the mother...."); Cole v. Cole, 23 Iowa 433, 447 (1867) (observing that American judicial decisions have tended to deny the father's presumptive right to custody, resting instead on a consideration of the child's best interests); Ahrenfeldt v. Ahrenfeldt, 1 Hoff. Ch. 497 (N.Y. Ch. 1840) (awarding custody to mother on the basis of the best interests of the child, in view of father's lack of financial wealth); Barrere v. Barrere, 4 Johns. Ch. 187 (N.Y. Ch. 1819) (awarding custody to the wife on the grounds that husband's cruelty to wife was presumed to be a bad influence on the children); Codd v. Codd, 2 Johns. Ch. 141 (N.Y. Ch. 1816); State v. Paine, 23 Tenn. (4 Hum.) 523, 535 (1843) (saying of the notion that fathers have a paramount right to custody, "if it were so, it is no longer.... [T]he court is not bound ... to deliver the child to the father....") Ironically, even though the court in *State v. Paine* specifically rejected that idea that fathers have a superior right to custody, and custody of a child was awarded to the mother, the case is cited in later decisions as authority for the proposition that the common law gave fathers an absolute right to the custody of their children. *See, e.g.*, Stubblefield v. State, 106 S.W.2d 558 (Tenn. 1937). 2 BISHOP § 529, *supra* note 146 (father's right to custody "is not an absolute one; and it is usually made to yield when the good of the child ... requires it should yield.")

[307] Mercein v. People *ex rel.* Barry, 25 Wend. 64, 105-06 (N.Y. 1840) (Bronson, J., concurring.) Iowa is an example of a state that followed the minority rule. In Hunt v. Hunt, 4 Greene 216, 219 (Iowa 1854), the Iowa Supreme Court declared that "[t]he law of England ... is in force here..." and that because the father has the exclusive duty to support children he has a right to custody of them. The court cited *De Manneville* as authority for its decision.

A few courts adopted the minority rule that a father should be entitled to the custody of his children because he alone was responsible for their support. These courts stated that this was what they believed to be the rule under English common law, and they said they therefore felt compelled to adopt it. Of course, this was not correct. States that adopted the common law of England as it existed prior to the American Revolution would not have been adopting a system of laws that gave fathers custody of children irrespective of what was in the children's best interests. In *Blisset's Case*,[308] an English case decided in 1774 just prior to the American Revolution, Lord Mansfield had refused to grant custody to the father. The father in that case was a bankrupt who had not provided proper care for his child. Mansfield explained that "the public right to superintend the education of its citizens necessitated doing what appeared best for the child, notwithstanding the father's natural right."[309] What Mansfield was saying was that the court's determination of what was in a child's best interests took precedence over fathers' rights. An American state that adopted English common law as it existed prior to the American Revolution, then, would not have adopted a father's rights approach. Rather, it would have adopted the "best interests of the child" standard articulated by Lord Mansfield in *Blisset's Case*.

Reviewing American custody decisions from the time of the Revolution to 1830, when New York enacted a "tender years" statute, a United States Circuit Court concluded that it had always been the law in America, even prior to that enactment, that "the judgment and discretion of the court is not to be controlled by any supposed legal right of the father in exclusion of that of the mother...." The court described this as being "substantially in consonance with the decisions in England antecedent to the Revolution." And it was consistent with New York state court decisions, too. The court summarized the relationship between English and American custody law as follows:

---

[308] Lofft 748, 98 Eng. Rep. 899 (K.B. 1774)

[309] *Id.*; *see also* Rex v. Delavel, 3 Burr. 1434, 97 Eng. Rep. 913 (K.B. 1763) (denying custody to father); Rex v. Smith, 2 Strange 982, 93 Eng. Rep. 983 (1735) (denying father's claim of a right to custody, and allowing aunt to retain custody, on the grounds that it was in the child's best interests to allow the child to choose whether to reside with his father or with his aunt, and he had chosen his aunt.)

[It has always been] the established law of this country that the court, or officer, were authorized to exercise a discretion, and that the father was not entitled to demand a delivery of the child to him, upon a habeas corpus, as an absolute right. This was also the law of England at the time of our separation from the mother country; though ... the decisions of the English courts since that period, appeared to have gone back to the principles of a semi-barbarous age.... [310]

The outcomes of custody cases varied from state to state, depending at least in part on the extent to which a particular court felt bound by English precedents, and the extent to which a particular judge possessed an adequate understanding of English common law as it existed prior to the American Revolution. Despite these variations, it is possible to identify at least one general principle upon which most courts agreed: neither parent had anything like a property right to children. Instead, courts awarded custody to either the mother or the father on the basis of a determination of what was in a child's best interests.[311] An unfit parent could be awarded

---

[310] *In re* Barry, 42 F. 113, 117, 34 L. Ed. 503 (U.S. 1844). Mercein v. People *ex rel.* Barry, 25 Wend. 64, 92 (N.Y. 1840). To similar effect, see McKim v. McKim, 12 R.I. 462, 464 (1879) ("In this country, the earlier English doctrine [referring to the "best interests" standard enunciated in *Blisset's Case*, *supra*] has generally been adopted.")

[311] *See, e.g., In re* Waldron, 13 Johns. 418, 421 (N.Y. 1816) (denying father custody, and placing children in custody of maternal grandparent instead because "[i]t is to the benefit and welfare of the infant, to which the attention of the court ought principally to be directed..."); Commonwealth v. Addicks, 5 Binn. 520 (Pa. 1813) (disapproving mother's adultery but awarding custody to her anyway, because "[i]t is to *them* [the children] that our anxiety is principally directed"); Threewits v. Threewits, 4 Des. 560 (S.C. 1815) (awarding custody to the mother); *see also* Miner v. Miner, 11 Ill. 43, 49 (1849) (awarding custody to the mother on the basis that parental rights "are subject to the control of the courts of chancery, and ... the best interests of the child must be primarily consulted"); Cowls v. Cowls, 3 Ill. (Gilm.) 435, 440-41 (1846) (affirming an award of custody to the mother on the basis that parental rights do not govern custody decisions and that "the best interests of the child must be consulted"); McBride v. McBride, 64 Ky. (1 Bush) 15, 16 (1866) (affirming custody to mother on the basis that consideration of all the facts and circumstances made maternal custody "appear most beneficial to the child"); Commonwealth v. Briggs, 33 Mass. (16 Pick.) 203 (1834) (holding that "the good of the child," not the father's rights, is "the predominant consideration"); State v. Stigall, 22 N.J.L. 286 (1849) (awarding custody of one child to mother and one to father on the basis of a determination that it was in their best interests); *Ex parte*

property in a divorce, but placement of children in the custody of an unfit parent was considered contrary to children's best interests, so an unfit parent would not be awarded custody.

In contests between fit parents, early American courts applied two rules: First, mothers had an exclusive right to custody of children born to them out of wedlock. Second, custody of the children of married parents was based on the individual judge's assessment of what was in the child's best interests. Guiding that assessment was an assumption that maternal sole custody was in the best interests of children of tender years, i.e., young sons, children of any age who were in poor health, and, in some states, daughters of any age. For older children, courts generally regarded the child's preference as controlling. In some states, paternal custody was assumed to be in the best interests of an older, healthy male child of married parents, provided he had not expressed a preference to reside with the mother.

Moral virtue and marital fault

Parental fitness was defined largely in terms of moral character. Poor moral character, in turn, could be inferred from conduct creating grounds for the divorce (e.g., adultery, habitual drunkenness, cruelty to wife) with the result that custody normally would be awarded to the innocent party in a divorce.

The rule that children would not be placed in the custody of an unfit parent also applied in situations where a court, though not granting a divorce, was called upon to decide custody (such as a writ of habeas corpus brought to test the custody of young children of separated parents, in those states where courts permitted the writ to be used in that way.) In those situations, courts looked for other indicia of unfitness (e.g., desertion, unlawful cohabitation, cruelty, child abuse, etc.)

Schumpert, 6 Rich. 344 (S.C. 1853) (holding award of custody to mother was in child's best interests); 2 BISHOP § 532, *supra* note 146 ("The courts have not laid down exact rules to guide their discretion.... The leading doctrine is to consult the good of the child rather than the gratification of the parents.")

Marital misconduct

As we have seen, most early American courts regarded the child's welfare, not fathers' rights, as the paramount consideration in custody cases. That is to say, they decided custody on the basis of what they believed was in the best interest of the child. Opinions about what was in children's best interests, however, were very different from those that prevail today.

Early American courts ascribed the greatest importance to a parent's moral character. In fact, judicial decisions from the period treated moral and religious fitness as the chief qualifications for parenthood. Extramarital sex, i.e., adultery, was regarded as a serious moral failing.[312] It not only furnished grounds for a divorce, but it also justified a conclusion that the offending spouse was not morally fit to parent. The result was that in a divorce, custody of children normally would be awarded to the innocent spouse, who presumably would be better qualified to instill proper morals in a child than the immoral parent would be.[313] This is why one of the very first recorded child custody decisions in the United States was an award of custody to a mother on the grounds of the father's commission of adultery.[314]

In states that recognized additional grounds for divorce or legal separation, such as desertion or a husband's extreme cruelty to his wife, those other grounds typically were equated with parental unfitness, too. Thus, a woman who obtained a divorce or separation because of her husband's cruelty toward her would be awarded custody of the children for that reason.[315] Likewise, in a state in which habitual drunkenness was

---

[312] *See, e.g.,* Commonwealth v. Addicks, 2 Serg. & Rawl. 174 (Pa. 1815) (describing a spouse's disbelief in the obligations of the marriage contract, as evidenced by the commission of adultery, as "a fundamental point of morals.")

[313] *See, e.g.,* Jeans v. Jeans, 2 Harr. 142 (Del. 1836); Kremelberg v. Kremelberg, 52 Md. 553 (Md. 1879); Holden v. Holden, 7 Wis. 256 (1858)

[314] Prather v. Prather, 4 Desau. 33 (S.C. 1809)

[315] Barrere v. Barrere, Johns. Ch. 187 (N.Y. Ch. 1819); Codd v. Codd, 2 Johns. Ch. 141 (N.Y. 1916); *see also* Becker v. Becker, 79 Ill. 532 (1875); Horning v. Horning, 65 N.W. 555 (Mich. 1895); Johns v. Johns, 57 Miss. 530 (1879); People v. Mercein, 8 Paige Ch. 47 (N.Y. Ch. 1839); Myers v. Myers, 6 S.E. 630 (Va. 1887). In many states, statutes offered women more grounds for divorce and separation than men were given. For example, statutes commonly made "cruelty to wife" grounds for a divorce or separation, but "cruelty to husband" was not. *See, e.g.,* MINN. GEN. STAT. ch. 62, §§ 30, 31 (1878) (superseded by MINN. STAT. § 518.06 (2012).)

recognized as grounds for divorce, it was also grounds for a denial of custody.[316] And in a state in which desertion was grounds for divorce, a spouse's unjustified desertion of the family furnished not only the grounds for a divorce, but also for denying him or her custody of the children.[317]

In short, the general rule of law that prevailed in many states in the nineteenth century was that custody of children should be awarded to the party not at fault for the breakdown of the marriage.[318] Generally, if the wife was at fault for the divorce or separation, then the husband was awarded custody of the children; if the husband was at fault, then the wife got custody.[319]

---

[316] *See, e.g.*, Brandon v. Brandon, 14 Kan. 342 (1875)

[317] *See, e.g.*, Bermudez v. Bermudez, 2 Mart. (O.S.) 180 (La. 1812); Commonwealth v. Briggs, 33 Mass. (16 Pick.) 203 (1834); People *ex rel.* Barry v. Mercein, 3 Hill. 399 (N.Y. Sup. Ct. 1842); Ahrenfeldt v. Ahrenfeldt, 4 Sand. Ch. 493 (N.Y. Ch. 1847); People *ex rel.* Brooks v. Brooks, 35 Barb. 85, 90-95 (N.Y. App. Div. 1861) (holding that a statute giving husbands and wives equal custody rights does not alter rule that spouse who unjustifiably left the family home normally was not entitled to custody of the children); People v. Humphreys, 24 Barb. 521 (N.Y. App. Div. 1857); Carr v. Carr, 22 Gratt. 168 (Va. 1872). Grounds for divorce varied from state to state. New Hampshire's first divorce statute, for example, gave married persons the right to obtain divorces on the grounds of adultery, incest, bigamy, abandonment for at least three years, or extreme cruelty. Laws of New Hampshire c. 94, 732-733 (1791). Under New York's first divorce statute, enacted in 1787, adultery was the only recognized grounds for divorce. By 1813, though, a wife could obtain a legal separation from her husband on the grounds of either adultery or extreme cruelty. Laws of New York, 1787, c. 69; Laws, 1813, c. 102, 197.

[318] Becker v. Becker, 79 Ill. 532 (1875); J.F.C. v. M.E., 6 Rob. 135 (La. 1843); Lambert v. Lambert, 19 P. 459 (Or. 1888). Rather than deciding on the basis of gender, early American courts generally decided custody cases on the basis of marital fault, with the innocent party being the one presumptively entitled to sole custody of the couple's children. *Id.* at 520 ("The children will be best taken care of and instructed by the innocent party"); *see generally* J. BISHOP, COMMENTARIES ON THE LAW OF MARRIAGE AND DIVORCE 518, 520 (Boston: Little, Brown & Co. 1852) ("The children will be best taken care of and instructed by the innocent party"); *cf. In re* Laplain, 8 So. 615 (La. 1890) (holding that custody normally should be granted to the innocent spouse, meaning that the one who obtains the divorce normally will also receive custody of the children, unless doing so would be contrary to the child's best interests.)

[319] *See, e.g.*, Hansford v. Hansford, 10 Ala. 561 (1846); State *ex rel.* Lynch v. Bratton, 15 Am. L. Reg. 359 (Del. 1876); Wilkinson v. Deming, 80 Ill. 342 (1875); Cole v. Cole, 23 Iowa 433 (1867); Small v. Small, 45 N.W. 248 (Neb. 1890); Waring v. Waring, 3 N.E. 289 (N.Y. 1885); Codd v. Codd, 2 Jons. Ch. 141 (N.Y. Ch. 1816); People v. Brooks, 35 Barb. 85 (N.Y. App. Div. 1861); People *ex rel.* Olmstead v.

Again, this was not a different standard from the "best interests of the child" test. It was an application of it during a time when a different set of moral values prevailed. It proceeded on the twin premises that (1) it is in a child's best interest to be raised by a parent who sets a good moral example;[320] and (2) the kinds of acts that justify a divorce (such as adultery, habitual drunkenness, desertion or cruelty to wife) are evidence of gross immorality. As such, they demonstrate a parent's lack of moral character. The thinking was that "if a father wrongs his wife, it is readily presumed that he will wrong his children likewise."[321]

Olmstead, 27 Barb. 9 (N.Y. App. Div. 1857); Uhlmann v. Uhlmann, 17 Abb. N. Cas. 236 (N.Y. 1885); Crimmins v. Crimmins, 64 How. Pr. 103 (N.Y. 1882); State v. Nishwitz, 1 Ohio Dec. Reprint 370 (1850) (granting custody to wife if she has "reasonable excuse" for living separately from husband); Jackson v. Jackson, 8 Or. 402 (1880); Commonwealth v. Addicks, 2 Serg. & Rawl. 174 (Pa. 1815); Prather v. Prather, 4 S.C. Eq. (4 Des.) 33 (S.C. 1809) (granting custody to wife if husband "drove" wife from home.) The concept of deciding custody and support issues on the basis of fault was sometimes incorporated into statutory provisions. *See, e.g.,* N.H. REV. STAT. § 148:12 (1842) (repealed) (authorizing courts to "[m]ake such further decree in relation to the ... custody ... of the children as shall be most conducive to their benefit, and...order a reasonable provision for their support to be made by or out of the estate of the guilty party.")

[320] *See, e.g.,* People *ex rel.* Olmstead v. Olmstead, 27 Barb. 9, 32 (N.Y. App. Div. 1857) (observing that the same result is reached whether a court applies a marital fault standard or a "best interests" test, because a parent who is guilty of marital misconduct is a bad influence on a child's morals); Commonwealth v. Addicks, 2 Serg. & Rawl. 174, 177 (Pa. 1815) (holding that custody of older children should not be awarded to the spouse whose marital misconduct was the cause of the breakdown of the marriage because the children would then conclude that such conduct is approved)

[321] SCHOULER, *supra* note 55 at 363; *see also* Cole v. Cole, 23 Iowa 433, 447 (1867) (awarding custody to the wife, where the husband had been guilty of inhumane treatment of the wife, holding that "a husband false to his marital vows will probably prove an unfit guardian for his children"); Latham v. Latham, 71 (30 Gratt.) 307, 333 (1878) ("court will enquire who is most to blame for the separation, giving the preference to the innocent party, because with such a party the infant is most likely to be cared for properly"); 2 BISHOP § 532, *supra* note 146 ("One who has conducted himself well or ill in a particular domestic relation, will conduct the same in another; and so, as a general practice, the courts give the custody to the innocent party; because with such party, the children will be more likely to be cared for properly."); *see also* People *ex rel.* Olmstead v. Olmstead, 27 Barb. 9, 32, 34 (N.Y. 1857) (observing that any other rule would work to "the punishment of the innocent, and the solace of the guilty" and that "public policy requires that the party sinned against shall not bear all the punishment....")

On the other hand, courts sometimes seemed to deny custody to the party at fault not so much out of a concern for the welfare of a child as from a desire to punish a man for his failings. Thus, in *Ahrenfeldt v. Ahrenfeldt*,[322] the court denied a father custody of his child on the basis of his nonsupport of his wife and child, opining that because "the present unhappy situation of the family, is the fault of the husband" it was "therefore, not an undue punishment to him, that his fault should deprive him of the custody of his daughter; while it would be cruel to the unoffending wife, to add to her misfortune, the deprivation of the society of her only child."

The 1834 Massachusetts case of *Commonwealth v. Briggs*[323] made another kind of connection between marital fault and the "best interests of the child" standard. There, the father won custody of the child because the court determined that the mother had unjustifiably deserted the family. The father was found to have been innocent of any wrongdoing. Rather than invoking English paternal custody precedents or the doctrine of coverture, the court instead insisted "the good of the child is to be regarded as the predominant consideration."[324] The court reasoned that it was in children's best interests for their parents to remain together; accordingly, a spouse who unjustifiably broke up the family was acting contrary to the best interests of their children, and for that reason should not be entrusted with their custody.

The rule was not an inflexible one. In its discretion, a court could award custody of a child to the guilty spouse if an award to the innocent spouse was thought to be "manifestly improper."[325] The custody of children of tender years was a situation in which an award of custody to anyone but the mother was regarded as "manifestly improper."[326] There

---

[322] 4 Sand. Ch. 493, 494-95 (N.Y. Ch. 1847)

[323] 33 Mass. (16 Pick.) 203, 205 (1834).

[324] *Id.*

[325] *See* Campbell v. Campbell, 37 Wis. 206, 210 (1875) (pointing out that a custody decision "may be influenced" by the cause of the divorce, "but it is not dependent on the right of divorce.")

[326] *See, e.g.*, Commonwealth v. Addicks, 5 Binn. 520 (Pa. 1813) (awarding custody of 10- and 7-year-old daughters to adulterous mother); *see also* Brandon v. Brandon, 14 Kan. 264 (1875) (awarding custody of 3- and 1-year-old children to the wife on the basis that children "need a mother's care," notwithstanding the fact that a divorce

were others – e.g., situations in which the innocent parent was incarcerated, or had used vulgarities in mixed company, etc.

The rule against awarding custody to the party guilty of marital misconduct applied to both husbands and wives. While cases can be found in which a court applied it very strictly against a mother, as a general matter courts tended to apply it at least as strictly against fathers. For example, as early as 1813 a mother was granted custody of children notwithstanding her commission of adultery.[327] Yet in 1890, courts were still regularly denying custody to fathers on the grounds of their commission of adultery or other marital fault.[328] Accordingly, it is not accurate to say, as some have, that marital fault ceased to be a bar to an award of custody sometime near the end of the nineteenth century. It is more accurate to say that by the end of the nineteenth century, marital misconduct was not often considered a valid reason to deny custody of a child to a mother, especially in cases involving children of tender years, but it was still considered a proper basis for denying a father custody of his children.

Paternal misconduct

While early American courts sometimes stated the English common law rule that fathers have a paramount right to the custody of their children (most likely because fathers' attorneys hoped that citing these cases might persuade judges to award custody to their clients), they most often applied that doctrine to the benefit of a father when the contest was between a father and a third party; it was not applied by too many courts in custody disputes between parents.[329] According to treatise writers from the period,

---

was granted to the husband on the basis of her habitual drunkenness.)

[327] Commonwealth v. Addicks, 5 Binn. 520 (Pa. 1813).

[328] *Compare* Small v. Small, 45 N.W. 248, 249 (Neb. 1890) (denying custody to the father on the basis that he alone had engaged in marital misconduct furnishing grounds for the divorce) *and* Umlauf v. Umlauf, 21 N.E. 600 (Ill. 1889) (awarding custody to the mother despite the fact that she alone had engaged in marital misconduct furnishing grounds for the divorce.) A spouse's commission of adultery was not necessarily a permanent bar to custody if all other things were equal and there was persuasive evidence of remorse and reform on the part of the adulterous spouse. 2 BISHOP § 533, *supra* note 146.

[329] *See, e.g.*, Ross v. Pick, 86 A.2d 463 (Md. 1852). Even as against nonparents, though, a father's right to custody was not always superior. *Ross v. Pick*, for example, recited the common law "paramount right of fathers" but proceeded to

the laws of every jurisdiction in the United States have always authorized awards of child custody to either mothers or fathers, the best interests of the child being the paramount consideration.[330] As we have seen, courts were awarding custody to mothers in some of the earliest reported custody decisions in the United States.

One reason for this is that in child custody cases, the court sat as a court of equity, applying principles that had been developed over the centuries by courts of chancery. One of those principles was that the paramount consideration in a child custody case was how the court, in its role as *parens patriae*, could best protect the interests of children. In America, the English common law right of a father to custody was not regarded as a limitation on the power of a court of equity to award custody to the mother -- or even to a third party -- if doing so served the child's best interests. "There are no bounds to the interference of the Court of Chancery with the rights of the father to the custody of his children whenever … his natural rights to the custody of them clash with their true interests."[331]

When attorneys for fathers cited the English paternal custody cases to them, American judges either refused to accept those cases as binding precedent, or they created or expanded exceptions to the rule.[332] If the mother was clearly at fault (e.g., in cases where she had committed adultery and had deserted the family home without justification, and the father was not guilty of any wrongdoing), then a court might cite the paternal custody rule in support of its decision to grant the father custody.[333] But if the father was at fault, then the court would reject the rule outright, apply an

---

award custody of a child to nonparents in preference to the father, on the basis of the court's conclusion that the child's best interests would be served by being placed in the custody of the nonparents rather than the father.

[330] *See, e.g.*, BISHOP, *supra* note 318 at 520.

[331] C.G. ADDISON, A TREATISE ON THE LAW OF TORTS (New York: James Cockcroft, 1876)

[332] *See, e.g.*, Prather v. Prather, 4 S.C. Eq. (4 Des.) 33 (1809), in which a judge refused to give a father custody of his children, preferring the mother instead. The judge observed that he was aware that the court was "treading on new … grounds," but "fe[lt] a consolation in the reflection that if it errs, there is a tribunal wherein the error can be redressed."

[333] HARTOG, *supra* note 1 at 212; *see* People *ex rel.* Olmstead v. Olmstead and Randell, 27 Barb. 9 (N.Y. App. Div. 1857); People *ex rel.* Sinclair v. Sinclair, 95 N.Y.S. 861 (Sup. Ct. 1905); Latham v. Latham, 71 Va. (30 Gratt.)(307 (1878)

exception, or create a new exception to the rule in order to award custody to the mother.[334]

The principal exception was that a father forfeited whatever right to custody he might otherwise have if, through his conduct, he caused the breakdown of the marriage or the couple's separation from each other. The kinds of conduct that were regarded as causing the breakdown of a marriage were set out in a state's divorce statute as the grounds upon which a petition for divorce or separation could be brought. Adultery was the most common one. Most states also recognized other grounds, too, principally desertion, habitual drunkenness, cruelty to wife, and nonsupport of wife.

The concept of fault, for child custody purposes, was extended very early in America's history to encompass many other kinds of misconduct on the part of the father. A father's right to custody, it was said, could be forfeited not only by marital misconduct, but also by any kind of conduct that might reflect adversely on his moral character.[335] Judicial interpretations were broad enough to reach conduct affecting the interests of the child even if the conduct in question was not responsible for the breakdown of the marriage or the couple's separation. For example, a father could lose custody of his children if he was guilty of blasphemy or "low and gross debauchery," or "atheistical or irreligious principles" or if he associated with people who tended to the "corruption and contamination"

---

[334] "In no case do I find this legal right of the father ... where a divorce has been granted for his fault or misconduct," Miner v. Miner, 11 Ill. 43, 50 (1843)

[335] HARTOG, *supra* note 1; *see, e.g.,* Cowls v. Cowls, 3 Ill. (Gil.) 435 (1846) (citing the father's cohabitation with a woman as a basis for an award of custody to the mother, even though the cohabitation began subsequent to the divorce and it was not the grounds for the divorce); Tarkington v. State, 1 Ind. 171 (1848); People v. Chegaray, 18 Wend. 637 (N.Y. 1836). In Codd v. Codd, 2 Johns. Ch. 141 (N.Y. Ch. 1816), the court granted custody to the mother on the basis that the father had a violent personality, although neither adultery nor cruelty to wife could be proven and, therefore, there were no grounds for divorce. *See also* Pawling v. Bird's Ex'rs, 13 Johns. 192 (N.Y. Sup. Ct. 1816); *In re* Hansen, 1 Edmonds' Select Cas. 9 (N.Y. Ch. 1834); Graves v. Graves, 2 Paige Ch. 62 (N.Y. Ch. 1830); Haviland v. Myers, 6 Johns. Ch. 25, 178 (N.Y. Ch. 1822); Barrere v. Barrere, 4 Johns. Ch. 187, 188, 191, 197 (N.Y. Ch. 1819); *In re* Wollstonecraft, 4 Johns. Ch. 79 (N.Y. Ch. 1819); Bedell v. Bedell, 1 Johns. Ch. 604 (N.Y. Ch. 1815); CHARLES EDWARDS, PLEASANTRIES ABOUT COURTS AND LAWYERS OF THE STATE OF NEW YORK 108-09 (New York, Richardson & Co. 1867).

of his children.[336] "Notorious impiety," profligacy, or "keeping low company" could work a forfeiture of the father's "right," as could his use of vulgar language in mixed company or in the presence of a child.[337]

A husband's expression of doubt about the paternity of a child born to his wife during the marriage was regarded as paternal misconduct so egregious and vile as to justify stripping him of custody – apparently even if he had valid reasons for his doubts.[338]

The concept of paternal misconduct was also broad enough to reach conduct that involved no willful wrongdoing, no moral culpability. For example, the law imposed upon fathers a legal obligation to support their wives and children financially. A father who was unable to do so was deemed unfit to have the custody of children even if his inability was due entirely to circumstances beyond his control. "In those American cases which uphold to the greatest extent the right of the father, it is conceded that it may be lost by his ill usage, immoral principles or habits, or by his inability to provide for his children."[339]

A nineteenth century legal scholar observed that among those courts that had not rejected the English paternal custody rule outright, the paternal misconduct exception had been interpreted so broadly that these courts were not really applying a paternal custody rule at all:

> [In these states,] the court of chancery will interfere to disturb the paternal rights only in cases of a father's gross misconduct; such misconduct seeming, however, to be regarded with reference rather to the interests of the child than the moral delinquency of the parent. If the father has so conducted himself that it will not be for the benefit of the infants that they should be delivered to him, or if their being

---

[336] JOSEPH STORY, COMMENTARIES ON EQUITY JURISPRUDENCE AS ADMINISTERED IN ENGLAND AND AMERICA, 529-33 (2d ed., Boston, C.C. Little & J. Brown 1839).

[337] Cooke v. Hannum, 39 Miss. 423 (1860); *see also* Cowls v. Cowls, 3 Ill. (Gilm) 435, 438 (1846); ADDISON, *supra* note 331.

[338] Harding v. Harding, 22 Md. 337 (1864)

[339] Mercein v. People *ex rel.* Barry, 25 Wend. 64, 101 (N.Y. 1840). *See, e.g.,* Ahrenfeldt v. Ahrenfeldt, 1 Hoff. Ch. 497 (N.Y. Ch. 1840) (awarding custody to the mother on the basis of the father's nonsupport of his wife and child.)

with him will injuriously affect their happiness, or if they cannot associate with him without moral contamination, or if, because they associate with him, other persons will share their society, the court will award the custody to another....[O]ur courts have required no [Talfourd Act] to prevent them from taking the custody of any child from one whose parental influence, by reason of immoral character or otherwise, is found to be injurious to the child's welfare....Our divorce jurisprudence, being...quite different from that of England, further opportunity has been furnished for a departure from the common law rules which favor the paternal right of custody...[and] the child's custody may be given to either parent or a third person, generally to the innocent parent, though with due regard to the child's welfare.[340]

In one reported case, the court cited the fact that the father had made the assertion, in his petition, that as a father he had a superior right to custody of his children, as being, in itself, paternal misconduct so egregious in nature as to warrant a denial of custody to him.[341]

In many states, it was not necessary to create or expand a paternal misconduct exception, because courts specifically rejected the English precedents that had asserted a rule favoring fathers. In *Mercein v. People ex rel. Barry*,[342] for example, a New York court declared that in America "the father has no paramount right to the custody of his child."[343] These courts

---

[340] SCHOULER, *supra* note 55 at 360-64; *see also* BISHOP, *supra* note 318 at 518, 520; AUGUSTUS LLOYD, A TREATISE ON THE LAW OF DIVORCE 241 (Boston and New York, Houghton Mifflin Co. 1887). A New Jersey court summarized the rule as follows: "[W]hen the children would be exposed to cruelty or gross corruption, immoral principles or habits, or the father is not of ability to provide for the support, education, and future prospects of the children ... the court will make no order granting the custody of the child to the father." State v. Stigall, 22 N.J.L. 286, 289 (1849)

[341] People v. Mercein, 3 Hill 399, 410 (N.Y. 1842)

[342] 25 Wend. 64 (N.Y. 1840)

[343] *Id.* at 102-03; *see also* Clark v. Bayer, 32 Ohio St. 299, 305 (Ohio 1877) (holding that courts have never been restrained by either parent's "supposed absolute right to custody," and instead "will direct the custody where the best and highest interests of the infant will be sub-served"); *but cf.* People *ex rel.* Olmstead v. Olmstead, 27 Barb. 9, 13-14 (N.Y. 1857), in which the court asserted that the rule

insisted instead that the overarching consideration in custody cases was not the rights of parents, but the interests of children.[344] To most courts, it was not necessary to find the father guilty of misconduct in order to justify an award of custody to a mother.[345] Custody of children could be awarded to a mother simply because doing so was in their best interests, whether the father was guilty of any wrongdoing or not.

The best interests of the child standard, under which it was common for a court to award custody of children to a mother, appears to have been the majority rule. The paternal rights doctrine, though frequently mentioned, appears, in practice, to have been the minority rule. After acknowledging the American cases in which courts had stated the paternal preference rule, the New York Court for Correction of Errors observed: "But the great principle which runs through nearly all the American and the earlier English cases, is … that the custody of infant children must always be regulated by judicial discretion, exercised in reference to their best interests."[346]

In one of its earliest reported opinions (1816), the New York court had refused to deliver custody of a child to the father, although no misconduct on his part had been alleged. In that case, the court specifically

---

that the father has a paramount right to custody of his children "exists in this state." The court in that case articulated two exceptions to the rule: (1) paternal misconduct (immoral habits, etc.); and (2) cases where the wife has grounds for a legal separation (e.g., the husband's inability to support wife and child financially.) *Id.* at 15. The court found that neither exception applied, and that the wife was the one who was at fault for the breakdown of the marriage. Reasoning that an award of custody to the party at fault for unjustifiably breaking up the family was not in children's best interests because such a custody arrangement would be a bad influence on them, and would unfairly reward the guilty parent while punishing the innocent one, the court proceeded to award custody to the father. *Id.* at 31- 32, 34. Accordingly, although the court recited the paternal custody rule in this case, the rule the court actually applied was that custody of children should be awarded to the innocent spouse.

[344] *Id.; see also* Miner v. Miner, 11 Ill. 43 n.2 (1849) (stating that equity courts are "to move only in the interest of the infant; not to be urged by consideration of the rights of parents….")

[345] Commonwealth *ex rel.* d'Hauteville v. Sears 289-90 (Phila., Pa. Ct. of General Sessions 1840) (observing that while some cases seem to suggest that a father's right to custody is defeasible only if he is guilty of misconduct, "the bulk of the cases embraces broader grounds.")

[346] Mercein v. People *ex rel.* Barry, 25 Wend. 64, 101 (N.Y. 1840).

rejected the contention that fathers have any special right to custody, explaining that "it is a matter resting in the sound discretion of the court, and not a matter of right which the father can claim at the hands of the court."[347] In short, most courts rejected the notion of a "paramount right of fathers to custody," and those courts that did not expressly reject it honored it more in the breach than in the observance.

Parental rights; third-party custody disputes

Although most American courts rejected, or refused to apply, the doctrine that fathers have a paramount right to custody in disputes between a father and a mother, they generally did claim to adhere to a belief in the paramount rights of parents to custody of their children in contests between a parent and a non-parent.[348]

When writing their decisions in cases involving contests between parents and non-parents, it was common for judges to speak in terms of "father's rights." In *McGlennan v. Margowski*,[349] for example (a custody contest between a father and a non-parent third party) the Indiana Supreme Court declared, "Other things being equal … the father of a legitimate infant child is entitled to the possession and control of the child's person as against any other claimant."[350]

---

[347] *In re* Waldron, 13 Johns. 418 (N.Y. 1816); Mercein v. People *ex rel.* Barry, 25 Wend. 64, 101 (N.Y. 1840). "The rights and interests of the parents must in all cases yield to the interests and welfare of the infant." *Id.* at 102. Some other examples of cases granting custody to the mother in preference to the father include United States v. Green, 26 F. Cas. 30 (C.C.D.R.I. 1824) (No. 15256); State v. Smith, 6 Greenl. 462 (Me. 1830); *In re* Wollstonecraft, 4 Johns. Ch. 80 (N.Y. 1819); Crawford v. Morrell, 8 Johns. 253 (N.Y. App. Div.); Commonwealth v. Addicks, 5 Binn. 520 (Pa. 1813); Commonwealth *ex rel.* d'Hauteville v. Sears (Phila., Pa. Ct. of General Sessions 1840.)

[348] While the custody rights of mothers, as parents, were also superior to those of third-party non-parents, under the coverture doctrine a married woman's rights were subsumed within the husband's during the marriage. The coverture doctrine also gave the husband the right to decide the residence and direct the upbringing of the children during the marriage. As a result, a suit for the return of a married couple's child from the custody of a third party (e.g., a petition for a writ of habeas corpus) needed to be prosecuted in the name of the husband, not the wife. Pierce v. Millay, 62 Ill. 133 (1871); Miner v. Miner, 11 Ill. 43 (1849)

[349] 90 Ind. 150 (1883).

[350] *Id.* at 155

Modern legal scholars and historians have have misinterpreted this kind of language as authority for the proposition that fathers' rights were superior even to mother's rights in the nineteenth century. As we have seen, though, when the contest was between the parents of the child, and not between a parent and a non-parent, most courts applied a "best interest of the child" standard, often actually favoring the mother, not the father.

The explanation for the "father's superior rights" language in third-party custody cases is the coverture doctrine. Under that doctrine, a married woman's rights were subsumed within the husband's during the marriage. The husband had the right to decide the residence and direct the upbringing of the children during the marriage. As a result, a suit for the return of a married couple's child from the custody of a third party (e.g., a petition for a writ of habeas corpus) was prosecuted solely in the name of the husband, not the wife.[351] Because the contest in third-party custody cases was styled as one between the father and the third party, judges spoke only in terms of the father's rights relative to the rights of third parties. When judges spoke about "fathers' rights" in contests between parents and non-parents, they were referring to the bundle of parental rights possessed by both spouses that was being managed by the husband during the marriage pursuant to the coverture doctrine. The coverture doctrine had no application in custody contests between two parents (such as during a divorce or separation proceeding.)

Like the preference for the innocent spouse, the preference for awarding custody to a parent rather than a non-parent was an application of the "best interests" standard. Courts presumed that it was normally in children's best interests to be raised by their parents, because it was believed that parents were children's natural protectors and providers. In other words, parents were presumed to act in their children's best interests.[352]

The presumption was rebuttable by showing that third-party custody of a child, rather than parental custody, was in the child's best interests in a

---

[351] Pierce v. Millay, 62 Ill. 133 (1871); Miner v. Miner, 11 Ill. 43 (1849)

[352] Cowls v. Cowls, 3 Ill. (Gilm.) 435, 437 (1846); Chapsky v. Wood, 26 Kan. 650 (1881) (explaining that the superior claim of parents to custody of their children "is, that it is a law of nature that the affection which springs from such a relation as that is stronger and more potent than any which springs from any other human relation.")

particular case.[353] Joseph Story, sitting on the federal circuit bench in 1824, explained it this way:

> As to the question of the right of the father to have the custody of his infant child, in a general sense it is true. But this is not on account of any absolute right of the father, but for the benefit of the infant, the law presuming it to be for his interest to be under the nurture and care of his natural protector, both for maintenance and education. When, therefore, the court is asked to lend its aid to put the infant into the custody of the father, and to withdraw him from other persons, it will look into all the circumstances, and ascertain whether it will be for the real, permanent interests of the infant; and if the infant be of sufficient discretion, it will also consult its personal wishes....It is an entire mistake to suppose the court is at all events bound to deliver over the infant to his father.[354]

Considering parents to have a presumptive claim to custody superior to that of any non-parent, some courts required a strong showing of some exceptional circumstance, something on the order of parental unfitness, before they would award custody to a non-parent in preference to a parent.[355] In other states, the presumption was rebuttable simply by showing that the child's interests would be better served by placement in another person's custody instead.[356] The kind of evidence needed to rebut the presumption generally was left to the "sound discretion" of the court.

---

[353] *See* State v. Richardson, 40 N.H. 272 (1860).

[354] United States v. Green, 26 F. Cas. 30 (C.C.D.R.I. 1824) (No. 15256).

[355] *See, e.g.,* Child v. Dodd, 51 Ind. 484, 485 (1875) (awarding custody to a father in preference to a grandparent, describing it a parent's right to custody of his children as a "universal law of all nations"); State *ex rel.* Shaw v. Nachtway, 43 Iowa 653 (1876) (granting custody to father despite older child's preference to reside with non-parent third party.)

[356] *See, e.g., In re* Toulmin, 1 Ga. (R.M. Charlton) 489 (Chatham Super. Ct. 1836); Bryan v. Lyons, 3 N.E. 880 (Ind. 1885); Jones v. Barnell, 2 N.E. 229 (Ind. 1885); State v. Kirkpatrick, 6 N.W. 588 (Iowa 1880); *In re* Cuneen, 17 How. Pr. 516 (N.Y. 1859); Sheers v. Stein, 43 N.W. 728 (Wis. 1889); *In re* Goodenough, 19 Wis. 274 (1865); SCHOULER, *supra* note 55 at 362; TIFFANY, *supra* note 178 at 268.

Some courts held that an award of custody to the mother permanently terminated the father's right to custody even in a subsequent contest between the father and an unrelated third party. In *Wilkinson v. Deming*,[357] the mother died after having been awarded custody of the children in a divorce. She had executed a will appointing a person other than the children's father as the guardian for the children. The father asked the court to grant him custody of the children notwithstanding the ex-wife's appointment of a third-party guardian. The court denied his request, holding that when a mother is granted custody of children in a divorce, "the infant is no longer the child of the divorced father...."[358] Evidently some nineteenth century courts conceived of a sole custody award as a complete termination of parental rights, rather than merely a partial or temporary suspension of parental rights.

When ruling against a parent in a custody case, American courts generally invoked the inherent *parens patriae* authority of courts of equity, observing that "[t]he rights of the parents must in all cases yield to the interests and welfare of the infant."[359] Courts sometimes mentioned the "common law" rule about "absolute" or "paramount" rights of parents, but they rarely decided cases on that basis alone unless doing so happened to coincide with what they believed was in a child's best interests. If it was believed that an award of custody to a parent was in a child's best interests in a particular case, then a judge was likely to couch his decision in language about the "absolute" or "paramount" rights of parents. If the court believed a child's best interests would be served by an award of custody to a non-parent, then it would say that the paramount consideration in custody cases was not the rights of the parent, but the court's independent determination of what was in the best interests of the child. [360]

---

[357] 80 Ill. 342 (1875)

[358] *Id.* at 343.

[359] *Id.*; *see also* Finlay v. Finlay, 240 N.Y. 429 (1925) (explaining that "[t]he chancellor in exercising his jurisdiction upon petition does not proceed upon the theory that the petitioner, whether father or mother, has a cause of action against the other or indeed against only one. He acts as parens patriae to do what is best for the interest of the child.")

[360] TIFFANY, *supra* note 178 at 268. Of course, as with most things, there was an occasional exception. In Hunt v. Hunt, 4 Greene 216, 219 (Iowa 1854), an Iowa court granted custody of an older daughter to the father on the basis of the father's supposed paramount right to custody, citing the *De Manneville* case.

As a rule, courts recognized a presumption that parents act in their children's best interests, so parental custody normally was presumed to be in children's best interests. A parent could lose the benefit of that presumption, however, if he or she abdicated parental responsibility by abandoning, abusing or neglecting a child, or by permitting a third party to raise the child for a number of years.[361]

Since a court does not take parental rights into consideration when it exercises its *parens patriae* power to make an award of custody on the basis of its own determination of what is in a child's best interests, it cannot really be said that courts regarded parents as having "rights" to their children, at least not "absolute" or "paramount" ones.[362] In disputes between parents, American judges, from the beginning, awarded custody of children to either the father or the mother on the basis of what they determined was best for the child. The Georgia Supreme Court, in 1836, described the custody of children as being "not a matter of right which the father can claim at the hands of the court, but a matter resting in the sound discretion of the court, to be guided by the interests of the child."[363] In disputes between a parent and a non-parent, courts sometimes determined that third-party custody was in a child's best interests, and when they did, they often would award custody to the third party.

---

[361] *See, e.g.,* Chapsky v. Wood, 26 Kan. 650 (1881) (awarding custody of child to third party in preference to father, where father had permitted the child to be raised by the non-parent for five years); Maples v. Maples, 49 Miss. 393 (1873); *cf.* Thompson v. Thompson, 72 N.C. 32 (1875) (awarding custody to mother despite the fact that the child had been residing with a grandparent for some time, where the placement was originally due to the mother's insanity and there was some evidence that her sanity had been restored.)

[362] Mercein v. People *ex rel.* Barry, 25 Wend. 64, 101 (N.Y. 1840) ("By the law of nature, the father has no paramount right to the custody of his child.")

[363] 3 Charlton 489 (Ga. 1836); ; *see also* Cornelius v. Cornelius, 31 Ala. 479 (1858) (holding that a court may award custody to the mother even if she is unable to establish any fault on the part of the father); Cowls v. Cowls, 8 Ill. (3 Gilm.) 435 (1846) (applying "best interests of the child" standard); Adams v. Adams, 62 Ky. (1 Duv.) 167 (Ky. 1864 (describing the father's right as existing only in the abstract, and that custody decisions are to be made on the basis of a determination of which parent is more capable and trustworthy.) In Wand v. Wand, 14 Cal. 512 (1860), one of the earliest custody cases decided in California, the court awarded custody to the mother on the basis of the "best interests of the child" standard.

The tender years doctrine

The tender years doctrine is a principle of law according to which it is deemed to be in the best interests of young children, and of daughters and unhealthy children of any age, to be placed in the sole custody of their mothers, unless the mother is proven to be unfit to parent in a particular case.[364]

The traditional account of custody law describes it as a late nineteenth or early twentieth century American innovation. As we have seen, though, the idea did not originate in America. It was a principle of law that was applied at earlier times in other countries. And American courts applied it throughout the nineteenth century, not just near the end of it.[365]

The tender years doctrine treats custody of very young children, like custody of children born out of wedlock, as a woman's natural right:

---

[364] *See, e.g.*, Miner v. Miner, 11 Ill. 43 (1849); State v. Stigall, 22 N.J.L. 286, 289 (1849). The rule remained virtually unchanged for well over a century. *See, e.g.*, Horst v. McLain, 466 S.W.2d 187 (Mo. Ct. App. 1971) (describing the rule as follows: "[B]efore a mother should be deprived of the custody of her young child [or] a girl, the evidence must show that she is demonstrably unfit to assume the child's proper care.")

[365] *See, e.g., In re* Barry, 42 F. 113 (C.C.S.D.N.Y. 1844); Commonwealth v. Addicks, 5 Binn. 520 (Pa. 1813); Prather v. Prather, 4 Des. 32 (S.C. 1809); *see also* State v. King, 1 Ga. Dec. 93 (1841); Cowls v. Cowls, 3 Ill. (Gilm.) 435, 440 (1846); Klein v. Klein, 11 N.W. 367 (Mich. 1882); State v. Stigall, 22 N.J.L. 286, 289 (1849); Clutch v. Clutch, 1 N.J. Eq. 474 (1831); Mercein v. People *ex rel.* Barry, 25 Wend. 64 (N.Y. 1840); Ahrenfeldt v. Ahrenfeldt, 1 Hoff. Ch. 497 (N.Y. Ch. 1840); Duhme v. Duhme, 3 Ohio Dec. Reprint 95 (Hamilton Ct. Common Pleas 1859); Commonwealth *ex rel.* d'Hauteville v. Sears (Phila., Pa. Ct. of General Sessions, 1840); McKim v. McKim, 12 R.I. 462, 464 (1879); State v. Paine, 23 Tenn. (4 Hum.) 523 (1843). The tender years doctrine was also part of the territorial law of those states that acquired statehood in the nineteenth century. MINN. REV. STAT. (Terr.) ch. 66, § 18 (ca. 1850), for example, required courts to have "due regard to the age and sex of children" when making custody decisions, language which courts have consistently interpreted as mandating application of the tender years doctrine. This provision of Minnesota's territorial laws was adopted, word for word, as part of Minnesota's public laws upon attaining statehood. *See* MINN. PUB. STAT. ch. 53, § 18 (1858); MINN. GEN. STAT. ch. 62 § 18 (1866) (superseded by MINN. STAT. § 518.17 (2012).) *see also* WIS. REV. STAT. ch. 79, § 19 (1849); WIS. REV. STAT. § 2362 (1878) (superseded by WIS. STAT. § 767.41 (2011))

[T]he law of nature has given to her an attachment for her infant offspring which no other relative will be likely to possess in an equal degree, and where no sufficient reasons exist for depriving her of the care and nurture of her child, it would not be a proper exercise of discretion in any court to violate the law of nature in this respect.[366]

In many cases, the judicial preference for keeping young children with their mothers did not conflict with the rule that the custody of children should be decided on the basis of marital fault. If the husband was at fault for the breakdown of the marriage, then custody of the children generally would be awarded to the mother regardless of how old the children were. The two doctrines came into conflict only when the mother of a very young child was the one who was at fault for the breakdown of the marriage (such as where she was the one who had committed adultery.) When such a conflict occurred, many courts resolved it in favor of the tender years doctrine, overlooking the mother's marital indiscretions if necessary in order to keep a young child with her mother. Thus, in 1813 a Pennsylvania court, while "expressing … disapprobation of the mother's conduct" (i.e., her commission of adultery) nevertheless concluded that "considering [the children's] tender age…we think it best, at present, not to take them from her."[367] In other words, while marital misconduct could work a forfeiture of a father's custody rights, it would not necessarily work a forfeiture of a mother's custody rights, at least not if the children were young.

---

[366] People v. Mercein, 3 Hill 399, 410 (N.Y. 1842); *see also* Krieger v. Krieger, 81 P.2d 1081, 1083 (Idaho 1938) (declaring that the tender years doctrine "arises out of the very nature and instincts of motherhood"); Helm v. Franciscus, 2 Bland Ch. 544, 563 (Md. Ch. 1830) ("It would violate the laws of nature to snatch an infant from an affectionate mother and place it in the coarse hands of the father"); Wojnarowicz v. Wojnarowicz, 137 A.2d 618, 620 (N.J. Super. Ct. Ch. Div. 1958) ("inexorable natural force"); Random v. Random, 170 N.W. 313, 314 (N.D. 1918) ("the most sacred ties of nature.")

[367] Commonwealth v. Addicks, 5 Binn. 520 (Pa. 1813); *see also* Brandon v. Brandon, 14 Kan. 264 (1875) (granting divorce to husband on grounds of wife's habitual drunkenness, but awarding custody of three- and one-year-old children to wife); Haskell v. Haskell, 24 N.E. 859 (Mass. 1890) (applying tender years doctrine in favor of a mother despite her commission of adultery and bigamy); Brown v. Brown, 53 Mo. Ct. App. 453 (1893) (awarding custody to mother guilty of indignities.)

The Philadelphia court of general sessions summarized the law as it was applied in early America as follows:

The reputation of a father may be stainless as crystal; he may not be afflicted with the slightest mental, moral, or physical disqualification from superintending the general welfare of the infant; the mother may have separated from him without the shadow of a pretense of justification; and yet the interests of the child may imperatively demand the denial of the father's right, and its continuance with the mother....

[E]very instinct of humanity unerringly proclaims that *no* substitute can supply the place of HER, whose watchfulness over the sleeping cradle or waking moments of her offspring, is prompted by deeper and holier feelings than the most liberal allowance of a nurse's wages could possibly stimulate[368]

In other words, the tender years doctrine trumped the marital fault doctrine.

---

[368] Commonwealth *ex rel.* d'Hauteville v. Sears (Phila., Pa. Ct. of General Sessions, 1840) (awarding custody to an adulterous wife, and observing: "All the American cases, without a single exception ... recognize to its fullest extent, the principle upon which, in the case of *Commonwealth v. Addicks and Wife* (citation omitted), Chief Justice Tilghman, refused to take the children from the mother, and remove them to the custody of the father...."); *see also,* McKim v. McKim, 12 R.I. 462, 465 (1879) (awarding custody of sickly child to mother, even though mother was at fault for the separation and the father was not guilty of wrongdoing.) The traditional account of American custody law asserts that marital fault, such as adultery, stopped being the basis for custody decisions sometime during the mid- or late-nineteenth century. This is not accurate. *See, e.g.,* Commonwealth v. Addicks, 5 Binn. 520 (Pa. 1813) (awarding custody of children of tender years to an adulterous wife); *see also* Miner v. Miner, 11 Ill. 43, 50 (1849) (explaining that it was because courts decide cases on the basis of a consideration of what is in children's best interests, not on the basis of parental rights, that children of tender years and daughters of any age were awarded to the mother, "even if the father is blameless.") Courts continued to apply moral and marital fault as a basis for denying custody to a father long after they stopped treating it as a basis for denying custody to a mother. *See, e.g.,* Small v. Small, 45 N.W. 248 (Neb. 1890) (denying custody to a father on the grounds that his commission of adultery rendered him unfit to parent.)

Placement of young children in their mother's care was sometimes rationalized as an application of the "best interests of the child" standard, the idea being that it is in young children's best interests to be cared for by their mothers rather than by their fathers.[369] In so ruling, courts applied a strong – and in some cases, conclusive -- presumption that men are inherently inferior to women when it comes to nurturing children. This was what the Pennsylvania Supreme Court was getting at when, in 1813, it held that children, "considering their tender age ... stand in need of that kind of assistance, which can be afforded by none so well as a mother."[370] Placement with the mother was seen as the only means of ensuring proper care for children.

> There may be cases in which the court, from a consideration of the child's welfare, would not award its custody to the father, even though no fault or neglect of duty could be imputed to him. A child of very tender years needs the care and attention of a mother, and even were she to desert the father, without any fault on his part, the child would not be taken from her.... [371]

---

[369] *See, e.g.*, State *ex rel.* Flint v. Flint, 65 N.W. 272, 273 (Minn. 1895) (affirming award of custody of child of tender years to the mother on the basis that "[t]he cardinal principle in such matters is to regard the benefit of the infant paramount to the claims of either parent." "the primary object of all courts, at least in America, is to secure the welfare of the child, and not the special claims of one or the other parent.")

[370] Commonwealth v. Addicks, 5 Binn. 520 (Pa. 1813)

[371]. TIFFANY, *supra* note 178 at 271, *citing* Miner v. Miner, 11 Ill. 43 (1849); *In re* Bort, 25 Kan. 308 (1881); Chandler v. Chandler, 24 Mich. 176 (1884); Scoggins v. Scoggins, 80 N.C. 318 (1879); Commonwealth v. Demott, 64 Pa. 305 (1893); Commonwealth v. Addicks, 5 Binn. 520 (Pa. 1813); McKim v. McKim, 12 R.I. 462 (1879); *Ex parte* Schumpert, 6 Rich. 344 (S.C. [n.d.]); State v. Paine, 23 Tenn. (4 Hum.) 523 (1843). *McKim v. McKim* was a habeas corpus proceeding on a father's petition for the return to his custody of a daughter whom the mother had taken with her when she separated from him without legal justification. Although the father was found to be fit for custody, and the mother was at fault for the breakup of the marriage, the court denied the father's request, holding that it was in the daughter's best interests to remain in her mother's care. *McKim, supra* at 464-65. It is not clear why legal historian Mary Ann Mason cites this case as standing for the proposition that "male children [were] more likely to be awarded to fathers." *See* MASON, *supra* note 1 at 204 n.58.

[I]t is well known by all men, no other love is quite so tender, no other solicitude quite so deep, no other devotion quite so enduring as that of a mother. Generally, the love, solicitude and devotion of a mother cannot be replaced by another and is worth more to a child of tender years than all other things combined and it should not be deprived of … mother if it can reasonably be avoided.[372]

Judges often waxed poetic in their expressions of the tender years doctrine. "There is but a twilight zone between a mother's love and the atmosphere of heaven," Hon. James F. Fulbright, writing for the Missouri Court of Appeals, opined, "And all things being equal, no child should be deprived of that maternal influence."[373]

According to the Iowa Supreme Court, "The mother is God's own institution for the rearing and upbringing of the child."[374]

States varied with respect to the age range to which the doctrine applied. Typically, children over the age of seven were deemed to have become untender, though courts sometimes cited the tender years doctrine in support of an award to the mother of custody of children older than seven, too.[375] On the other hand, cases can be found in which a court ruled that a child as young as four or five years of age was no longer tender.[376]

It has been suggested that the tender years doctrine was the product of a heightened exaltation of motherhood incidental to the Industrial Revolution of the nineteenth century.[377] While it is debatable whether the Industrial Revolution can really be said to have caused a division of labor along sexual lines, there is little doubt that it intensified it. Industrialization created a demand for a work force that was willing and able to work long hours outside the home, in factories and mines, building railroads, houses,

---

[372] Ellis v. Johnson, 260 S.W. 1010, 1012 (Mo. Ct. App. 1924)

[373] Tuter v. Tuter, 120 S.W.2d 203, 205 (Mo. Ct. App. 1938)

[374] Hines v. Hines, 185 N.W. 91, 92 (Iowa 1921)

[375] *In re* Barry, 42 F. 113 (C.C.S.D.N.Y. 1844); Baird v. Baird, 18 N.J. Eq. 194, 198 (N.J. Ch. 1867) ; Bennet v. Bennet, 13 N.J. Eq. 118 (N.J. Ch. 1860)

[376] *See, e.g.*, Hunt v. Hunt, 4 Greene 216, 219 (Iowa 1854) (five); Latham v. Latham, 71 Va. (30 Gratt.) 307 (1878) (four.)

[377] *See, e.g.*, RICHARD A. WARSHAK, THE CUSTODY REVOLUTION: THE FATHER FACTOR AND THE MOTHERHOOD MYSTIQUE 29-31 (1992).

highways and so on. This was not considered safe or suitable work for pregnant women or for women nursing newborn babies. It is not difficult to see how this could have reinforced the notion that a woman's place is in the home raising children, while a man's place is to work outside the home to provide for and protect women and children.

At one point, the idealized view of the proper roles of women and men led the United States Supreme Court to declare that allowing women to practice law instead of staying home and raising children was against the will of God:

> The constitution of the family organization, which is founded in the divine ordinance, as well as in the nature of things, indicates the domestic sphere as that which properly belongs to the domain and functions of womanhood. The harmony, not to say identity, of interests and view which belong, or should belong, to the family institution is repugnant to the ideas of a woman adopting a distinct and independent career from that of her husband.... The paramount destiny and mission of woman are to fulfill the noble and benign offices of wife and mother. This is the law of the creator.[378]

The sexual division of labor put women at a disadvantage in terms of securing employment outside the home, but it gave them an advantage in terms of securing custody of children. At the same time, men came to have an advantage with respect to securing employment outside the home, but they were at a disadvantage in terms of forming and maintaining parent-child attachments and winning custody of children.

> [Fathers] had to make [a parenting time] commitment and at the same time honor their obligation to earn the family bread. And it was just this dual responsibility that put fathers at a relative disadvantage. Children needed and wanted both love and money; mothers supplied healthy doses of the former, but fathers by and large were the sole suppliers of the latter. Consequently, children looked to their mothers

---

[378] Bradwell v. Illinois, 83 U.S. 130, 141 (1873)

as emotional caretakers and to their fathers as combination playmates and bankers.[379]

In scores of court decisions throughout the nineteenth century, courts regularly denied fathers custody of their young children on the basis that caring for young children was the exclusive province of mothers. It was "women's work." According to nineteenth century American courts, children needed to be placed in the custody of their mothers because men as a class lacked the capacity to love their children enough to care for them properly. Indeed, a court committed reversible error if it placed a young child in a father's custody.[380]

Older children

While mothers were presumptively entitled to custody of daughters and of young or infirm sons, courts generally gave great weight to the preference of older male children as to their custody. If an older child desired to remain with his mother, then a court might be inclined to place him in the custody of his mother.[381] If an older son preferred to be in his father's custody, then a court might be inclined to place him in the custody of his father.[382]

Courts placed more emphasis on the influence of parents as role models for their children in cases involving older children than in cases involving younger children. A court might be willing to overlook a mother's marital or other moral misconduct in the case of children of tender years, but would give such things more serious consideration when it came to the custody of older children.[383] A court might order a different custodial

---

[379] Robert L. Griswold, *Ties That Bind and Bonds That Break: Children's Attitudes Toward Fathers, 1900-1930, in* SMALL WORLDS: CHILDREN & ADOLESCENTS IN AMERICA, 1850-1950, at 273 (E. West & P. Petrik, P. eds., 1992).

[380] *See, e.g.,* Smith v. Smith, 46 P. 234 (Wash. 1896)

[381] *See, e.g.,* Baird v. Baird, 18 N.J. Eq. 194 (N.J. Ch. 1867) (awarding custody of older children to mother, based on their expressed preference); *In re* Wollstonecraft, 4 Johns. Ch. 80 (N.Y. Ch. 1819) (respecting wish of 13-year-old girl to reside with her mother instead of her father.)

[382] State v. Paine, 23 Tenn. (4 Hum.) 523, 535 (1843). This was consistent with English common law. *See* King v. Greenhill, 4 Adolp. & Ellis 624, 111 Eng. Rep. 922 (K.B. 1836)

arrangement than would be called for by either the tender years doctrine or the child's preference if the otherwise preferred parent was unfit, guilty of marital or other misconduct, or a potentially bad influence on the child for some other reason.

In *Commonwealth v. Addicks*,[384] the Pennsylvania Supreme Court ruled that it was in the best interest of the children, who were then ten and seven years of age, to be in the custody of their mother notwithstanding her commission of adultery. The father renewed his request for custody later, when the children were thirteen and ten years of age. This time, the court ruled in the father's favor. The court reasoned that a parent's adultery, although not a concern when children are younger, becomes more important as children become older. Older children, needing positive role models for adulthood, benefit from being protected from a parent's immoral practices.[385]

Consistent with the view of parents as role models, many courts applied a rule that if all other things were equal (i.e., if both parents were fit), then older children should be in the custody of the parent who was of the same sex as the child.[386] That is to say, so long as a married parent was not guilty of marital or other misconduct, then courts tended to assume that placing an older child in the custody of the parent who was of the same sex as the child was in the child's best interests.[387] Courts recognized an

---

[383] *See, e.g.*, Latham v. Latham, 71 Va. (30 Gratt.) 307, 335 (1878) (awarding custody of child who is "past nursing stage" to the father, where the mother was at fault for the breakdown of the marriage, because "the time for moral training and impressions has arrived.")

[384] 5 Binn. 520 (Pa. 1813)

[385] Commonwealth v. Addicks, 5 Binn. 520 (Pa. 1813); Commonwealth v. Addicks, 2 Serg. & Rawl. 174, 1777 (Pa. 1815).

[386] *See, e.g.*, Miner v. Miner, 11 Ill. 43, 51 (1849) (holding that even if a father is innocent of any wrongdoing and presents no danger of harm to the child, daughters normally should be placed in the custody of their mothers because they need a maternal role model, and because mothers are more vigilant and tender than fathers are); Conn v. Conn, 57 Ind. 323 (1877) (awarding younger children to mother, older children to father); Hunt v. Hunt, 4 Greene 216 (Iowa 1854) (awarding younger daughter to mother, older sons to father); State v. Stigall, 22 N.J.L. 286 (1849) (awarding custody of child of tender years to mother, and custody of older male child to father); Duhme v. Duhme, 3 Ohio Dec. Reprint 95 (Hamilton Ct. Common Pleas 1859) (same); Prather v. Prather, 4 Des. 32 (S.C. 1809) (awarding younger child to mother, older child to father)

exception for unhealthy children of either sex, as to whom maternal care generally was deemed superior to paternal care in all cases.

Of course, these two principles – the preference for the parent of the same sex as the child, on one hand, and respect for an older son's preference, on the other – could come into conflict if an older son wished to stay with his mother. The same-sex role-model approach would suggest that placement with the father would be in his best interests, while the "older child's preference" rule would suggest that placement with the mother would be best for him. No clear rule for resolving this kind of conflict appears to have emerged, at least not one of general applicability throughout the country. A possible explanation for this is that the issue probably did not arise very often. Older boys might not have felt comfortable expressing a preference to remain with their mothers in lieu of entering the workforce with their fathers, as doing so could make them appear immature and unmanly. When issues like these did come before a court, judges invoked their "wide discretion" to decide what would be best for a child on a case-by-case basis. Often, some other factor bearing on parental fitness could be found to tip the balance in favor of one or the other parent, thus nullifying the "if all other things are equal" condition precedent to the application of either rule.

Although not cited in case reports as the rationale for their decisions, it is likely that the intensified sex role stratification attendant to the Industrial Revolution had something to do with how judges decided cases, in practice. Women increasingly were expected to stay at home and raise children while men were expected to work outside the home in factories, mills and so on. Fathers were expected to teach their sons a trade, and mothers were expected to teach their daughters how to tend to their families. Since boys began working outside the home at an early age (seven or eight, for example) — often alongside their fathers — it is not difficult to understand why a judge might conclude that keeping an older male child with his father would be in his best interests. This would also explain how a judge could conceive of a seven- or eight-year-old boy as "old."

---

[387] *See, e.g.*, People *ex rel.* Ordonaux v. Chegarey, 18 Wend. 637 (N.Y. 1836) (denying writ of habeas corpus to wife who sought custody of older male children while she was residing separately from her husband.)

The maternal preference

When it was not rejected outright (as many courts did from the beginning) the supposed "paramount right of the father" to the custody of his children was subject to six major exceptions: (1) children born out of wedlock; (2) young children; (3) weak, disabled or unhealthy children; (4) daughters; (5) older male children who expressed a preference to reside with their mothers; and (6) cases where the father was guilty of marital or moral misconduct, concepts which were defined very broadly in cases where a father sought custody of a child. Except when a married mother was determined to be unfit to parent, then, there were not many situations to which a "paramount right of fathers to custody" actually applied. The exceptions nearly swallowed the rule, in those few states where such a rule was actually applied at all.

What this meant was that, in practice, the courts of every state – those that had openly rejected the "fathers' rights" doctrine from the beginning, and those that had given it lip service while effectively nullifying it through the application of broad exceptions – decided custody on the basis of the best interests of the child, with a strong presumption that maternal custody was in a child's best interests.[388]

The maternal preference was based on strongly held beliefs about the natural superiority of women and the inferiority of men, as a class, with respect to child-rearing. For example, the Illinois Supreme Court, in 1849, issued this sweeping generalization:

The mother, from her natural endowments, her position in society, and her constant association with [children], can give them that care, attention and advice so indispensable to their welfare, which a father, if the same children were left to his supervision, would be compelled in a great degree to confide to strangers.[389]

---

[388] *See* Commonwealth *ex rel.* d'Hauteville v. Sears 279 (Phila., Pa. Ct. of General Sessions 1840) (concluding, on the basis of a review of early American custody cases, that "[t]he common law of the United States is in favour of the mother's custody")

[389] Miner v. Miner, 11 Ill. 43, 50 (1849)

Although the maternal preference was more ardently and eloquently expressed in cases involving younger children, it manifested itself in the rules courts applied to the custody of older children, too. For example, the near-absolute rights of mothers to custody of children born out of wedlock, and of daughters, and of weak, disabled or unhealthy children, applied irrespective of the ages of such children.

Maternal unfitness

The custody rights of parents were never absolute. A mother, like a father, could be denied custody if it was determined that she was unfit to be a parent.[390] The kinds of things that a court would accept as evidence of a mother's unfitness differed considerably from what would suffice for a father, though. In general, it may be said that the grounds for declaring a mother unfit were more limited than what would suffice to declare a father unfit. And over the course of the century, this double standard became increasingly pronounced.

One double standard had to do with the child support obligation. The law only imposed support obligations on men. Women were not expected to be breadwinners for a family. It is sometimes suggested that this was an aspect of the coverture doctrine, the idea being that the person who has all the rights should also have all the responsibilities. The support obligation was exclusively a male one even when coverture was not applicable, though. Support obligations were imposed on unwed fathers who possessed no rights of coverture, and they were imposed exclusively on men even after a marital unity had been dissolved by a divorce.[391]

Because courts only imposed support obligations upon men, a mother's inability to support her children financially normally was not held

---

[390] *See generally* AMERICAN BAR ASSOCIATION, *supra* note 303 at 172 (observing that "[b]y the mid-1800's, most states had come to exhibit a strong preference for the mothers in issues of custody.")

[391] Gilley v. Gilley, 9 A. 623 (Me. 1887); Logan v. Murray, 6 Serg. & Rawl. 175 (Pa. 1820); Campbell v. Campbell, 37 Wis. 206 (1875) (holding that a divorce may terminate a husband's right to custody but it does not terminate his obligation to support his wife and children.) *see generally* EPAPHRODITUS PECK, THE LAW OF PERSONS OR DOMESTIC RELATIONS 253-60, 278 (1913).

to be grounds for denying her custody of children, even though courts readily denied custody to fathers who either could not or did not adequately provide for his children financially.

Another clear example of the double standard was marital infidelity. Courts often treated a father's commission of adultery as grounds for denying him custody of a child but a mother's commission of adultery did not necessarily preclude an award of custody to her, especially if the child in question was young.

Moreover, regardless of the age of the child, a mother's commission of adultery was not a bar to custody if she had undergone a moral reformation. And courts typically would infer a woman's complete moral reformation simply from her termination of an adulterous relationship.

Victorian mores were such that women were seen as naturally innocent and asexual. Therefore, any demonstration of an interest in sex or of a lack of moral virtue on a woman's part was thought to be merely a temporary fall from the pedestal. The fall was assumed to have happened as a result of having been pushed by a man. Accordingly, if a married woman simply renounced her interest in the man who had led her astray, then she was immediately entitled to reclaim her position on the pedestal, and all order was restored to the Victorian world.[392] Men rarely were afforded such beneficent dispensation. There was an underlying current of opinion that men who strayed from their marital obligations did so of their own free will, and were virtually assured of doing it again: Once a scoundrel, always a scoundrel, it seemed.

The principal grounds upon which a mother might be deemed to be unfit to parent were habitual drunkenness (though this did not always prevent a court from awarding her custody of a child of tender years);[393] mental illness; and severe child abuse.[394]

---

[392] Of course, if she refused to abandon her paramour, then the court would have no basis for a finding of moral reformation, and most likely would proceed to find her unfit to parent.

[393] *See, e.g.*, Brandon v. Brandon, 14 Kan. 264 (1875)

[394] AMERICAN BAR ASSOCIATION, *supra* note 303.

17. MOTHERS' RIGHTS LEGISLATION

The Women's Movement

During the first half of the nineteenth century, American women had few legal rights other than those relating to support and child custody. State laws prohibited women from serving on juries and voting in elections, and prevented married women from entering into contracts without their husbands' signatures. Although the coverture doctrine gave women the right to be supported by men, it gave men the right to control and manage the couple's money and property.

To address these inequities, women's groups led by Lucretia Mott and Paulina Wright David began meeting in Philadelphia in 1846. In that year, the New York State Assembly enacted a Married Women's Property Act. It gave women the right to retain property they had brought into or acquired during a marriage, and it prohibited a husband's creditors from seizing a wife's property to satisfy a debt. Married women's property acts patterned after the New York statute were enacted in other states throughout the remainder of the century.

In July 1848, two years after the Philadelphia meeting, Mott and a woman named Elizabeth Cady Stanton organized a convention at Seneca Falls, New York, to discuss women's issues and concerns again, and to formulate a list of demands for reforms of the law on behalf of women.[395] A number of resolutions were passed at the convention including, among others, the following:

> *Resolved*, That such laws as conflict, in any way, with the true and substantial happiness of a woman, are contrary to the great precept of nature, and of no validity; for this is superior in obligation than any other.

> *Resolved*, That all laws which prevent woman from occupying such a station in society as her conscience shall dictate, or which place her in a position inferior to that of man, are contrary to the great precept of nature, and therefore of no force or authority.

> *Resolved*, That it is the duty of the women of this country to secure to themselves their sacred right to the elective franchise.[396]

The convention ultimately yielded a Declaration of Sentiments. "The history of mankind," it declared, "is a history of repeated injuries and usurpations on the part of man toward woman, having in direct object the establishment of an absolute tyranny over her."[397] It then proceeded to detail the ways in which men, as a class, were said to have injured and usurped women, as a class. The most pertinent to the history of custody law were these:

---

[395] Ironically, Lucretia Mott argued against giving women the right to vote. The inclusion of women's suffrage in the early feminist platform was largely the result of the efforts of one of the men in attendance at the convention, Frederick Douglass.

[396] *Report of the Women's Rights Convention, Held at Seneca Falls, N.Y., July 19th and 20th, 1848* (Rochester, 1848), 1 SELECTED PAPERS OF ELIZABETH CADY STANTON AND SUSAN B. ANTHONY (Ann. D. Gordon ed. 1997)

[397] *Id.*

Having deprived her of this first right of a citizen, the elective franchise, thereby leaving her without representation in the halls of legislation, he has oppressed her on all sides.

He has made her, if married, in the eye of the law, civilly dead.

He has made her, morally, an irresponsible being, as she can commit many crimes with impunity, provided they be done in the presence of her husband. In the covenant of marriage, she is compelled to promise obedience to her husband, he becoming, to all intents and purposes, her master....

He has so framed the laws of divorce, as to what shall be the proper causes of divorce; in case of separation, to whom the guardianship of the children shall be given; as to be wholly regardless of the happiness of women – the law, in all cases, going upon the false supposition of the supremacy of man, and giving all power into his hands.[398]

As can be seen from the first quoted paragraph, the women's movement of the nineteenth century was concerned with the civic equality of men and women. It sought to secure for women a right to vote in elections. As the middle two paragraphs make clear, it also sought to abolish the coverture doctrine. Finally, the last paragraph demonstrates that it also was concerned with reforming the laws of divorce and child custody.

The complaints about voting laws and coverture were legitimate. These things clearly had unfavorable consequences for women. The grievance that divorce laws placed all power in men's hands in preference to women, "wholly regardless of the happiness of women," however, was not quite as defensible. As we have seen, early American divorce laws made marital offenses, such as adultery, grounds for divorce whether committed by the husband or by the wife. And women had two special grounds for divorce or legal separation that were denied to men: cruelty and nonsupport. In the nineteenth century, only husbands were legally obligated to support their spouses; and during the first part of the century, cruelty to wife was grounds for divorce, but cruelty to husband was not.

---

[398] *Id.*

The grievance that child custody laws gave men all the power "wholly regardless of the happiness of women" also is not quite as supportable as the others are. *De Manneville v. De Manneville*, the British case in which a married woman who separated from her husband was not able to obtain a custody order because she did not seek or state grounds for divorce or legal separation, is the case that was (and continues to be) most frequently cited by women's rights advocates as "proof" that child custody laws were unfair to women. *De Manneville*, though, was a British decision that was decided in 1804, after both the American Revolution and the enactment of the U.S. Constitution. It was not binding on American courts, and in fact, many American courts had explicitly rejected it. Again, American courts had been favoring mothers for custody of children, especially young children, at least since 1813, and probably earlier. Nevertheless, there were still a few courts which, although creating broad exceptions to avoid its application, had never expressly rejected the "paramount right of a father to custody" for which Lord Blackstone and others had claimed *De Manneville* stood. The Seneca Falls grievance about child custody laws makes sense only if it is understood as an indictment against these particular judges, and not as a grievance against the many other judges who were already openly expressing a preference for mothers in custody cases.

The resolutions quoted above make it clear that first-wave feminism was not entirely, or even primarily, an "equal rights" movement. Although an equal right to vote was part of the platform, the ultimate objective seems to have been to ensure women's primacy in the law, not equality. Hence the resolution that the obligation of the law to make women happy was "superior" (not merely equal) to all others. The declaration that child custody should always be decided in a way that makes a woman happy was contrary to the judicially developed principle that the custody of children should be decided solely on the basis of a determination of what was in a child's best interests. Taken together with the resolution that the "superior obligation" of the law was to ensure the happiness of women, it is clear that the prevailing belief among these early feminists was that judges, when making custody decisions, should dedicate themselves to making women happy rather than trying to protect children's best interests. That would be consistent with Stanton's supremacist views about women and men. According to her, "We [Women] are, as a sex, infinitely superior to men, and if we were free and developed, healthy in body and mind, as we should be under natural conditions, our motherhood would be our glory."[399]

Feminists made no effort to extend the child support obligation to women. They were content to leave that a male-only obligation. Rather, they were committed to advancing and promoting sex-based stereotypes according to which women's naturally superior and proper role was that of child-raiser, while men's only legitimate function was to provide material comforts for women and children. This form of supremacism was congruent with the sexist judicial philosophies that had spawned the tender years and maternal preference doctrines, and it helped cement those doctrines more firmly in the law than they already were.

Implementation

The maternal preference doctrine was easily applied in cases involving never-married, divorced or divorcing parents. In many states, it was also applied in cases involving separated spouses. In some states, though, it was not applied in cases in which a married woman unjustifiably separated from a husband, taking the children with her. In these states, courts reasoned that because the coverture doctrine gave the husband the right to choose the family's residence, a wife who opted not to reside with him was guilty of desertion, unless her decision was justified on the basis of the husband's maltreatment of her, his inability to support her, or some other misconduct or shortcoming on his part. Unjustified desertion was grounds for divorce and a decree of separation, but those kinds of relief could only be granted to the innocent spouse. Accordingly, a woman who committed adultery, or who deserted her husband without good cause, and took the children with her would not have a remedy in the courts of these states.

To address this and other incidents of the coverture doctrine that had undesirable consequences for married women, several states in the middle and late nineteenth century enacted laws and state constitutional amendments ensuring that a married woman's rights would never be treated as inferior to a married man's rights. This was usually done by means of a law or set of laws abolishing coverture, and establishing the rights of

---

[399] Diary of 27 December 1890, published in STANTON, ELIZABETH CADY, ELIZABETH CADY STANTON AS REVEALED IN HER LETTERS, DIARY AND REMINISCENCES 270 (Theodore Stanton and Harriot Stanton Blatch eds., 1922.)

married women to enter into contracts and own, transfer and devise property independently of their husbands. Although arguably unnecessary, in view of the inherent power of courts of equity to award custody of children to mothers, some of these enactments also protected women's rights to custody of their children.[400]

IOWA CODE § 2241 (1876) is an example of an equal rights custody statute that was enacted during this period. It provided that "the parents are the natural guardians of their minor children, and are equally entitled to the care and custody of them."

In many states, statutes enacted during this period not only gave mothers equal rights, but actually gave them superior rights with respect to the custody of children. They typically required courts to award custody of children of tender years (defined as children under seven years of age in some states, or as old as twelve years of age in other states) to the mother in every case, leaving courts discretion to apply a general maternal preference or to develop some other rule for deciding what was in children's best interests in other kinds of cases.[401] Where such statutes had been enacted, courts generally construed them as mandating an award of custody of children of tender years to the mother even if she was the one who was at fault for the divorce or separation.[402]

---

[400] "Even in the absence of such legislation the courts of equity exercised ... their inherent jurisdiction by awarding custody of minor children to the mother upon separation of the parents if they felt this to be in the best interests of the child." C.T. Drechsler, Annotation, *Award of Custody of Child to Parent Against Whom Divorce Is Decreed*, 23 A.L.R.3d 6, 15 (1969). For an example of a state constitutional provision that was enacted during this period, see KAN. CONST. art. 15, §6. Enacted in 1859, it provides: "The legislature shall provide for the protection of the rights of women ... and shall also provide for their equal rights in the possession of their children." *Id.*; *see generally* PECK, *supra* note 391 at 261-62

[401] *See, e.g.*, LA. CIV. CODE art. 146 (1888) (requiring courts to award provisional custody of the children to the wife in every case, unless a strong reason for declining to do so existed); 1860 N.J. Laws, Act of March 20, 1860 (requiring courts to award custody of children under seven years of age to the mother in every case in which the wife and the husband were living separate and apart from each other for any reason, unless the mother was an unfit parent.) The Michigan statute gave the mother the right to custody of children under ten years of age, and gave the father the right to custody of children who were at least twelve years of age. 1879 Mich. Pub. Acts 163.

[402] *See, e.g.*, Bennet v. Bennet, 13 N.J. Eq. (2 Beasl.) 114, 117 (1860)

A few states enacted a different kind of statute, one which, on its face, appeared to give mothers and fathers equal rights in custody cases. This kind of statute authorized courts to award custody to either the mother or the father on the basis of the best interests of the child, subject only to the requirement that courts have "due regard" for the age and sex of the child.[403] Courts interpreted this kind of statute, however, as simply clarifying that husbands and wives have an equal right to *ask* a court for an award of custody upon divorce or separation, not as giving men and women a right to be free from discrimination in the course of a custody proceeding. The requirement that courts give "due regard" to a child's age and sex was intended to ensure that courts would continue to apply the tender years doctrine.

The net effect of these statutes was to remove any doubt that courts were free – and in some states, they were required – to award custody of children to mothers, and to continue to apply the judicially-developed maternal preference doctrine.[404]

State variations

Although all states eventually enacted laws abolishing coverture, and giving men and women equal guardianship and custody rights of their children, they did not all do it at the same time, or in the same way. By the end of the century, Colorado, Connecticut, Illinois, Kansas, Maine, Massachusetts, Nebraska, New York, Oregon, Washington, and the District of Columbia had expressly given married women and men equal custodial and guardianship rights. Louisiana gave mothers a superior claim to custody while a divorce was pending. Mississippi prohibited husbands from divesting their wives of custody rights by will. Pennsylvania gave married women equal rights to custody provided they contributed labor or support toward the children's education or care. On the other hand, there were still several states at the turn of the century that authorized husbands to appoint a testamentary guardian for their children, while not authorizing, or remaining silent about, a wife's appointment of a testamentary guardian. [405]

---

[403] *See, e.g.,* OR. CIV. CODE § 497, subd. 1, p. 211 (1880)

[404] *See, e.g.,* People *ex rel.* Brooks v. Brooks, 35 Barb. 85, 90-95 (N.Y. App. Div. 1861).

[405] 4 THE HISTORY OF WOMAN SUFFRAGE (Susan B. Anthony and Ida Husted

Of course, even without this kind of legislation, a married woman could obtain custody rights by securing a divorce or separation from her husband, but only if grounds for a divorce existed. Grounds varied from state to state. By the end of the century they included (depending on the state): habitual drunkenness; adultery; desertion; felony conviction; cruelty; husband's nonsupport of wife or children; fraud; prolonged absence; ungovernable temper; "outrages;" indignities; insanity; notorious immorality of the husband prior to the marriage, if unknown to the wife; concealed pregnancy of the wife by another man prior to the marriage; fugitive from justice; gross misbehavior or wickedness; gross neglect of duty; wife's refusal to live with her husband; membership in a religious society that does not believe the marriage relationship is lawful; inability to live in peace and union; husband's vagrancy; or "excesses."[406]

Harper eds., 1902.)
[406] *Id.* at 459.

18. CHILDREN BORN OUT OF WEDLOCK

While early American courts departed from the English with respect to the custody of children of married couples, they followed Roman law and English common law with respect to children born out of wedlock. Like the Roman and English common law systems, nineteenth century American law treated children of unmarried mothers as the property of their mothers. Unmarried fathers did not have parental rights.[407]

Although Louisiana was unlike the rest of the country in that it was the only state to adopt the civil law system of France, fathers of children born out of wedlock had no rights there, either. The civil law of France, like the common law of England, also denied parental rights to fathers of children born out of wedlock.[408]

---

[407] *See, e.g.*, Friesner v. Symonds, 20 A. 257 (N.J. Eq. 1890); Bustamento v. Analla, 1 N.M. 255 (1857); Robalina v. Armstrong, 15 Barb. 247 (N.Y. 1853); Timmins v. Lacy, 30 Tex. 116 (1867) (holding that only a mother could authorize the apprenticeship of a child born out of wedlock; the father could not); 2 BISHOP § 550, *supra* note 146 ("The father of a bastard child has no right, as father, to its custody; the parental right, in this case, is with the mother.")

[408] SCHOULER, *supra* note 55 at 418

The parental rights of mothers of children born out of wedlock were not subject to conditions precedent or subsequent. Even if she later became married to the child's father, she was entitled by law to retain sole custody of the child in the event of a divorce or separation.[409]

The parental rights of the father of a child conceived as a result of sexual intercourse with a woman to whom he was not married received recognition only if he "legitimated" the child by becoming married to the mother prior to the child's birth. Doing so prevented the child from being born out of wedlock.

Having no parental rights, the father of a child born out of wedlock did not get custody of his children if their mother died.[410] This meant that the mother could appoint someone other than the father as the testamentary guardian for her children upon her death. Except in Texas, an unwed father had no legally enforceable right to guardianship of his child upon the death of the mother.[411]

Nineteenth century judicial decisions usually described the rights of fathers of children born out of wedlock as non-existent.[412] Some cases, though -- particularly near the end of the century -- described the mother's right as "superior" to the father's: "As between the putative father and the mother of illegitimate children, it is well settled that the mother's right of custody is superior, and the father's right, if any such exists, is secondary."[413]

---

[409] Wright v. Wright, 2 Mass. 109 (1806); Bustamento v. Analla, 1 N.M. 255, 261 (1857); Robalina v. Armstrong, 15 Barb. 247 (N.Y. 1853); 2 Bishop § 550, *supra* note 146

[410] *See, e.g.*, Freisner v. Symonds, 46 N.J. Eq. 521 (Prerog. 1890) (holding that a child born out of wedlock becomes an orphan upon the mother's death, as the father has no right to custody.)

[411] SCHOULER, *supra* note 55 at 418.

[412] *See, e.g.*, Wright v. Wright, 2 Mass. 109 (1806); Carpenter v. Whitman, 15 Johns. 208 (N.Y. 1818); Robalina v. Armstrong, 15 Barb. 247 (N.Y. App. Div. 1852); People v. Kling, 6 Barb. 366 (N.Y. App. Div. 1849); McGunigal v. Mong, 5 Pa. 269 (1847); *see generally* 4 VERNIER, *supra* note 303 at 19 (describing nineteenth century and early twentieth century American common law as "giving the mother the exclusive right" of custody.)

[413] B. Finberg, Annotation, *Right of mother to custody of illegitimate child*, 98 A.L.R.2d 417, 431 (1964); *see also* Graham v. Bennet, 2 Cal. 503 (1852); Marshall v. Reams, 14 So. 95 (Fla. 1893); Alfred v. McKay, 36 Ga. 440 (1867); Henderson v. Shiflett, 31 S.E. 186 (Ga. 1898); Wright v. Bennett, 7 Ill. 587 (1845): Young v. State, 53 Ind.

This implied that an unmarried father might have at least some rights.

Judges also sometimes said that the father's right was inferior to the mother's, but superior to all others.[414] In theory, then, it seemed that in the view of at least some courts near the end of the century, an unwed father might have standing to assert a claim to custody of his children if the mother had died, or if she was found to be unfit to care for children.

An example of the inferiority of fathers' rights was the legal doctrine that a father could be declared unfit to parent because of his commission of an immoral act, but a mother's immoral conduct would not support a finding of her unfitness to have the care and custody of children born to her out of wedlock.[415]

Consistent with the view that fathers of children had no parental rights, nineteenth century courts generally did not grant visitation rights to putative fathers.

---

536 (1876); Dalton v. State, 6 Blackf. 357 (Ind. 1842); Dehler v. State, 53 N.E. 850 (Ind. Ct. App. 1899); Pratt v. Nitz, 48 Iowa 33 (1878); Allen v. Allen, 8 Bush. 491 (Ky. 1871); Baker v. Winfery, 15 B. Mon. 499 (Ky. 1854); Acosta v. Robin, 7 Mart. (N.S.) 387 (La. 1829); Ramsay v. Thompson, 18 A. 592 (Md. 1889); Petersham v. Dana, 12 Mass. 429 (1815); Somerset v. Dighton, 12 Mass. 383 (1815); Wright v. Wright, 2 Mass. 109 (1806); State v. Nestaval, 75 N.W. 725 (Minn. 1898); Hudson v. Hills, 8 N.H. 417 (1836); Freisner v. Symonds, 20 A. 257 (N.J. 1890); State v. Stigall, 22 N.J.L. 286 (1849); Bustamento v. Analla, 1 N.M. 255 (1857); Carpenter v. Whitman, 15 Johns. 208 (N.Y. 1818); Robalina v. Armstrong, 15 Barb. 247 (N.Y. App. Div. 1852); People *ex rel.* Heilbronner v. Hoster, 14 Abb. Pr. (n.s.) 423 (1873); Pote's Appeal, 106 Pa. 574 (1884); McGunigal v. Mong, 5 Pa. 269 (1847) (father has no right of custody of children under the age of seven); Moritz v. Garnhart, 7 Watts 302 (Pa. 1838); Commonwealth v. Fee, 6 Serg. & Rawle 255 (Pa. 1820); Hope's Petition, 34 A. 994 (R.I. 1896); Austin v. M'Cluney, 36 S.C.L. (5 Strobh.) 104 (1850); King v. Johnson, 11 S.C. Eq. (2 Hill) 624 (1837); Lawson v. Scott, 1 Tenn. (Yerg.) 92 (1825); Timmins v. Lacy, 30 Tex. 116 (1867).

[414] *See, e.g., In re* Doyle, Clarke Ch. 154 (N.Y. 1839); People *ex rel.* Trainer v. Cooper, 8 How. Pr. 288 (N.Y. 1853); Moritz v. Garnhart, 7 Watts 302 (Pa. 1838); Pote's Appeal, 106 Pa. 574 (1884); King v. Johnson, 11 S.C. Eq. (2 Hill) 624 (1837)

[415] Bustamento v. Analla, 1 N.M. 255 (1857).

The general rule in the nineteenth century and throughout most of the twentieth century was that mothers had an exclusive right to the custody of any children born to them out of wedlock. Fathers did not have parental rights; they had support obligations.

19. SLAVES AND INDENTURED SERVANTS

Slaves were the property of their owners. They could be bought and sold, and slave-owners had legal recourse to the courts for the enforcement of their claimed rights.

Children of slaves were the property of the slave-owner, too. One consequence of this was that an owner could sell children separately from their parents.[416]

> One of these sale days, I saw a mother lead seven children to the auction-block. She knew that some of them would be taken from her; but they took all. The children were sole [sic] to a slave-trader, and their mother was by a man in her own town. Before night her children were all far away. She begged the trader to tell her where he intended to take them; this he refused to do. How could he, when he knew he would sell them, one by one, wherever he could command the highest price? I met the mother in the street, and her wild, haggard face lives

---

[416] Margaret A. Burnham, *An Impossible Marriage: Slave Law and Family Law*, 5 L. & INEQUALITY 187-225 (July 1987); George L. Christian and Frank W. Christian, *Slave-Marriages*, 1 VA. L.J. 641-52 (November 1877).

to-day in my mind, She wrung her hands in anguish, and exclaimed, 'Gone! All gone! Why don't God kill me?' I had no words wherewith to comfort her. Instances of this kind are of daily, yea, hourly occurrence.[417]

A child's status as free or slave was determined by the status of his mother; the father's status was irrelevant. A 1662 Virginia statute, for example, provided: "Whereas some doubts have arisen whether children got by any Englishman upon a negro woman should be slave or free. Be it therefore enacted…that all children born in this country shall be held bond or free only according to the condition of the mother." [418] If the mother was a slave, then her children were, too, even if the father was not. If the father was a slave but the mother was free, then the children were free, too.

Although a slave mother did not have a legally enforceable right to custody of her children, officials entrusted with responsibility for enforcing the laws sometimes were disposed to keep mothers and children together irrespective of the slave-owner's claimed legal rights. For example, in an 1811 Kentucky case in which a slave-owner asserted a legal right to sell slave parents and children separately, the judge nevertheless approved the sheriff's sale of a mother and child slave together. In so ruling, he wrote, "The mother and child were indeed physically divisible, but morally they were not so; and the sheriff in selling them together certainly acted in conformity to the dictates of humanity…."[419] Evidently some courts were disposed to apply a form of the maternal preference doctrine in cases involving slave children a well as in cases involving free children.[420]

A judicial preference for keeping slave mothers and their children together would have been consistent with the common law principle that unwed mothers possess the exclusive right to custody of the children born to them out of wedlock. Before the Civil War, slave marriages were not

---

[417] HARRIET ANN JACOBS, INCIDENTS IN THE LIFE OF A SLAVE GIRL 15 (2010)

[418] 2 WILLIAM W. HENING, STATUTES AT LARGE, BEING A COLLECTION OF ALL THE LAWS OF VIRGINIA, FROM THE FIRST SESSION OF THE LEGISLATURE IN THE YEAR 1619, at 170 (Richmond, Samuel Pleasants 1821)

[419] Lawrence v. Speed, 2 Bibb. 401 (Ky. 1811)

[420] Cf. Bell v. Pharr, 7 Ala. 807, 812 (1845) (stating, in dictum, that the law will not require children of slaves to be separated from their mothers.).

valid or legally enforceable.[421] Children born into a slave marriage, therefore, would have been considered children born out of wedlock, in the eyes of the law.[422]

The institution of slavery was abolished in 1865.[423]

Indentured servants

In both pre- and post-Revolutionary America, it was not uncommon for parents who were too poor to raise their children to bind them out to live with and serve other people or families. If accomplished by means of a contract of indenture, the child was called an *indentured servant*. When this occurred, the parent would then have no greater right to the custody and control of the child than what was provided in the contract. The rights of the parent of an indentured servant child were treated as purely contractual rights, applied and interpreted in accordance with contract law, not natural law.

Involuntary servitude, like slavery, was abolished in 1865.[424]

---

[421] 4 ALBERT H. PUTNEY, POPULAR LAW LIBRARY (1908).
[422] Allen v. Allen, 8 Bush 491 (Ky. 1871).
[423] U.S. CONST. AMEND. 13
[424] *Id.*

20. NATIVE AMERICAN CHILDREN

As the United States Supreme Court acknowledged early in the nineteenth century, Native American tribes are sovereign states. As such (and except to the extent a treaty or Congressional enactment provides otherwise), they retain the same power of self-governance that they possessed before the United States was established.[425] Their sovereign powers include, among others, the rights to determine tribal membership and to regulate domestic relations among members of the tribe. This includes the right to regulate the custody of children.

When the federal government has not intervened, custody of Native American children historically has been decided in accordance with the customary laws of the tribe (or, more recently, tribal codes patterned after state law codes.) While each tribe's customs and traditions are different, as a general matter it may be said that many of them have tended to be organized around a clan system rather than the nuclear family system familiar to Western cultures. A typical clan consisted of a child's parent and extended relatives. In such a system, placement with a particular parent may

---

[425] Cherokee Nation v. Georgia, 30 U.S. (5 Pet.) 1 (1831); Worcester v. Georgia, 31 U.S. (6 Pet.) 515 (1832)

have been considered less important than ensuring continuity of care by members of the child's clan.[426]

The Dawes Act

The development of Native American customary law on the subject of child custody was severely disrupted by federal legislation in the nineteenth century. The federal constitution gave Congress authority to "regulate Commerce with the Indian Tribes."[427] Construing this power very broadly, almost as if the constitution had granted it blanket power to regulate Indian tribes (as distinguished from power to regulate "commerce with" tribes) Congress proceeded to enact a series of laws that had the effect – and, some would say, the purpose – of breaking up Native American families. The General Allotment Act of 1887, also known as the Dawes Act, was one of these laws.

Federal policy with respect to the regulation of tribes has alternated between attempts to assimilate Native Americans into non-Native populations, on one hand, and efforts to preserve tribal self-determination, on the other.[428] The focus in the nineteenth century was on assimilation. A key component of the nineteenth century federal policy of assimilation was to abolish the tribal system of communal ownership of land. The Dawes Act attempted to do this by dividing reservations into parcels of land and then allotting individual parcels of land to individual Indians and their families. In addition, some of the reservation land was allotted to non-Natives, the plan being for these non-Natives to "civilize" the Natives by teaching them modern farming methods and such.

The leading proponent of allotment was Senator Henry L. Dawes, after whom the General Allotment Act of 1887 was named. While some historians portray him as a humanitarian concerned with the long-term welfare of Native Americans, his writings reflect a somewhat different kind of concern. "It was plain," he wrote, "that if [a Native American] were left alone, he must of necessity become a tramp and beggar with all the evil

---

[426] *In re* Custody of A.M.C., 8 Navajo Rptr. 825 (Chin. Fam. Ct. 2004).

[427] U.S. CONST. art. I, §8

[428] F. COHEN, HANDBOOK OF FEDERAL INDIAN LAW, WITH REFERENCE TABLES, AND INDEX (1972)

passions of a savage, a homeless and lawless poacher upon civilization and a terror to the peaceful citizen"[429]

Federal assimilation policy in the late nineteenth century went far beyond eliminating communal land ownership and teaching Native Americans modern farming methods. Federal lawmakers also embarked upon a grand experiment in social engineering that involved taking children from the custody of their parents and placing them in government-run boarding schools.

Throughout the late nineteenth century, federal policymakers viewed Native American children as the solution to "the Indian problem" because they were more malleable and teachable than adult Natives were. It was believed that if Native children could be reached early enough, then it would be possible to prevent their development into uncivilized "savages" like their parents. This was the rationale for the government-run boarding school program.

To ensure the success of the program, children were not permitted to speak in their native tongues, to practice their native religions or spiritual beliefs, or even to look like Native Americans. As the 1886 Commissioner of Indian Affairs explained:

> [T]he adult savage is not susceptible to the influence of civilization, and we must therefore turn to his children, that they might be taught how to abandon the pathway of barbarism and walk with a sure step along the pleasant highway of Christian civilization.... They must be withdrawn, in their tender years, entirely from the camp and taught to eat, to sleep, to dress, to play, to work and to think after the manner of the white man.[430]

The success of this program is debatable.

---

[429] Henry L. Dawes, *Have we failed with the Indian*, 84 ATLANTIC MONTHLY 280 (1899)

[430] quoted in L. George, *The challenge of permanency planning in a multicultural society*, 5 J. MULTICULTURAL SOC. WORK 165, 166 (1997)

The children were usually kept at boarding school for eight years during which time they were not permitted to see their parents, relatives or friends. Anything Indian — dress, language, religious practices, even outlook on life … was uncompromisingly prohibited. Ostensibly educated, articulate in the English language, wearing store-bought clothes and with their hair cut short and their emotionalism toned down the boarding school graduates were sent out either to make their way in a white world that did not want them or to return to a reservation to which they were now foreign.[431]

Federal policy began to shift toward preservation of Native American customs, traditions, and self-determination in the 1930's with the Indian Reorganization Act, and then again in 1978 with the Indian Child Welfare Act. By 1971, less than 18% of school-aged Native children were being removed from their homes and placed in federal boarding schools.[432] Today, the custody of Native American children is governed by a complex system of state, federal and tribal jurisdictional, procedural and substantive laws. And courts today are no longer permitted to indulge an assumption that removal of children from the custody of their Native American parents is in their best interests.

---

[431] PETER FARB, MAN'S RISE TO CIVILIZATION AS SHOWN BY THE INDIANS OF NORTH AMERICA 257-59 (1968)

[432] B. J. JONES, THE INDIAN CHILD WELFARE ACT HANDBOOK: A LEGAL GUIDE TO THE CUSTODY AND ADOPTION OF NATIVE AMERICAN CHILDREN (1995

21. RECIPROCITY OF CUSTODY AND SUPPORT

Nineteenth century American courts did not decide custody disputes between parents on the basis of parental rights. Instead, judges viewed the proper role of the courts to be to protect children's best interests. To that end, some courts sometimes expressed a preference for awarding custody to the person whom they believed was most able to provide material comforts for a child, even if this meant awarding custody to a non-parent rather than a parent.

On the other hand, courts could and did award custody of children to the mother even in cases where the father was in a better position to support them financially, or where the mother was financially dependent on others for her support. Custody rights did not always correlate positively with support obligations or a party's ability to support a child.

Nevertheless, early nineteenth century English law courts, and sometimes an American judge, occasionally made broad statements to the effect that the person who is responsible for the support of a child also has a right to custody. These pronouncements often are misunderstood to mean that nineteenth century courts treated custody rights and support obligations as residing in the same person.

> [A parent's right to custody] springs from two sources: one is, that he who brings a child, a helpless being, into life, ought to take care of that child ... and because of this obligation ... arises a reciprocal right to the custody and care of the offspring whom he must support; and the other reason is, that it is a law of nature that the affection which springs from such a relation as that is stronger and more potent than any which springs from any other human relation.[433]

The notion that a parent's custody rights correlate positively with his or her support obligations was most consistently applied in disputes between a father and a third party. Fathers were legally required to care for, and support, their children; unrelated third parties were not. Accordingly, it made sense in those kinds of cases for judges to say, as they sometimes did, that custody rights "sprang from," or were "reciprocal" to the parental obligation to support their children.

The principle was not consistently applied in disputes between parents, though. It was explicitly *not* followed in the case of children born out of wedlock. The law imposed an obligation upon the father of a child born out of wedlock to support the child, but gave him no right to custody of the child. Mothers had exclusive rights to sole custody of such children. Fathers acquired no rights by virtue of either possessing or fulfilling support obligations.

The principle also was not consistently followed in disputes between divorcing or separated married couples. Most American courts distinguished the issue of custody from the issue of responsibility for support. Custody issues would be decided on the basis of the best interests of the child, with the age and sex of the children and the parents, and the

---

[433] Chapsky v. Wood, 26 Kan. 650, 652 (1881); *see also* Hewitt v. Long, 76 Ill. 399, 408 (1875) ("The right of the father springs from the obligation of the father, by the common law, to provide for the maintenance of his children"); Hunt v. Hunt, 4 Greene 216, 219 (Iowa 1854) (justifying an award of custody of an older child to the father, in part, on the basis that "it is his right to see to the proper adjustment and disposal of his means," since it is a father's exclusive obligation to support children financially); *see generally* 2 J. KENT, COMMENTARIES ON AMERICAN LAW (12th ed., Boston: Little, Brown & Co. 1873)

parents' relative moral fitness, playing a major role in that determination. Liability for support was determined on the basis of a separate set of considerations: (1) the nature of the legal relationship between the child and the party seeking support; and (2) the sex of the parent.

Courts typically would deny support to a person whose relationship with the child was such as to entail no legal right to custody. For example, a court might deny a request for child support if it was made by a non-parent third party who was keeping a child from a parent in violation of the parent's natural right to custody. [434]

While most courts imposed a support obligation on the noncustodial parent following a divorce, courts in a few states sometimes declined to do so. These courts felt that doing so would be "doubly oppressive, depriving a man entirely of his child while still imposing responsibility for support on him." [435] Even in these states, however, courts found nothing "doubly oppressive" about depriving a man of his child while still imposing responsibility for support on him in cases where the child had been born out of wedlock. Even in England, courts did not recognize any right of custody "springing" from a father's obligation to support his children born out of wedlock. [436] Moreover, the general rule in most American states in the nineteenth century was that fathers, whether married, divorced, or never-married, were responsible for the support of their children whether they had custody of them or not.

Support as an exclusively male obligation

In the nineteenth century, only men were held legally responsible for the support of their families.

---

[434] *See.* Fitler v. Fitler, 2 Phila. 372 (Pa. 1857) (declining to enforce child support obligation against custodial father from whom child was being wrongfully withheld); *cf.* McClary v. Warner, 69 Ill. App. Ct. 223 (1897) (holding that a father is liable for child support if he is at fault for wife's separation from him); McMillen v. Lee, 78 Ill. 443 (1875) (holding that a father is liable for child support if the mother lives separately from him, with the children, with his consent.)

[435] 2 J. KENT, *supra* note 433; *see also* Finch v. Finch, 22 Conn. 411 (1853); Husband v. Husband, 67 Ind. 583 (1879); Burritt v. Burritt, 29 Barb. 124, 129-30 (N.Y. Sup. Ct. 1859)

[436] Rex v. Soper, 5 T.R. 278, 101 Eng. Rep. 156 (1793)

Fathers were responsible for the support of the children born to them during marriage, and they were responsible for the support of any children born out of wedlock, too. Early English common law did not impose a support obligation on the putative father of a child born out of wedlock, but the Act of 1576[437] decreed that children born out of wedlock should be supported by their putative fathers, and courts ordered them to do so. The Bastardy Act of 1733 gave courts the specific power to imprison a putative father until he either provided financial support for his children or agreed to marry the mother. Most American colonies enacted laws patterned after the English laws imposing support obligations on the fathers of children born out of wedlock, as did most states either prior to or shortly after attaining statehood.[438]

A man's failure to support his wife or child was punishable both criminally and civilly.[439]

Married and divorced men

For married men, this obligation was bound up with the doctrine of coverture, which made a husband solely responsible for all debts, obligations and liabilities incurred by any member of his family during the marriage. A husband was required to pay for anything his wife might purchase; to pay for any necessaries a third party might provide to her or to his children; to compensate third parties for whatever injuries his wife or

---

[437] 18 Eliz. C. 3

[438] Gilley v. Gilley, 9 A. 623 (Me. 1887); Logan v. Murray, 6 Serg. & Rawl. 175 (Pa. 1820); Commonwealth v. Murray, 4 Binn. 487 (Pa. 1812); PECK, *supra* note 391 at 253-54; SCHOULER, *supra* note 55 at 257, 344; Anthony Camp, *Records of illegitimate children*, 17 FAM. TREE MAG. (UK) 7-9 (May 2001). On the history of "bastardy" laws in America, see generally BASTARDY AND ITS COMPARATIVE HISTORY (Peter Laslett et al. eds., 1980); JENNY TEICHMAN, ILLEGITIMACY: A PHILOSOPHICAL EXAMINATION (1982); TIFFANY, *supra* note 178 at 250. Because most states enacted statutes imposing support obligations on putative fathers either prior to or very shortly after attaining statehood, the question whether a putative father had a common law obligation to support his children was not often addressed in American cases, except in dictum. In Doughty v. Engler, 211 P. 619 (Kan. 1923), a case raising the issue squarely, the Kansas Supreme Court declared that in America, a putative father does have a common law duty to support his children even in the absence of statute. The extent of the obligation, however, is controlled entirely by statute. *See, e.g.,* Simmons v. Bull, 21 Ala. 501 (1852)

[439] PECK, *supra* note 391 at 257.

his children may cause them; and to bear sole responsibility for supporting the family financially.[440]

Rather than treat the support obligation as an incident of the right of custody (i.e., as an obligation of the custodial parent alone), the majority of American courts required fathers to pay child support to the mother in those cases where she was awarded custody of the children. That is to say, courts extended the husband's family support obligation beyond the termination of the marriage. The result was an explicit double standard in the law: If a mother was awarded custody of the children in a divorce or separation, the father was required to pay child support to her, but if custody was awarded to the father, the mother was not required to pay child support to him, even if she had the means.[441] A woman's marital obligations terminated upon the dissolution of her marriage; a man's did not. His obligation to support his wife and children continued to exist even after the marital unity had been dissolved.

In most states, a man continued to be liable for the support of his family regardless of who was awarded custody of the children.[442] Although a few states recognized an exception for cases in which the mother had been guilty of marital misconduct, in most states a man remained liable for support even if his wife left the marriage for no just cause, even if she had been guilty of extreme cruelty toward him, and "however wanton or disobedient she might have been."[443]

---

[440] HARTOG *supra* note 1; ROLLIN C. HURD, A TREATISE ON THE RIGHT OF PERSONAL LIBERTY, AND ON THE WRIT OF HABEAS CORPUS AND THE PRACTICE CONNECTED WITH IT: A VIEW OF THE LAW OF EXTRADITION OF FUGITIVES 25 (2d ed., Albany, N.Y., W.C. Little & Co. 1876) (1858).

[441] *See, e.g.*, Courtright v. Courtright, 40 Mich. 633 (1879); Spencer v. Spencer, 97 Minn. 56 (1906); Ahrenfeldt v. Ahrenfeldt, 1 Hoff. Ch. 497 (N.Y. Ch. 1840) (awarding custody of the children to the wife and ordering the husband to pay child support); 2 BISHOP § 552, *supra* note 146; SCHOULER, *supra* note 55 at 345; PECK, *supra* note 391 at 258.

[442] *See, e.g.*, Barrere v. Barrere, 4 Johns. Ch. 187, 197 (N.Y. Ch. 1819) (awarding custody to the mother and ordering the father to pay her child support); Campbell v. Campbell, 37 Wis. 206, 210 (1875)

[443] HARTOG, *supra* note 1 at 165; *see also* Hanberry v. Hanberry, 29 Ala. 719 (1857); M'Gahey v. Williams, 12 Johns. 293 (N.Y. Sup. Ct. 1815); M'Cutchen v. M'Gahey, 11 Johns. 281 (N.Y. Sup. Ct. 1814); Fenner v. Lewis, 10 Johns. 38 (N.Y. Sup. Ct. 1813); Hay v. Warren, 8 Paige Ch. 609 (N.Y. Ch. 1841); Pomeroy v. Wells, 8 Paige Ch. 406 (N.Y. Ch. 1840); Sykes v. Halstead, 3 N.Y. Super. (1 Sand.) 483 (1848);

Adultery was a partial exception to this rule. In most states a court would not require an ex-husband to support (i.e., pay alimony to) an ex-wife who had committed adultery, at least not where she had left her husband to take up residence with her lover. A father had an obligation to continue to support his children, though, regardless of the mother's conduct.[444]

Women, by contrast, had no duty to support their husbands or their children under any circumstances, whether the husband had been faithful or not.[445] Again, family support was the sole responsibility of men whether they were married or divorced, and whether they had custody or access to their children or not.

Women's rights included new laws or changes in the old laws which would improve the lives of women but would not necessarily require...equality with men....Women were granted the chance of custody... [b]ut women's rights reformers did not attempt to remove the obligation of men to support [them].[446]

Unwed fathers

The doctrine of coverture did not apply to unwed parents, and early English common law did not impose a support obligation on the putative father of a child born out of wedlock. This changed in 1576 when an Act of Parliament[447] decreed that children born out of wedlock should be

---

ANONYMOUS, A TREATISE OF FEME COVERTS: OR, THE LADY'S LAW 91 (The Savoy, E. & R. Nutt, & R. Gosling (assigns of B. Sayer, Esq.) for B. Lintot 1732); JAMES CLANCY, A TREATISE OF THE RIGHTS, DUTIES AND LIABILITIES OF HUSBAND AND WIFE, AT LAW AND IN EQUITY 24-47 (2d Amer. ed., New York, The Law Press 1837); TAPPING REEVE, THE LAW OF BARON AND FEMME, OF PARENT AND CHILD, OF GUARDIAN AND WARD, OF MASTER AND SERVANT, AND OF THE POWERS OF COURTS OF CHANCERY 164 (New Haven, Oliver Steele 1816)
[444] HARTOG, *supra* note 1 at 160.
[445] Gilley v. Gilley, 9 A. 623 (Me. 1887); Gladding v. Follett, 2 Dem. Surr. 58 (N.Y. 1883), *aff'd*, 95 N.Y. 652 (1883); *In re* Hippert's Estate, 1 Chester Co. Rep. 66, 12 Lanc. Bar 68 (Pa. 1880)
[446] MARY ANN MASON, THE EQUALITY TRAP 37 (2002). On the other hand, a few courts declined to require a father to pay child support to a person who was wrongfully withholding or concealing his children from him. PECK, *supra* note 391 at 257.

supported by their putative fathers, and courts ordered them to do so. The Bastardy Act of 1733 gave courts the power to imprison a putative father until he either provided financial support for his children or agreed to marry the mother.[448]

Most American colonies enacted similar kinds of laws imposing support obligations on the fathers of children born out of wedlock, as did most states either prior to or shortly after attaining statehood.[449] Accordingly, the question whether a putative father had a common law obligation to support his children has not often been addressed in American judicial decisions except in dictum. In *Doughty v. Engler*,[450] a rare case raising the issue squarely, the Kansas Supreme Court declared that in America, unlike in England, a putative father does indeed have a common law duty to support his children even in the absence of statute. The specific attributes of the obligation (such as the formula for calculating the amount of money required to be paid, for example) are controlled by statute.[451]

Parents vs. non-parents

American judicial decisions from the earliest published reports to the present day have always recognized the superior right of parents, both mothers and fathers, to custody of their children. This was true in both the nineteenth and twentieth centuries, long before courts began imposing child support obligations on mothers and well as fathers. Accordingly, it cannot really be said that there was ever a time when courts viewed custody rights as things that "spring from" the support obligation.

Independence of custody and support obligations

Until very recently, the law in every state was that men, but not women, were responsible for the support of their children, whether the children were born during marriage or not, and this rule applied even if the law or a court divested the man of rights of custody and access to his

---

[447] 18 Elizabeth C. 3 (1576)
[448] Camp, *supra* note 438 at 7-9
[449] *See generally* BASTARDY AND ITS COMPARATIVE HISTORY, *supra* note 438; TEICHMAN, *supra* note 438; TIFFANY, *supra* note 178.
[450] 211 P. 619 (Kan. 1923)
[451] *See, e.g.*, Simmons v. Bull, 21 Ala. 501 (1852).

children through no fault of his own. The double standard endured, to varying degrees in different states, for over a century after the nineteenth century enactment of "equal rights" legislation that is said to have abolished the coverture doctrine and put men and women on an "equal" footing. In short, the assertion that custody rights "spring from" the support obligation was merely dictum. It was something judges sometimes said to justify a decision to grant a father custody of his children in preference to a non-parent third party, but it never operated as a bar to a mother's right to custody of her children.

22. VISITATION RIGHTS

Throughout the nineteenth century, courts regularly granted visitation rights (sometimes called "access" rights) to a parent when they made an award of custody of a child to someone other than the parent.[452]

The rationale for visitation was that "[t]he law has such regard for the affections of parents, … even the guilty party will not be wholly deprived of the society of the children, but provision will be made for such party to visit them at all reasonable times."[453]

---

[452] *See, e.g.*, People *ex rel.* Odronaux v. Chegaray, 18 Wend. 637, 644 (N.Y. 1836); Prather v. Prather, 4 Des. 32 (S.C. 1809); 2 BISHOP § 536, *supra* note 146 ("whoever has the custody, both the parents are generally permitted access to them.")

[453] Hewitt v. Long, 76 Ill. 76 Ill. 399, 412 (1875); *see also* Miner v. Miner, 11 Ill. 43, 51 (1849) (holding that a parent deprived of custody "must not be wholly deprived of its society, but must be allowed access to it upon all reasonable occasions"); Hill v. Hill, 49 Md. 450 (1878) (granting visitation rights to adulterous parent); Baird v. Baird, 18 N.J. Eq. 194, 204 (N.J. Ch. 1867) (granting father visitation rights notwithstanding statute requiring courts to award exclusive custody of children under the age of seven to the mother); People *ex rel.* Ordonaux v. Chegarey, 18 Wend. 637, 644 (N.Y. 1836); Ahrenfeldt v. Ahrenfeldt, 4 Sandf. Ch. 497 (N.Y. Ch. 1847); Prather v. Prather, 4 Des. 32 (S.C. 1809)

As the quoted passage suggests, early visitation orders typically granted the noncustodial parent a right to visit the child "at all reasonable times."[454] Sometimes courts simply granted a "right of access" or a "right to visit and see" the child.[455] It was contemplated that the specific days and hours would be selected by the noncustodial parent.[456] Occasionally, a court would prescribe a specific visitation schedule.[457]

The amount of visitation time that nineteenth century courts deemed to be reasonable would be considered rather minimal by today's standards. It might consist of one afternoon per week;[458] a couple of hours per week;[459] or even as little as a couple of times per year.[460] Sometimes a court would order more liberal visitation, though. In *State ex rel. Flint v. Flint*,[461] for example, the noncustodial parent was granted a right to visit the child three times per week, and five hours on Sundays.

It was not uncommon for a court to order visitation to take place in the custodial parent's home.[462] This kind of restriction appears to have been imposed principally upon fathers, not mothers.[463] Reasons typically were not given in the order. In view of prevailing beliefs about the unique suitability of mothers for child-raising, it is likely that the mother's presence during the father's time with the child was felt to be necessary to ensure that the children would be properly cared for while the father was visiting with them.

---

[454] *See, e.g.*, Prather v. Prather, 4 Des. 32 (S.C. 1809); *see also* Hansford v. Hansford, 10 Ala. 561 (1846).

[455] *See, e.g.*, Cole v. Cole, 23 Iowa 433, 449 (1867); Duhme v. Duhme, 3 Ohio Dec. Reprint 95 (Hamilton Co. C.P. 1859)

[456] *See, e.g.*, Hill v. Hill, 49 Md. 450 (1878); Commonwealth v. Addicks, 5 Binn. 520 (Pa. 1813)

[457] *See, e.g.*, Ahrenfeldt v. Ahrenfeldt, 4 Sand. Ch. 493, 495 (N.Y. Ch. 1847); Campbell v. Campbell, 37 Wis. 206 (1875)

[458] *See, e.g.*, Campbell v. Campbell, 37 Wis. 206 (1875)

[459] *See, e.g.*, State *ex rel.* McDonough v. O'Malley, 80 N.W. 1133 (Minn. 1899)

[460] *See, e.g.*, Hill v. Hill, 49 Md. 450 (1878)

[461] 65 N.W. 272 (Minn. 1895)

[462] *See, e.g.*, State *ex rel.* McDonough v. O'Malley, 78 Minn. 163 (Minn. 1899)

[463] *Compare* Hill v. Hill, 49 Md. 450 (1878), in which the court allowed the noncustodial mother to select the times and places for visitation, *with* State *ex rel.* McDonough v. O'Malley, 78 Minn. 163 (Minn. 1899), in which the court required the noncustodial father to conduct all visitations in the mother's home, giving no reason for imposing this restriction.

In some cases, a court would impose other restrictions on a parent's visitation, or deny it altogether, in order to protect a child from physical or moral harm. For example, to protect a child from moral harm, a court might deny visitation rights to a parent who had been found guilty of adultery[464]

Nineteenth century jurists generally viewed visitation and access as rights or privileges that only parents could seek. Courts normally did not grant visitation rights to grandparents or other third parties. At common law, parents were regarded as having a moral obligation to allow their children to visit with extended family members, but the obligation generally was not legally enforceable.[465]

Although courts sometimes described visitation and access as parental rights, not all parents were entitled to them, not even if such rights could be shown to be in a child's best interests in a particular case. Visitation was a mother's natural right in all cases where she was not awarded custody of her children, but it was a father's legal right only if he had entered into a marriage with the mother before the birth of the children. Courts did not grant visitation rights to fathers of children born out of wedlock.

Visitation and access are aspects of the broader right to the preservation of the parent-child relationship. In the nineteenth century, the law viewed this as a right belonging to parents (or more precisely, a specified subset of parents), not to children. The twentieth century would see a series of progressive reforms aimed at advancing and improving the rights and interests of children. Surprisingly, after a full century of these reforms, the law continues to treat parents, not children, as possessing the basic right to the preservation of the parent-child relationship. Children are said to have an interest in the preservation of a relationship with both

---

[464] *See, e.g.,* Codd v. Codd, 2 Johns. Ch. 141 (N.Y. Ch. 1816) (denying visitation rights to an adulterous father); Crimmins v. Crimmins, 64 How. Pr. 103 (N.Y. 1882) (denying visitation rights to an adulterous mother)

[465] Succession of Reiss, 15 So. 151, 152 (La. 1894); *In re* Goldfarb, 70 A.2d 94, 96 (NJ. Super. Ct. Ch. Div. 1949); 2 H. CLARK, THE LAW OF DOMESTIC RELATIONS IN THE UNITED STATES § 20.7 (2d ed. 1987); NAOMI KARP, *Introduction to* GRANDPARENT VISITATION DISPUTES: A LEGAL RESOURCE MANUAL (Ellen C. Segal & Naomi Karp eds., 1989); *but cf. Ex parte* Ralston, R.M. Charlton 119 (Ga. 1821) (giving the grandmother, in that case, a right "to have access to the infant on her request, and at convenient periods.")

parents, but it is not an independently enforceable right of the child.[466] It is possible that as the relatively recently introduced "shared parenting" model increasingly supplants the "custody rights" model that treats adults as having something akin to property rights in children, a new understanding of the preservation of the parent-child relationship as a child's right may begin to emerge.

---

[466] A court might appoint a guardian *ad litem* to provide independent representation for a child in a custody proceeding, but the guardian *ad litem*'s charge, normally, is to advocate for whatever she believes to be in the child's "best interests." Courts normally do not charge them with responsibility to protect a child's right to a continuing relationship with both parents

PART IV. MODERN AMERICA

23. EARLY CUSTODY STATUTES

By the beginning of the twentieth century, most states had enacted statutes addressing the subject of child custody. For the most part, these statutes did not change the legal standards the courts had developed in the nineteenth century for the decision of custody cases. They simply codified them.

Many of these statutes expressed the idea that marital fault should be the principal basis for custody decisions. They directed courts to award custody to "the innocent party" or to "the party not at fault."[467]

A few statutes specifically directed courts to decide custody on the basis of the best interests of the children.[468] Even in the absence of such a statute, though, courts continued to hold that the paramount consideration in custody cases was the welfare of the child, not the rights of the parents.[469]

---

[467] *See, e.g.,* N.D. COMP. L. 4371 (1913); *see generally* Einhorn, *Child Custody in Historical Perspective: A Study of Changing Social Perceptions of Divorce and Child Custody in Anglo-American Law,* 4 BEHAV. SCI. & L. 119 (1986)

[468] *See, e.g.,* ARIZ. REV. STAT. § 3870 (1913) (superseded by ARIZ. REV. STAT. §25-403 (2012)); FLA. COMP. LAWS § 1938 (1914) (superseded by Fla. Stat. § 61.13 (2012)); ILL. REV. STAT. § 13 (1917) (superseded by 750 ILL. COMP. STAT. § 5/602 (2010)); MASS. REV. LAWS § 28 (1902) (superseded by MASS. GEN. LAWS ch. 208, § 31 (2011)).

Most statutes also directed courts to have "due regard for the age and sex of the child."[470] This language was intended to require courts to continue to apply the tender years doctrine.

It was not uncommon for a statute to authorize courts to sidestep the marital fault doctrine for other reasons, too. A statute of this kind directed courts to award custody to the party not at fault unless doing so would be "manifestly improper."[471] This codified the judicial discretion to consider other factors besides marital fault. This could include not only the age and sex of the child and the parents, but also such things as child abuse, moral character, use of vulgar language in the presence of a woman or child, and so on.

Early twentieth century statutes generally did not address joint custody. Instead, they required courts to award custody to "the" party not at fault, or to "the" party who would best care for the child, simply assuming that one or the other party had to be declared "the winner" in every case.

American custody statutes remained relatively unchanged throughout the century. Efforts to establish gender-neutral, non-fault-based standards did not begin until the no-fault movement of the 1970's.

---

[469] *See, e.g.,* McDonald v. Short, 130 N.E. 536, 537 (Ind. 1921); Hild v. Hild, 157 A.2d 442, 446 (Md. Ct. App. 1960); Wood v. Wood, 77 A. 91 (N.J. Eq. 1910); PECK, *supra* note 391 at 261 (asserting that "the material and moral welfare of the child, as it will be affected by giving its control to one or the other parent" as the "controlling consideration" in custody disputes between parents; TIFFANY, *supra* note 178 at 268, 380 (observing that although courts might allude to a father's "right" to custody, the rule they actually applied was a "best interests of the child" standard that does not give preference to fathers)

[470] *See, e.g.,* 1909 Wis. Laws, ch. 223, § 2362

[471] *See, e.g.,* OR. CODE § 402 (1911)

24. THE DEMISE OF MARITAL FAULT

For the first two-thirds of the twentieth century, marital fault was an important factor in custody cases. By law, the innocent spouse enjoyed a prima facie right to custody of the children in the event of a divorce or separation.[472] Judges believed marital fault to be a good indicator of moral character. Moral character, in turn, was considered an important component of parental fitness. The Maryland Court of Appeals, in 1960, explained it this way:

> [C]ustody of the child is usually awarded to the innocent party, not as a matter of punishment or reward, but because it is assumed that the child will be reared in a cleaner and more wholesome moral

---

[472] *See, e.g.*, GA. CIV. CODE § 2971 (Park, 1914) (superseded by GA. CODE § 19-3-3 (2012)) (specifying that the party not at fault is entitled to custody); IDAHO COMP. LAWS § 4623 (1919) (superseded by IDAHO CODE § 32-717 (2011)) ("to the innocent party"); OR. LAWS § 513 (1920) (superseded by OR. REV. STAT. § 107.137 (2011)) ("having due regard to the age and sex of the children, and unless otherwise manifestly improper, giving the preference to the party not in fault"); P.R. CIV. CODE § 175 (1902) (superseded) (requiring courts to award custody to the mother unless she is at fault for the divorce.)

atmosphere…. [It is harmful to a child to be raised by one who demonstrates a] flagrant disregard of the law of the land, including the sanctity of an oath, as well as the moral code, which is well-nigh universally accepted by our society. Such a person should not be entrusted to guide the physical, spiritual and moral development of the child. [473]

From an early twentieth century family law treatise: "If the question is between husband and wife, the court will consider the cause of the estrangement between them, and the question which was at fault in the separation, as proper factors in determining the custody of the children…."[474]

The prima facie right of the innocent spouse to custody could be defeated by proof that a child's best interests would be served by awarding custody to the guilty spouse in a particular case.[475] In the case of daughters, disabled or unhealthy children, and young children of either sex, the presumption reflected in the tender years doctrine defeated the presumption that custody should be awarded to the innocent spouse. The tender years doctrine established a presumption that it was in the best interests of children in any of these categories to be placed in their mother's custody irrespective of any marital misconduct on her part.[476]

Another way to look at the state of custody law during the first part of the twentieth century is that marital fault created only a presumption that the innocent party should have custody. The presumption could be

---

[473] Hild v. Hild, 157 A.2d 442, 447-48 (Md. Ct. App. 1960). In this case, the court of appeals reversed an award of custody to an adulterous mother on the basis of the presumption against awards of custody to the guilty spouse. The court distinguished cases in which a parent evidences moral reform by terminating the affair, indicating that in such cases the presumption against an award of custody to the guilty party would be deemed rebutted. *Id.* at 447. Marriage to one's paramour subsequent to a divorce from the spouse against whom one committed adultery was not necessarily sufficient to establish moral reform. Pangle v. Pangle, 106 A. 337 (Md. 1919). *See also* Carter v. Carter, 156 M. 500, 507 (1929) (denying custody to spouse who unjustifiably deserted the marriage and had concealed the children from the innocent spouse.)

[474] PECK, *supra* note 391 at 261.

[475] TIFFANY, *supra* note 178 at 273-74.

[476] *Id.* at 271, 274; *see also* Dinkel v. Dinkel, 322 So. 2d (Fla. 1975).

rebutted with evidence that the party who had engaged in the marital misconduct was female (i.e., the mother.) That would trigger the maternal preference. The maternal preference, in turn, was rebuttable by proving that the mother was actually a danger to the child.

The idealization of maternal care that dominated child custody jurisprudence in nineteenth and twentieth century America led many courts to extend the maternal preference embodied in the tender years doctrine to every custody case irrespective of the age of the child. This general maternal preference, like the tender years presumption, was rebuttable only by proof that the mother was actually a danger to the child.[477] Thus, in many states the evolution of the tender years doctrine into a general maternal preference effectively eliminated the relevance of marital fault in contests between a mother and a father. Its relevance, in many states, increasingly became limited to cases in which a third party sought to divest a father of custody.

No-fault divorce

In the 1960's and 1970's, America experienced, simultaneously, a sexual revolution and a second wave of feminism. Together, these movements yielded significant changes in family law.

Before the women's movement of the 1960's and 1970's, a general societal expectation existed in the United States that a woman should abstain from sexual intercourse until she became married, and then should have sexual relations with only one man, her husband. 1960's feminists viewed the expectation that a woman should "save herself" for marriage, and then commit herself exclusively to one man for life, as emblematic of men's enslavement of women.[478] These societal expectations, they argued, prevented women from realizing their full human potential.[479] Sexual

---

[477] *See, e.g.,* Hild v. Hild, 157 A.2d 42 (Md. 1960) (reversing trial court's award of custody to an adulterous mother, and holding that the tender years doctrine will not overcome the presumption against an award of custody to an adulterous spouse if the mother, in addition to being adulterous, is also a danger to the child's emotional health and development due to her interference with the other parent's visitation rights and her disparagement of the other parent to the child.)

[478] *See* BETTY FRIEDAN, THE FEMININE MYSTIQUE (1963). "A liberated woman," Gloria Steinem wrote, "Is one who has sex before marriage and a job after." *Newsweek* (March 28, 1960)

[479] FRIEDAN, *supra* note 478.

liberationists concurred, at least with respect to the view that chastity and monogamy prevented women from leading fulfilling lives. Sexual liberals believed that women should be encouraged to enjoy sex, and to enjoy it with as many different partners as they desired.[480]

Leading feminists of the time viewed marriage as an oppressive institution, one by which men ensured their perpetual dominance over women. Beginning with Betty Friedan in 1963, they argued that it was a form of slavery, and that, at best, it stifled women's creativity and ambitions, draining all love, meaning and value from their lives.[481] "Since marriage constitutes slavery for women," Sheila Cronan wrote, "It is clear that the women's movement must concentrate on attacking this institution. Freedom for women cannot be won without the abolition of marriage."[482] Further, "the institution of marriage 'protects' women in the same way that the institution of slavery was said to 'protect' blacks--that is, that the word 'protection' in this case is simply a euphemism for oppression."[483] Germaine Greer, in her influential book, *The Female Eunuch*, declared: "If women are to effect a significant amelioration in their condition it seems obvious that they must refuse to marry."[484] Kate Millett declared the goal of feminism to be "the complete destruction of traditional marriage and the nuclear family."[485] Ti-Grace Atkinson referred to married women as "hostages."[486] "Marriage," it was said, "remains thoroughly tainted by being a long-standing buttress for the patriarchal domination of women."[487] Picketing the New York City Marriage License Bureau in September 1969, a N.O.W. splinter group under the leadership of Robin Morgan distributed

---

[480] Steinem, *supra* note 478. Probably the most famous literary convergence of the women's liberation movement with the sexual liberation movement was the 1973 book, *Fear of Flying*, by Erica Jong. Best known today for its glorification of what she called "the zipless f**k," i.e., a casual, no-strings-attached sexual encounter (what today would be called a "hook-up"), the book sold over 20 million copies

[481] FRIEDAN, *supra* note 478.

[482] Sheila Cronan, in RADICAL FEMINISM – "MARRIAGE" 219 (Koedt, Levine, & Rapone eds., 1973).

[483] *Id.* at 214.

[484] GERMAINE GREER, THE FEMALE EUNUCH 317 (1971)

[485] .KATE MILLETT, SEXUAL POLITICS 35 (1970).

[486] ALICE ECHOLS, DARING TO BE BAD: RADICAL FEMINISM IN AMERICA 1967-1975 at p. 178 (1989).

[487] Merran Toerien & Andrew Williams, *In Knots: Dilemmas of a Feminist Couple Contemplating Marriage*, 13 FEMINISM & PSYCHOL. 434 (November 2003)

pamphlets declaring: "All the discriminatory practices against women are patterned and rationalized by this slavery-like practice. We can't destroy the inequities between men and women until we destroy marriage."[488] Ms. Morgan went on to become editor of *Ms. Magazine*. The New York Public Library lists her book, *Sisterhood Is Powerful*, in which the quoted statement appears, as one of the most influential books of the twentieth century.[489]

> Marriage has existed for the benefit of men; and has been a legally sanctioned method of control over women…. Male society has sold us the idea of marriage…. Now we know it is the institution that has failed us and we must work to destroy it. The end of the institution of marriage is a necessary condition for the liberation of women. Therefore it is important for us to encourage women to leave their husbands and not to live individually with men….[490]

Although they did not succeed in abolishing the institution of marriage completely, second wave feminists did succeed in securing reforms that would make it possible for women to leave their marriages irrespective of whether they had been faithful to their husbands or not. Beginning in 1970 with California[491] states began eliminating the requirement of showing that one's spouse was guilty of marital wrongdoing before a court could grant a party's request for a divorce. At the same time, states also eliminated the requirement that the party seeking the divorce had to be innocent of any marital wrongdoing herself. In short, states began reforming their divorce laws to make marital fault irrelevant.

---

[488] SISTERHOOD IS POWERFUL: AN ANTHOLOGY OF WRITINGS FROM THE WOMEN'S LIBERATION MOVEMENT 537 (Robin Morgan ed., 1970)

[489] THE NEW YORK PUBLIC LIBRARY'S BOOKS OF THE CENTURY (Elizabeth Diefendorf ed., 1996).

[490] NANCY LEHMANN & HELEN SULLINGER, DECLARATION OF FEMINISM (1971)

[491] There is some dispute about whether California was the first state to enact no-fault divorce legislation. If "living separate and apart" for a specified period of time is included within the meaning of "no-fault" divorce, then several states, such as New York and Maryland, enacted no-fault divorce legislation before California did. And in 1968, Delaware enacted legislation authorizing divorces for couples that had experienced a two-year period of incompatibility. Denese Ashbaugh Vlosky & Pamela A. Monroe, *The Effective Dates of No-Fault Divorce Laws in the 50 States*, 51 FAM. REL. 317, 322 Table 2 (Oct. 2002)

The women's liberation movement and the sexual revolution were not the only sources of opposition to fault-based divorce. Social scientists criticized it for protracting children's exposure to acrimony between their parents.[492] Legal commentators, for their part, argued that fault-based divorce systems tainted the integrity of the justice system because they induced married people to commit perjury and falsify evidence in order to get around strict statutory obstacles to divorce.[493]

States varied with respect to the kinds of no-fault legislation they enacted. Many completely replaced fault-based grounds for divorce with no-fault grounds, such as "irreconcilable differences" and/or "irretrievable breakdown of the marriage." Who was at fault for the inability to reconcile and the breakdown of the marriage was irrelevant.

Other states, such as New York, retained fault-based grounds, but added no-fault grounds to them. In these states, a person seeking a divorce could choose to pursue either a fault-based or a no-fault divorce.

Still other states effected no-fault divorce reform by making the fact of living separate and apart for a specified period of time (such as six months) grounds for divorce without any need for proof that the separation was justified due to a party's misconduct.

By 1987, all fifty states had enacted some form of no-fault divorce legislation.[494]

Impact of no-fault legislation on child custody standards

No-fault divorce legislation generally only removed the requirement of fault-finding from the process of deciding whether a divorce should be granted or not. This did not necessarily mean that fault could not be considered in connection with other issues. In fact, courts continued to consider certain kinds of marital misconduct in connection with other issues. For example, a party's commission of adultery might preclude an

---

[492] *Id.* at 317

[493] M. RHEINSTEIN, MARRIAGE, DIVORCE, STABILITY AND THE LAW (1971); Thomas B. Marvell, *Divorce rates and the fault requirement*, 23 LAW & SOC'Y REV. 543-567 (1989); S.E. Stanley & J.J. Berman, *Changing from fault to no-fault divorce: An interrupted time series analysis*, 7 J. APPLIED SOC. PSYCHOL. 300-312 (1977).

[494] Vlosky & Monroe, *supra* note 491 at 323, Table 3.

award of alimony to that spouse. Similarly, a father's nonsupport of his wife or children could be considered in connection with the issue of custody, since judicial precedents had established that it was relevant to a father's parental fitness.

Nevertheless, the removal of marital fault as the grounds for a divorce made the application of statutes directing courts to award custody to "the party not at fault for the divorce" problematic. Influenced by the women's movement to enable women to leave their husbands and still keep their children even if they had not been faithful to their husbands, and by the liberalization of sexual mores wrought by the sexual revolution, the legislative solution was to articulate a new set of factors, independent of marital fault, for deciding the custody of children in a divorce. Some of the factors included were similar to ones that had been developed by the courts over the years. Others were new. Only a very small handful of states included any reference to moral character among their statutory "best interest" factors. (The development of statutory "best interest" factors is described in more detail in Chapter 30, *infra*.)

Although it does not appear that any court has completely ruled out the possibility of considering marital fault in connection with custody issues, it no longer occupies anything close to the central position it once did. Today, only a small handful of states authorize courts to consider a child's moral development, or the potential impact of a parent's marital misconduct on a child's moral character. In most (but not all) states, evidence of marital misconduct is relevant only to the extent a party can demonstrate that it adversely affects a child's physical, psychological, or emotional development.

No-fault legislation, as of 1998[495]

State	Exclusively no-fault	Both fault and no-fault	Separation for a specified time
Alabama		X (1971)	2 years (1947)
Alaska		X (1963)	
Arizona	X (1973)		
Arkansas		X	18 months
California	X (1970)		3 years

---

[495] adapted from Vlosky & Monroe, *supra* note 491 at 322-23, Table 2.

Colorado	X (1972)		
Connecticut		X (1973)	18 months
Delaware	X		
Florida	X (1971)		
Georgia		X (1973)	
Hawaii	X (1972)		2 years
Idaho		X (1971)	
Illinois		X (1984)	2 years
Indiana		X (1973)	
Iowa	X (1970)		
Kansas		X (1969)	
Kentucky	X (1972)		
Louisiana		X	1 year
Maine	X (1973)		
Maryland		X	2 years
Massachusetts		X (1975)	
Michigan	X (1972)		
Minnesota	X (1974)		
Mississippi		X (1976)	
Missouri		X (1974)	1-2 years
Montana	X (1973)		180 days
Nebraska	X (1972)		
Nevada		X (1967)	1 year
New Hampshire		X (1971)	2 years
New Jersey		X	18 months
New Mexico		X (1973)	
New York		X	1 year
North Carolina			1 year
North Dakota		X (1971)	
Ohio		X	1 year
Oklahoma		X	
Oregon	X (1971)		
Pennsylvania		X (1980)	2 years
Rhode Island		X (1975)	3 years
South Carolina		X	1 year
South Dakota		X (1985)	
Tennessee		X (1977)	2 years
Texas		X (1970)	3 years
Utah		X (1987)	3 years
Vermont		X	6 months
Virginia		X	1 year
Washington	X (1973)		
West Virginia		X (1977)	1 year
Wisconsin	X (1978)		
Wyoming	X (1977)		

25. THE MATERNAL PREFERENCE

The maternal preference that was established in the nineteenth century continued to be the principal standard of decision in custody cases throughout most of the twentieth century. "It is universally recognized that the mother is the natural custodian of her young. Accordingly, the mother is ordinarily awarded the custody of children of tender age, especially girls, unless it is clearly shown that she is not a fit and proper person."[496] Some jurisdictions codified it.[497] In others, courts applied a judicially-created presumption that maternal sole custody is in every child's best interests.

---

[496] Comwell v. Comwell, 224 A. 2d 870 (Md. 1966); *see also* HARTOG *supra* note 1 at 306 ("In 1950 (and still in 1960 and even in 1970), much of the nineteenth century law of husband and wife remained.")

[497] LA. REV. CIV. CODE art. 146 (1912) (superseded by LA. CIV. CODE art. 131 (2011)) (requiring courts to award custody to the wife even if she is at fault for the divorce); N.H. STAT. ch. 176 § 4 (superseded by N.H. REV. STAT. § 458:16 (2011)) (authorizing only wives, not husbands, to get orders for temporary custody of children during the pendency of a divorce); R.I. GEN. LAWS ch. 245, § 1 (1909) (superseded) (declaring that a married woman has sole custody if she lives separately from her husband for a year); UTAH COMP. LAWS § 3004 (1917) (superseded by UTAH CODE § 30-3-10 (2012)) (requiring courts to award custody to the mother unless she is proven to be "immoral or otherwise incompetent"); P.R. CIV. CODE §§ 166, 175 (1902) (superseded) (requiring courts to award custody to the wife unless she is at fault for the divorce.)

In all states, it was a firmly established rule of law throughout most of the twentieth century that the mother was entitled to custody of the children in a divorce or separation unless she was proven to be unfit to parent. "The mother of an illegitimate child is entitled to its custody unless she be unfit therefore. And the same rule as to custody of legitimate children is applied to the custody of illegitimate children, and the courts are controlled and actuated by the same considerations."[498] As late as 1976, *American Law Reports* reported that "the vast majority of the jurisdictions continue to follow" the maternal preference, viewing the mother as the "natural custodian of her young" because "her love for her child is irreplaceable."[499]

Prior to the 1980's, judges simply assumed that mothers were imbued with a natural instinct for child-rearing, and that this instinct was lacking in fathers. Courts explained their refusal to grant custody to fathers this way: "To deprive [a] child of the society, companionship and the instinctive and natural maternal love of her mother ... would hardly be to the interests of the child."[500]

Sometimes courts characterized the mother-child bond as "sacred." [501] The father-child bond was not. As the Wisconsin Supreme Court explained:

[No father's love] can be an adequate substitute for mother love – for that constant ministration required during the period of nurture that only a mother can give because in her alone is duty swallowed up in desire; in her alone is service expressed in terms of love.[502]

---

[498] Pierce v. Jeffries, 137 S.E. 651 (W. Va. 1927).

[499] Thomas R. Trenkner, Annotation, *Modern Status of Maternal Preference Rule or Presumption in Child Custody Cases*, 70 A.L.R.3d 262 (1976).

[500] Pitts v. Pitts, 29 A. 2d 300, 305 (Md. 1942). Freudian dogma held that women were naturally suited for child-raising and had an inherent nurturing ability that men lacked, thereby making the mother-child relationship more important to children than the father-child relationship is. *See* Roth, *supra* note 2)

[501] *See, e.g.,* Waldron v. Childers, 148 S.W. 1030 (Ark. 1912) (holding that "the natural affection of a mother ... is stronger and more sacred than that of any other....")

[502] Jenkins v. Jenkins, 181 N.W. 826, 827 (Wis. 1921)

In 1972, the Maryland Court of Appeals candidly expressed its bias in favor of mothers in the following terms:

> The maternal tie is so primordial that it should not be lightly severed or attenuated. The appreciation of the visceral bond between mother and child will always be placed upon the balance scales, and all else being equal or nearly so, will tilt them.[503]

From article of faith to rule of reason

In 1973, Joseph Goldstein and Albert Solnit teamed up with Sigmund Freud's daughter, Anna Freud, to publish a book called *Beyond the Best Interests of the Child*.[504] It espoused a psychoanalytic approach to determining what is in a child's best interests, one that relied heavily on Sigmund Freud's psychoanalytic theories and John Bowlby's attachment theory, which also was grounded in Freudian theory.

Freud and her colleagues observed that an infant develops a psychological attachment to an adult who is personally and emotionally involved with him. They theorized that the attachment consisted of the baby's superimposition of its libidinal interests on the events of bodily care (feeding and diaper-changing, for example.) They postulated that because of this early attachment, it is vitally important to a child's psychological well-being for this first bond to remain uninterrupted.

> Such primitive and tenuous first attachments form the base from which any further relationships develop. What the child brings to them next are no longer only his needs for body comfort and gratification but his emotional demands for affection, companionship, and stimulating intimacy. Where these are answered reliably and regularly, the child-parent relationship becomes firm, with immensely productive effects on the child's intellectual and social development.[505]

---

[503] Kirstukas v. Kirstukas, 286 A.2d 535 (Md. Ct. App. 1972)
[504] JOSEPH GOLDSTEIN ET AL., BEYOND THE BEST INTERESTS OF THE CHILD (1973).
[505] *Id.* at 18.

"Unlike adults, who are generally capable of maintaining positive emotional ties with a number of different individuals," they asserted, "Children lack the capacity to do so."[506] Since mothers are the ones who are biologically equipped to nurse their babies, it is easy to see how Freud's theoretical framework could have been thought to support a preference for making awards of sole custody to mothers.

The difficulty with using Freud's psychoanalytical libido-superimposition theory as a justification for a judicial preference for mothers is that it is not necessarily true that the mother is the one upon whom the child superimposes its libido in every case. If a particular father does a greater share of the feeding, diapering and comforting of the baby than the mother, then the theory would support a preference for making an award of sole custody to the father rather than the mother in that case. The theory is not sufficient, by itself, to support a maternal preference or presumption specifically in favor of mothers.

Moreover, there was very little basis for Freud's assumptions that children are incapable of forming psychological attachments to more than one person, or that multiple attachments are detrimental to a developing child's psychological health. In fact, available empirical evidence contradicted those assumptions. For example, researchers H. Rudolph Schaffer and Peggy E. Emerson found that from birth to three months of age, babies respond and attach equally to any caregiver; between four and nine months, a baby tends to have a primary attachment to one person, but also maintains secondary attachments to others; and that by nine months babies form multiple attachments. In addition, they found that attachment correlates closely with the person who responds most accurately to the baby's needs and desires, not the person who spends the most time with the baby. Further, they reported that at eighteen months, a child's main attachment figure was the mother for only about half of the children studied, and the father was the main attachment figure for nearly all of the rest. Finally – and contrary to Freud's libidinal-superimposition theory -- they found that the most important factor in forming attachments is not who feeds and diapers a child, but who plays and communicates with her.[507]

---

[506] *Id.* at 13.

[507] H. Rudolph Schaffer and Peggy E. Emerson *The Development of Social Attachments*

Nevertheless, late-twentieth century judges, custody evaluators, and family law policy-makers increasingly cited Freud's theory, as expounded in *Beyond the Best Interests of the Child*, as the justification for their preference for maternal sole custody, and for permitting children to have only very brief periods of visitation with their fathers.[508] By the end of the century, Freudian attachment theory had supplanted both God and the maternal instinct as the doctrinal basis for the judicial preference for mothers.

Maternal unfitness

The maternal preference was never absolute. A father could rebut the presumption that custody should be awarded to the mother by proving that she was unfit to be a parent. Courts construed the concept of parental unfitness very narrowly when considering the fitness of a mother to parent, though. The double standard they had developed in this respect in the nineteenth century continued into the twentieth.

A father's insolvency or poverty was sufficient to support a finding of his unfitness for custody. In *Bryant v. Dukehart*,[509] the mother died and the trial court, instead of leaving the children in the custody of their father, awarded them to the guardian the mother had appointed in her will. Acknowledging that the surviving parent normally has a right to custody of the couple's children when one of the parents dies, the appellate court nevertheless affirmed the award of custody to the guardian rather than the father. In support of its decision, the court cited the fact that the father had entered into a lump-sum child support settlement at the time of the parties' divorce. The court held that a father's attempt to enter into a one-time lump-sum settlement of his child support obligation at the time of the divorce evidenced an intention to evade the obligation of a father to support women and children financially with periodic payments of money throughout their lives. That intention rendered him unfit to be a parent.

A mother's insolvency or poverty, by contrast, was deemed irrelevant to her fitness to parent. If a woman was not able to support her child, the

---

in Infancy, 29 MONOGRAPHS OF THE SOC'Y FOR RES. IN CHILD DEV. no. 94 (1964)
[508] Kathryn L. Mercer, *A Content Analysis of Judicial Decision-Making: How Judges Use Primary Caretaker Standard to Make a Custody Determination*, 5 WM. & MARY J. WOMEN & L. 73 (1998)
[509] 210 P. 454, 457, 459 (Or. 1922).

courts reasoned that her financial difficulties could be ameliorated by ordering the father to pay alimony and child support to her. So long as she was not habitually drunk, did not suffer from a serious mental illness, and was not guilty of severe physical child abuse, a mother would be considered sufficiently fit for child-raising.[510]

In most states, a mother's commission of adultery would not support a finding the she was unfit to parent. A few states did treat adultery or other marital misconduct as evidence of parental unfitness.[511] Even in these states, though, a mother's termination of the adulterous relationship sufficed to restore her to full fitness.[512]

Other courts applied a more general double standard. These courts treated a father's commission of adultery, desertion or other marital misconduct as conclusive evidence of his unfitness to parent, but held that a mother's commission of these kinds of things did not necessarily render her unfit to parent, especially if the custody of a daughter, a disabled or unhealthy child, or a young child, was at stake. To these courts, the tender years doctrine overrode the presumption of parental unfitness that otherwise would arise upon proof of marital fault.

In most states, the fact that the mother was the one who was at fault for the divorce did not prevent a court from awarding her custody of the children, no matter how egregious her behavior had been. In *Crabtree v. Crabtree*,[513] the wife had cut a five-inch slit in her husband's throat with a razor blade, intending to kill him, and then chased him down and stabbed him again as he was running away. Upon his release from the hospital, he petitioned for divorce on the grounds of extreme cruelty. The court found that the wife's attempt to kill him was not justified, her reason apparently having been simply her displeasure with his "sullen" attitude, and her anger at him for trying to get away from her. The court found that he had not

---

[510] AMERICAN BAR ASSOCIATION, *supra* note 303 at 172

[511] *See, e.g.,* Palmer v. Palmer, 207 A.2d 481 (Md. 1965)

[512] As one family law treatise from the period put it: "the mother is preferred as their custodian...and this though she may have been guilty of delinquencies in the past [provided] there is no evidence that she was delinquent at the time of determining the matter by the court." FRANK H. KEEZER, KEEZER ON THE LAW OF MARRIAGE AND DIVORCE (3d ed., John W. Morland ed., 1946)

[513] 242 S.W. 804 (1922)

been guilty of any wrongdoing, so he was indeed entitled to a divorce on the grounds of extreme cruelty, and then proceeded to award custody of the children to the wife because she was their mother.

Judicial beliefs and attitudes at the end of the century

In the twentieth century, the vast majority of cases involving the custody of children were settled without trial. These settlements almost always provided sole custody for the mother. Judges said this was because "many men recognize that their children will be better cared for by the mother."[514] It is also possible that many men simply recognized that judges were predisposed to believe that children are better cared for by mothers than by fathers. Even today, many attorneys advise their male clients that regardless of how qualified they may be as parents, they are not likely to be awarded custody of their children unless they can prove the mother is unfit.

A survey of judges in Alabama, Louisiana, Mississippi and Tennessee conducted near the end of the century found a clear preference among judges for maternal custody.[515] A survey commissioned by the Minnesota Supreme Court found that a majority (56%) of the state's judges, both male and female, agreed with the statement, "I believe young children belong with their mother." Only a few of them indicated that they would need more information about the mother before they could answer. Fathers, one judge explained, "must prove their ability to parent while mothers are assumed to be able."[516] Another judge commented, "I believe that God has given women a psychological makeup that is better tuned to caring for small children."[517]

Judges' self-reporting of their prejudices against fathers was consistent with practicing attorneys' impressions of them. 69% of male attorneys and 40% of female attorneys had come to the conclusion that judges always or

---

[514] Carl A. Weinman, *The Trial Judge Awards Custody*, 10 L. & CONTEMP. PROBS. 721, 723 (1944).

[515] Leighton Stamps, *Maternal Preference in Child Custody Decisions*, 37 J. DIVORCE & REMARRIAGE 1, 7 (2002) ("Overall, ... the means indicated a preference toward mothers over fathers, which are consistent with the theory of maternal preference.").

[516] MINNESOTA SUPREME COURT TASK FORCE FOR GENDER FAIRNESS IN THE COURTS, FINAL REPORT 23 (1989)

[517] *Id.* at 23-24.

often assume from the outset (i.e., before being presented with any evidence) that children belong with their mothers. Nearly all attorneys (94% of male attorneys and 84% of female attorneys) said that all judges exhibited prejudice against fathers at least some of the time.[518]

Similar findings have been made in court-sponsored gender bias studies conducted in other states.[519] Surveys of judges in Maryland, Missouri, Texas and Washington found that a majority of judges were unable to say that they usually give fathers fair consideration in custody cases.[520] This matched the perception of members of the bar.[521]

The Georgia Commission on Gender Bias in the Judicial System uncovered judicial beliefs that mothers are always better parents than fathers; that children need to be with their mothers, but not necessarily with their fathers; and that a father cannot be a nurturing parent if he works outside the home. In addition, the commission uncovered a reluctance to deny custody of children to mothers out of fear that doing so will "brand" the mother as unfit or unworthy.[522] No judge expressed any comparable concern for the reputation or well-being of fathers.

---

[518] *Id.* at 24.

[519] *See, e.g.,* MARYLAND SPECIAL JOINT COMMITTEE ON GENDER BIAS IN THE COURTS, GENDER BIAS REPORT (1989); MARYLAND SELECT COMMITTEE ON GENDER EQUALITY, RETROSPECTIVE REPORT (2001)

[520] Douglas Dotterweich & Michael McKinney, *National Attitudes Regarding Gender Bias in Child Custody Cases,* 38 FAM. & CONCILIATION CTS. REV. 212 (2000).

[521] *Id.* at 213.

[522] COMMISSION ON GENDER BIAS IN THE JUDICIAL SYSTEM: GENDER & JUSTICE IN THE COURTS: A REPORT TO THE SUPREME COURT OF GEORGIA (1991), *reprinted in* 8 GA. ST. U. L. REV. 539, 657-60 (1992).

26. GENDER NEUTRALIZATION

Ironically, the maternal preference for which women had fought in the nineteenth century ultimately would be dismantled by women in the twentieth. While nineteenth century feminists had characterized the *paternal* preference of the English common law as a male conspiracy to subjugate women, twentieth century feminists characterized the *maternal* preference as a male conspiracy to subjugate women.

Referring to the English paternal custody rule, nineteenth century feminists had declared that "[t]he history of mankind is a history of repeated injuries and usurpations on the part of man toward woman.... He has so framed the laws of divorce, as...to whom the guardianship of the children shall be given, as to be wholly regardless of the happiness of women...."[523] Evidently, they assumed that child-rearing was essential to women's happiness, but not to men's. After the desired reforms were achieved and the maternal preference doctrine had become firmly cemented in the law of custody, it came to be seen as a burden, not a pleasure: "Caretakers of the ideology of motherhood ... perpetuate the existing

---

[523] THE DECLARATION OF SENTIMENTS, SENECA FALLS CONFERENCE (1848), *reprinted in* 1 ELIZABETH CADY STANTON, A HISTORY OF WOMAN SUFFRAGE 70-71 (Elizabeth C. Stanton, et al., eds., Rochester, N.Y., Susan B. Anthony 1889).

structure of male-female relationships, legitimating women's relegation to the responsibility for the domestic sphere by an emphasis on the biological mother as the primary caretaker for her children during the early years."[524] Despite the fact that women had been the ones who fought for a strong maternal preference in the law of custody in the nineteenth century, twentieth century anthropologist Margaret Mead described the exaltation of motherhood inherent in the maternal preference as a "form of anti-feminism in which men – under the guise of exalting the importance of maternity – are tying women ... tightly to their children...."[525]

Feminists of the 1960's and 1970's were similar to their nineteenth century predecessors in the sense that they, like their predecessors, were focused on the advancement of women's interests. Nineteenth century feminists had sought to advance women's interests by securing civic equality for them with respect to property rights and voting, as to which men had an advantage at the time. At the same time, they had sought to preserve and secure preferential treatment for women with respect to matters as to which women either had, or were believed to be entitled to have, an advantage, such as the custody of children.

A flexible concept of women's rights...rather than...equality was the focus of most organized women's activities in the nineteenth century....Women's rights included new laws or changes in the old laws which would improve the lives of women but would not necessarily require...equality with men....Women [wanted] custody... [b]ut women's rights reformers did not attempt to remove the obligation of men to support [them]. [526]

---

[524] BETSY WEARING, THE IDEOLOGY OF MOTHERHOOD: A STUDY OF SYDNEY SUBURBAN MOTHERS 198 (1983).

[525] Margaret Mead, *Some Theoretical Considerations of the Problems of Mother-Child Separation*, 24 AM. J. ORTHOPSYCHIATRY 24 (1954), *quoted with approval in* State *ex rel.* Watts v. Watts, 350 N.Y.S.2d 285 (Fam. Ct. 1973). *See also* ANN DALLY, INVENTING MOTHERHOOD (1982) (arguing that the maternal preference doctrine was deployed to restrict women's roles to the domestic sphere so that men would have greater employment opportunities.)

[526] MASON, *supra* note 446 at 37.

Unlike their predecessors, feminists of the 1960's and 1970's opposed sex-based stereotypes, and challenged the sex-based division of labor that resulted from them. A principal focus of this wave of feminism was to achieve social equality between the sexes. Thus, the 1967 founding statement of the National Organization for Women (N.O.W.) declared:

> We reject the current assumption that a man must carry the sole burden of supporting himself, his wife, and family, and that a woman is automatically entitled to lifelong support by a man upon her marriage, or that marriage, home and family are primarily woman's world and responsibility--hers to dominate--his to support. We believe that a true partnership between the sexes demands a different concept of marriage, an equitable sharing of the responsibilities of home and children and of the economic burdens of their support....[527]

Influential feminist writers of the period saw the maternal preference and tender years doctrines as limiting women's opportunities.[528] Although these doctrines had become established in the law at the insistence of an earlier generation of women, the new generation portrayed these laws as strictures that men had invented to keep women "in their place," i.e., at home, bearing and raising children. This is probably what Simone de Beauvoir had in mind when she wrote to one of her contemporaries that "as long as ... the myth of ... the maternal instinct [is] not destroyed, women will still be oppressed."[529]

State and federal legislators responded by enacting laws designed to end sex discrimination. Some states amended their constitutions to

---

[527] BETTY FRIEDAN, NATIONAL ORGANIZATION FOR WOMEN'S STATEMENT OF PURPOSE (1966), *reprinted in* UP FROM THE PEDESTAL 368 (Aileen S. Kraditor ed., 1970).

[528] "Many feminists feared that the motherhood connection would restrict their opportunities for equal treatment in the workplace. Asking for special consideration for motherhood could shut the door to the male professions even tighter." MARY ANN MASON, THE CUSTODY WARS: WHY CHILDREN ARE LOSING THE LEGAL BATTLE, AND WHAT WE CAN DO ABOUT IT 3 (1999); see also DALLY, *supra* note 525.

[529] Letter to Betty Friedan, *quoted in* JIM FORDHAM & ANDREA FORDHAM, THE ASSAULT ON THE SEXES 437-38 (1977).

guarantee equal rights to women; and numerous laws, at both the state and federal levels, were enacted to prohibit discrimination on the basis of sex.

During this time, state legislatures also made efforts to gender-neutralize their laws by removing gendered pronouns, and by enacting laws specifying that wherever a masculine pronoun appeared in a law it was to be construed as including the feminine, and vice versa. In many states, custody laws were amended to require courts to put women and men on an equal footing, at least in theory. Some states enacted laws specifically prohibiting judges from deciding custody cases solely on the basis of the sex of the parent.

Even without prodding from the legislature, some judges rejected the maternal preference doctrine simply because they no longer believed that it met the criteria for a valid presumption. In 1973, a New York judge declared, "The simple fact of being a mother does not, by itself, indicate a capacity or willingness to render a quality of care different from that which the father can provide."[530] This was a radical departure from the maternal preference that judges theretofore uniformly had applied.

Not all judges were as ready to let go of the maternal preference as the New York judge quoted above was, though. Upon determining that a gender-neutral application of the "best interest" factors supported an award of custody to the father, a different judge declared, "I don't care what the state law says today; we all know that a little girl's interests are best served by being with her mother, and as long as I am judge, children...will be placed with their mother."[531]

By the end of the century, judicial protestations notwithstanding -- and subject to two important exceptions (children born out of wedlock, and very young children) -- most states, either by judicial decision or statute, had stopped using the maternal preference as an explicit basis for the decision of custody cases.[532]

---

[530] State *ex rel.* Watts v. Watts, 350 N.Y.S. 2d 285, 289 (Fam. Ct. 1973).

[531] ROBERT H. WOODY, PH.D., SC.D., GETTING CUSTODY: WINNING THE LAST BATTLE OF THE MARITAL WAR 60-61 (1973).

[532] *See, e.g.*, ARK. STAT. § 9-13-101 (2008) (requiring courts to decide custody "without regard to the sex of a parent"); DEL. CODE tit. 13, § 701 (2010) ("[Neither parent has] any right, or presumption of right or fitness, superior to the right of the

Survey of state laws abolishing sex-based preferences

States that have abolished sex-based preferences or presumptions, either by statute or by judicial decision, include: Alabama, Arizona, Arkansas, California, Colorado, Delaware, Georgia, Indiana, Iowa, Kansas, Maine, Maryland, Massachusetts, Mississippi, Missouri, Nebraska, New Hampshire, New Jersey, New York, North Carolina, North Dakota, Ohio, Oklahoma, Pennsylvania, South Carolina, South Dakota, Tennessee, Texas, Vermont, Virginia, Washington, Wisconsin.[533] There may be others.

---

other concerning such child's custody"); DEL. CODE tit. 13, § 722 (2010) ("The court shall not presume that a parent, because of his or her sex, is better qualified than the other parent"); GA. CODE § 19-9-3 (2010) ("There shall be no presumption in favor of any particular form of custody, legal or physical, nor in favor of either parent"); MD. CODE (FAM. LAW) § 5-203 (2010) ("Neither parent is presumed to have any right to custody that is superior to the right of the other parent"); MASS. GEN. L. ch. 208 § 31 (2011) ("[T]he rights of the parents shall, in the absence of misconduct, be held to be equal"); N.J. STAT. § 9:2-4 (2011) ("[R]ights of the parents shall be equal"); N.C. STAT. § 50-13.2 (2010) ("Between the mother and father, whether natural or adoptive, no presumption shall apply as to who will better promote the interest and welfare of the child"); S.D. CODIFIED LAWS § 25-5-7 (2010) ("[F]ather and mother of any minor child born in wedlock are equally entitled to the child's custody..."); TEX. FAM. CODE § 153.003 (2011) (requiring courts to decide custody "without regard...to the sex of the party or the child"); WASH. REV. CODE § 26.16.125 (2009) ("The rights and responsibilities of the parents in the absence of misconduct shall be equal"); Elza v. Elza, 475 A.2d 1180 (Md. 1984); Watts v. Watts, 337 A.2d 350 (N.H. 1975); State *ex rel.* Watts v. Watts, 350 N.Y.S.2d 285 (Fam. Ct. 1973); Commonwealth *ex rel.* Spriggs v. Carlson, 368 A.2d 635 (Pa. 1977); *see generally* C. Buehler & J.M. Gerard, *Divorce law in the United States: A focus on child custody*, 44 FAM. REL. 439-58 (1995); Kelly, *supra* note 53. Courts in some states held the application of a maternal preference presumption in final custody determinations to be unconstitutional, usually as a violation of a state's equal rights amendment. *See, e.g., Ex parte* Devine, 398 So. 2d 686 (Ala. 1981); McAndrew v. McAndrew, 39 Md. Ct. App. 1 (1978)

[533] ARIZ. REV. STAT. § 25-403.01 (2011); ARK. CODE § 9-13-101 (2008); CAL. FAM. CODE §§ 3010, 3040 (2011); COLO. REV. STAT. § 14-10-124 (2011); DEL. CODE tit. 13, §§ 701, 722 (2010); GA. CODE § 19-9-3 (2011); IND. CODE § 31-17-2-8 (2011); KAN. STAT. § 23-3204 (2011); ME. REV. STAT. tit. 19A, § 1653 (2011); MD. FAM. LAW CODE § 5-203 (2006); MASS. GEN. L. ch. 208 § 31 (2011); MISS. CODE § 93-5-24 (2011); MO. REV. STAT. § 452.375 (2011); NEB. REV. STAT. 42-364 (2011); N.H. REV. STAT. § 461-A:6 (2011); N.J. REV. STAT. § 9:2-4 (2012) N.C. GEN. STAT. § 50-13.2 (2011); N.D. CENT. CODE § 14-09-29 (2011); OHIO REV. CODE § 3109.03 (2011); 23 OKLA. STAT. tit. 43, § 112 (2011); PA. CONS. STAT. §§ 5327, 5328 (2012); S.C. CODE § 63-15-10 (2011) (expressly abolishing the tender years doctrine); S.D. CODIFIED LAWS § 25-5-7 (2010); TENN. CODE § 36-6-101 (2011); TEX. FAM.

The Texas statute applies to children over three years of age.[534]

States that prohibit the determination of custody "solely" on the basis of sex include: Minnesota, Nevada, New Mexico, Oregon, Utah and Wyoming.[535]

Maine's statute, although prohibiting courts from applying a preference on the basis of the sex of the parent, requires a court to take into consideration the fact that a child under one year of age is being breastfed.[536]

Although no longer permitted to apply a presumption in favor of mothers, Mississippi appellate courts have held that courts may continue to use the maternal preference as "a factor" in custody decisions.[537] The Nebraska Supreme Court's 1998 list of "best interest" factors includes the sex of the parents.[538]

CODE § 153.003 (2011); VT. STAT. tit. 15, § 665 (2011); VA. CODE § 20-124.2 (2011); WASH. REV. CODE § 26.16.125 (2009); WIS. STAT. § 767.41 (2011); *In re* Marriage of Murphy, 592 N.W.2d 681 (Iowa 1999); Elza v. Elza, 475 A.2d 1180 (Md. 1984); *In re* Custody of Kali, 792 N.E.2d 635 (Mass. 2003); Watts v. Watts, 337 A.2d 350 (N.H. 1975); State *ex rel.* Watts v. Watts, 350 N.Y.S.2d 285 (Fam. Ct. 1973); Commonwealth *ex rel.* Spriggs v. Carlson, 368 A.2d 635 (Pa. 1977); Berger v. Van Winsen, 743 N.W.2d 136 (S.D. 2007); Hubbell v. Hubbell, 702 A.2d 129 (Vt. 1997). Alabama's highest court, in *Ex Parte* Devine, 398 So. 2d 686 (Ala. 1981), held the application of a maternal preference presumption in final custody determinations violates the Equal Protection Clause, but an Alabama statute continues to specifically authorize courts to issue temporary custody orders only to mothers. *See* ALA. CODE 30-3-2(b) (2012).

[534] TEX. FAM. CODE §§ 153.003, .251 (2011)

[535] MINN. STAT. § 518.17 (2012); NEV. REV. STAT. § 125.480 (2011); N.M. STAT. § 40-4-9.1 (2011); OR. REV. STAT. § 107.137 (2011); UTAH CODE § 30-3-10 (2012); WYO. STAT. § 20-2-201 (2011)

[536] ME. REV. STAT. tit. 19-A, § 1653 (2011).

[537] Copeland v. Copeland, 904 So. 2d 1066 (Miss. 2004); Street v. Street, 936 So. 2d 1002 (Miss. Ct. App. 2006)

[538] Davidson v. Davidson, 576 N.W.2d 779 (Neb. 1998)

27. THE TENDER YEARS DOCTRINE

The tender years doctrine (the rule that disabled, unhealthy or young children should be placed in the custody of their mothers unless the mother is shown to be unfit in a particular case) that had been applied by the courts in the nineteenth century was firmly in place in every state in the United States throughout most of the twentieth century.

As applied in the twentieth century, the "tender years" generally consisted of the period from birth through ten years of age. Children as old as twelve years of age, however, were sometimes held to be "of tender years." As in the nineteenth century, some courts applied the tender years doctrine to unhealthy children, and to daughters of any age, too.[539]

As we shall see, the drafters of the model no-fault divorce statute (the Uniform Marriage and Divorce Act), which was adopted in 1970, intended

---

[539] Hudson v. Hudson, 295 So. 2d 92 (La. Ct. App. 1974); Commonwealth *ex rel.* Grillo v. Shuster, 312 A.2d 58 (Pa. Super. 1973); TIFFANY, *supra* note 178 at 271, 289-90; Trenkner, *supra* note 499 and cases collected therein at 274-76. "Since the mother is the natural custodian of the young and immature, custody is ordinarily awarded to her … in contests between parents … even when the father is without fault, provided the mother is a fit and proper person…" Hild v. Hild, 157 A.2d 442 (Md. Ct. 1960).

the tender years doctrine to survive the enactment of facially objective "best interest" factors. Nevertheless, by the end of the century, many states had abolished the doctrine -- by statute, judicial decision, or both.

Some state courts declared it unconstitutional because it discriminates on the basis of sex in violation of the Equal Protection clause of the Fourteenth Amendment, or a comparable provision of a state constitution.[540]

At the same time, courts in other states utilized loopholes in their nondiscrimination statutes to hold onto their preference for mothers to the fullest extent possible. In these states, statutes purporting to prohibit the determination of custody on the basis of sex were worded in a way that left courts room to continue to apply a generalized preference for mothers. A statute prohibiting a court from deciding custody "solely" on the basis of sex, it was said, allows a court to decide cases partially on the basis of sex.[541] In states that have this kind of statute, the tender years doctrine is not as likely as it once was to be cited as the exclusive basis for a custody decision, but a judge might apply it in combination with one or more gender-neutral factors.[542]

---

[540] *See, e.g., Ex parte* Devine, 398 So. 2d 686, 697 (Ala. 1981) ("[T]ender years presumption represents an unconstitutional gender-based classification which discriminates between fathers and mothers in child custody proceedings solely on the basis of sex"); State *ex rel.* Watts, 350 N.Y.S.2d 285, 288 (1973) (holding that the tender years presumption is based on "outdated social stereotypes" and violates the Fourteenth Amendment); Buehler & Gerard, *supra* note 532; Kelly, *supra* note 53.

[541] *See, e.g.,* Ryg v. Kerkow, 207 N.W.2d 701 (Minn. 1973) (applying the tender years preference for mothers as a tie-breaker, even after the Minnesota legislature had enacted a statute prohibiting courts from deciding custody cases "solely on the basis of sex"); *see also* Ettinger v. Ettinger, 383 P.2d 261 (N.M. 1963) (construing statutory enactment giving both the mother and the father "equal rights" as if it does not prohibit courts from applying a preference for mothers in custody cases); *cf.* Erwin v. Erwin, 505 S.W.2d 370 (Tex. Civ. App. 1974) (ruling that the Texas statute requiring custody decisions to be made "without regard to the sex of the parent" effectively abolished the maternal preference doctrine in Texas); State *ex rel.* Watts v. Watts, 350 N.Y.S.2d 285 (1973) (construing New York statute that "there shall be no prima facie right to custody in either parent" as abolishing the maternal preference in New York.)

[542]*See, e.g.,* Hollon v. Hollon, 784 So. 2d 943, 947 (Miss. 2001) (affirming the use of the maternal preference as a factor along with other evidence concerning the child's best interests.)

Originally, the tender years doctrine meant that a court was required to award custody exclusively to the mother (not to the father, and not to the mother and father jointly) even if she was the guilty spouse, unless she was proven to be unfit, with "unfit" being construed very narrowly to mean that she presented an actual danger of serious harm to the child.[543] By the end of the century, however, most courts no longer required a showing of actual danger in order to rebut the presumption. It could be rebutted by showing that an award of sole custody to the mother was not in the child's best interests in a particular case.[544]

Today, very few judges are likely to make an explicit reference to the tender years doctrine in their custody decisions. Nevertheless, unspoken beliefs about the special capacity and disposition of mothers to meet the needs of young children most likely continue to influence judicial decisions *sub silentio*.

---

[543] TIFFANY, *supra* note 178 at 274.

[544] *See, e.g.*, Di Biano v. Di Biano, 252 A.2d 735 (N.J. Super. 1969) and cases collected in Trenkner, *supra* note 499 at 279-81; *cf.* Mollish v. Mollish, 494 S.W.2d 145 (Tenn. Ct. App. 1972). In some states, it came to be treated as a tiebreaker, applied to justify an award of custody to the mother when all other the "best interests" factors were equal. *See* Glasgow v. Glasgow, 426 P.2d 617 (Alaska 1967), Commonwealth *ex rel.* Grillo v. Shuster, 312 A.2d 58 (Pa. Super. 1973) and cases collected in Trenkner, *supra* note 499 at 282-84.

28. CHILDREN BORN OUT OF WEDLOCK

Throughout the twentieth century, courts applied a maternal preference of one kind or another to determine the custody of children born out of wedlock.[545] During the first part of the twentieth century, it took the form of a presumption that the mother was entitled to sole custody unless proven to be unfit to parent; and a rule that fathers' rights were either subordinate to the mother's rights, or non-existent.[546]

---

[545] *See, e.g.*, Fowler v. Bright, 4 F. Supp. 565, 566 (D. Wash. 1933); Lewis v. Crowell, 97 So. 691 (Ala. 1923); Lipsey v. Battle, 97 S.W. 49 (Ark. 1906); *In re* Gille, 224 P. 784 (1924); Glansman v. Ledbetter, 130 N.E. 230 (Ind. 1920); *In re* Penny, 189 S.W. 1192 (Mo. Ct. App. 1916); Ousset v. Eurrad, 52 A. 1110 (N.J. 1902); Baylis v. Baylis, 101 N.E. 176 (1913); Pierce v. Jeffries, 137 S.E. 651 (W. Va. 1927).

[546] *See, e.g.*, Waldron v. Childers, 148 S.W. 1030 (Ark. 1912) (describing mother's right as "superior to that of any one else" defeasible only upon a showing that she is incompetent or unfit to parent); Lipsey v. Battle, 97 S.W. 49 (Ark. 1906) ("The mother's right to the custody and control of her illegitimate child is superior to that of anyone else."); *In re* Gille, 224 P. 784 (Cal. App. 1923); Ousset v. Euvrard , 52 A. 1110 (N.J. Ch. 1902) ("The father has hardly any right at all of custody, if he has any at all which the law recognizes. His position is largely that of a stranger, an outsider, having no natural relation to the child or children"); Cleaver v. Johnson, 212 S.W.2d 197 (Tex. Civ. App. 1948); Fowler v. Bright, 4 F. Supp. 565 (Wash. 1933); PECK, *supra* note 391 at 283 ("the mother ... has a right to their custody and control superior to that of the putative father as well as that of all other persons"); TIFFANY, *supra* note 178 at 247; A.L. Frechette, Annotation, *Right of Putative Father to Visit Illegitimate Child*, 15 A.L.R.3d 887 (1967) ("[T]he mother of a bastard child is

In the second half of the twentieth century, several states enacted laws that eliminated the parental rights of unwed fathers altogether. Typically, this was done by defining only the mother of a child born out of wedlock as the parent of the child. The purpose of these enactments was to facilitate unilateral adoption placements by unwed mothers. If classified as a "parent," then the father would have fundamental rights under the Due Process clause of the Fourteenth Amendment to notice and a hearing before his parental rights could be terminated.[547] Defining only the mother as a parent obviated the need to get the father's consent to the adoption, or even to notify him of it. Courts applied these statutes as a basis for denying unwed fathers standing to pursue custody of their children.[548]

State supreme courts generally upheld the constitutionality of these enactments.[549] Then, in 1972, the United States Supreme Court issued its landmark decision in *Stanley v. Illinois*.[550] In that case, the Court held, for the first time, that fathers of children born out of wedlock, like mothers of children born out of wedlock, have parental rights; that the parental right of custody is a fundamental natural right protected by the Fourteenth Amendment even when the parent in question is male; and that statutory schemes that unreasonably discriminate against unwed fathers with respect to the custody of children are unconstitutional.

Following the decision in *Stanley v. Illinois*, most states amended their statutes to provide some protections for the rights of putative fathers. They did not completely eliminate the maternal preference, however. Most states

---

the natural guardian of such child and, if suitable, has a legal right to custody, care, and control, superior to that of the father or any other person..."); *see also* Annotation, *Right of Mother to Custody of Illegitimate Child*, 98 A.L.R.2d 417, 431 (1964) ("[I]t is well established that the mother's right of custody is superior [to all others] and the father's right, if any such exists, is secondary.") The rationale for the rule was said to be that "the natural love and affection of a mother for such a child would probably be greater than that of any one else...." Lipsey v. Battle, 97 S.W. 49 (Ark. 1906).

[547]Mullane v. Central Hanover Trust Co., 339 U.S. 306, 314 (1950); Stanley v. Illinois, 405 U.S. 645 (1972)

[548] *See, e.g.,* Day v. Hatton, 83 S.E.2d 6 (Ga. 1954).

[549] *See, e.g.,* State *ex rel.* Lewis v. Lutheran Soc. Srv. 178 N.W.2d 56 (Wis. 1970) (holding that the abolition of putative fathers' common law parental rights by statute defining only the mother as a parent does not violate the constitution.)

[550] 405 U.S. 645 (1972)

left intact the rule that mothers possess the exclusive right to sole legal and physical custody of children born to them out of wedlock until there is a formal judicial declaration of paternity, at which time the father may have an opportunity to petition a court for an "award" of parental rights. In Minnesota, the exclusive maternal right to custody continues to exist even if the father has signed a Recognition of Parentage having the same legal force and effect as an adjudication of paternity. He may acquire rights of visitation or legal or physical custody only by commencing a court proceeding and convincing a judge that permitting him contact with his child is in the child's best interests.[551]

In most states, the maternal preference is now supposed to disappear, and courts are supposed to apply a "best interests" test to determine custody once paternity has been adjudicated and a father has commenced a proceeding to establish either custody or visitation ("parenting time") rights.

Courts originally interpreted the maternal preference in cases involving children born out of wedlock as continuing to apply even if the only reason for the birth being "out of wedlock" was that the parents' marriage had been annulled on the basis that an attempted marriage was either void or voidable.[552] By the end of the century, courts had come to apply the same facially gender-neutral "best interests" standard in all cases irrespective of the reason for the child being born out of wedlock, provided paternity had been acknowledged or established and a proceeding for the establishment of custody or visitation rights had been properly commenced.

Post-*Stanley* limitations on the rights of putative fathers

The Court returned to the question of the constitutional rights of unwed fathers six years later, in *Quilloin v. Walcott.*[553] In that case, the Court held that it is not always a violation of the federal constitution to treat an unwed father as having no greater right to the custody of his child than a

---

[551] *In re* Custody of J.J.S., 707 N.W.2d 706 (Minn. Ct. App. 2006); *see* MINN. STAT. § 257.541 (2012) (giving the mother the sole right to custody of children born out of wedlock.) In many states, the courts apply a "best interests" test to determine custody once paternity has been adjudicated.

[552] *See, e.g.*, Baylis v. Baylis, 101 N.E. 176 (N.Y. 1913)

[553] 434 U.S. 246 (1978)

non-parent has, while treating the mother's right as superior to either of them. To earn constitutional protection as an individual with the fundamental rights of a parent, a person must either be born female and give birth to a child; or, being male, do at least one of the following things: (1) marry the mother before the child is born; (2) adopt the child; or (3) assume either actual custody or significant responsibility for the child's rearing. In other words, the Supreme Court constitutionalized the common law principle that only women have natural rights as parents. Fathers' rights are conditional; they must be earned through works.

A year later, in *Caban v. Mohammed*[554] the Court held that if an unwed father does, in fact, prove himself worthy, then his parental rights acquire the same level of constitutional protection as are accorded to the rights of a mother. In short, the Court reaffirmed the principle it had enunciated in *Quilloin*, that unwed fathers have an inchoate interest in their children, but no constitutional rights. They can transform that interest into a constitutionally protected right only by assuming substantial parental responsibilities. The Court left open the question whether a different rule might apply in the case of newborn infants.

---

[554] 441 U.S. 380, 392 (1979).

29. THE PRIMARY CARETAKER STANDARD

At the beginning of the twentieth century, the division of labor in America was very starkly defined along gender lines: men worked outside the home; women stayed at home and raised children. Only 6% of married women worked outside the home — and then usually only because their husbands were unemployed. Employment outside the home spiked during World War II, when many men entered into military or alternative service, and then declined sharply, dropping to 12% by 1950.[555]

In the 1950's and 1960's, it was considered the norm for a woman either to become a housewife upon getting married, or to quit working and become a stay-at-home mother upon having a baby, if she was able to do so (i.e., if her husband had adequate financial means to support the family himself, or if she was independently wealthy.) Unmarried women, meanwhile, had sole custody of their children by law, and in several states, unwed fathers were not even defined in the law as parents. The result was that mothers almost always were the primary caretakers of children. Prohibited from overtly deciding custody on the basis of sex, judges used

---

[555] U.S. Census Bureau, Historical Statistics of the United States, Colonial Times to 1970, Bicentennial Edition (1975); U.S. Census Bureau, Statistical Abstract of the United States (1984)

this information to fashion a rule of decision that would seem gender-neutral on its face, but that would, in practice, continue to favor mothers: the primary caretaker standard.[556]

The primary caretaker standard was simply a presumption that a child's best interests are served by being placed in the sole custody of the person who historically has been the child's primary caretaker. Buttressed by the recent publication of *Beyond the Best Interests of the Child*,[557] a book advocating placement of children in the sole custody of the parent with whom they have formed the closest psychological attachment (as a result of bonding during a parent's performance of caretaking functions), several courts simply replaced the maternal preference with a presumption in favor of a child's primary caretaker.[558]

The problem with the primary caretaker presumption, from a feminist point of view, was that it did not work to the advantage of working women. This became a significant concern during the last quarter of the century, when the percentage of married women with children pursuing employment outside the home sharply increased. Less than one in four married women with children worked outside the home in the 1960's. By 1980, nearly half did; and by the end of the century, a majority did. Feminists therefore complained that the rule penalized working women.[559] (That it had always disadvantaged men in exactly the same way, and for exactly the same reason, apparently was not thought to have been of any great consequence.) Accordingly, most states that had adopted the primary caretaker presumption quickly scrapped it. Today, the question as to which parent has been a child's primary caretaker is just one of several factors a court may take into consideration when deciding what kind of custody arrangement is in the child's best interests.

---

[556] Garska v. McCoy, 278 S.E.2d 357 (W. Va. 1981); *see also* Pikula v. Pikula, 374 N.W.2d 705 (Minn. 1985)

[557] GOLDSTEIN ET AL., *supra* note 504.

[558] David Chambers, *Rethinking the Substantive Rule for Custody Disputes in Divorce*, 83 MICH. L. REV. 477 (1984)

[559] *cf.* F.M. Deutsch & S.E. Saxon, *The double standard of praise and criticism for mothers and fathers*, 22 PSYCHOL. WOMEN Q., 665-683 (1998)

30. "BEST INTEREST" FACTORS

The Uniform Marriage and Divorce Act

With the demise of marital fault and moral character as guiding principles for custody decision-making, and with questions being raised about the validity and constitutionality of the maternal preference, there was a need for a new set of standards. The National Conference of Commissioners on Uniform State Laws attempted to fill this need by drafting what they hoped would be an objective standard that would leave less room for the operation of the subjective moral judgments of individual judges, thereby promoting greater consistency and predictability of custody outcomes. They did this by articulating a set of gender-neutral considerations that they deemed relevant to a child's well-being and healthy development. They incorporated this set of considerations into the final draft of a Uniform Marriage and Divorce Act (UMDA), which they adopted in 1970.[560]

---

[560] UNIF. MARRIAGE & DIVORCE ACT § 402 (1970, amended in 1971 and 1973) This Act is now called the Model Marriage and Divorce Act.

SECTION 402. [Best Interest of Child.] The court shall determine custody in accordance with the best interest of the child. The court shall consider all relevant factors including:

(1) the wishes of the child's parent or parents as to his custody;

(2) the wishes of the child as to his custodian;

(3) the interaction and interrelationship of the child with his parent or parents, his siblings, and any other person who may significantly affect the child's best interest;

(4) the child's adjustment to his home, school, and community; and

(5) the mental and physical health of all individuals involved.

The court shall not consider conduct of a proposed custodian that does not affect his relationship to the child.[561]

The Comment to this section explained that courts "need not be limited to the factors specified" and:

Although none of the familiar presumptions developed by the case law are mentioned here, the language of the section is consistent with preserving such rules of thumb. The preference for the mother as custodian of young children when all things are equal, for example, is simply a shorthand method of expressing the best interest of children-
-and this section enjoins judges to decide custody cases according to that general standard. The same analysis is appropriate to the other common presumptions: a parent is usually preferred to a non-parent; the existing custodian is usually preferred to any new custodian because of the interest in assuring continuity for the child; preference is usually given to the custodian chosen by agreement of the parents....[562]

---

[561] *Id.*
[562] *Id.*

Adoption of a "best interest factors" statute, then, was not intended to supplant the tender years doctrine.

Section 402 was, however, intended to prohibit, or at least severely curtail, a court's consideration of marital misconduct when deciding the custody of children. The language, "The court shall not consider conduct of a proposed custodian that does not affect his relationship to the child" reflected the Commissioners' rejection of the practice of awarding custody of children to the spouse who was not at fault for the breakdown of the marriage. To ensure there was no doubt about this, the Commissioners appended the following Comment to the section:

> The last sentence of the section changes the law in those states which continue to use fault notions in custody adjudication. There is no reason to encourage parties to spy on each other in order to discover marital (most commonly, sexual) misconduct for use in a custody contest. This provision makes it clear that unless a contestant is able to prove that the parent's behavior in fact affects his relationship to the child (a standard which could seldom be met if the parent's behavior has been circumspect or unknown to the child), evidence of such behavior is irrelevant.[563]

A majority of states adopted this section of the UMDA.[564] Most states also added several more factors of their own to the list. The most common of these was domestic violence. Today, every state has added domestic violence – or at least its impact on the child – to its list of "best interest" factors, or has enacted a statute requiring courts to consider it, or both. Disposition to permit or encourage the child's contact and relationship with the other parent is another factor that many states have added to their lists.

Today, it is not uncommon for a state's "best interests" statute to enumerate a dozen or more factors that courts may or must consider..

---

[563] *Id.*
[564] Roth, *supra* note 2.

The American Law Institute's approximation rule

A significant shortcoming of the UMDA, and "best interest factors" statutes in general, is that they provide no guidance as to how the factors are to be applied in particular cases. That decision is simply left to each individual judge's discretion. This defeats the goals of uniformity and predictability. It also leaves plenty of room for the continued operation of the subjective biases and prejudices of individual judges. A judge who wishes to award custody to the mother in every case can usually find at least one statutory "best interest" factor in her favor, and then cite it as the basis for the decision. By the same token, a judge who is more critical of a mother than a father for pursuing a career rather than choosing to be a stay-at-home parent might be able to find at least one "best interest" factor to support his decision to award custody to the father.

Partly in response to these kinds of concerns about the indeterminacy of the "best interest factors" approach, the American Law Institute (ALI), in 2000, suggested a different approach: an "approximation rule."

The ALI proposed that courts should "allocate custodial responsibility so that the proportion of custodial time the child spends with each parent approximates the proportion of time each parent spent performing caretaking functions for the child prior to the parents' separation or, if the parents never lived together, before the filing of the action."[565]

The rule was subject to some exceptions. For example, exceptions were made for cases in which a different allocation was desirable in order to protect a child from harm, or to keep siblings together, or where an older child expressed a reasonable preference for a different arrangement, or where the parties had agreed to a different arrangement.

So far, only West Virginia has adopted the ALI's approximation rule.[566] All other states have retained one or another version of the open-ended "best interest factors" approach.

---

[565] AMERICAN LAW INSTITUTE, PRINCIPLES OF THE LAW OF FAMILY DISSOLUTION § 2.08 (2000)
[566] W. VA. CODE § 48-11-106 (2007)

31. PARENTAL AND THIRD-PARTY RIGHTS

Except in custody contests between a parent and a non-parent, twentieth century courts expressly disavowed any concern for parents' rights when deciding the custody of a child. They asserted, instead, that their sole concern was with the welfare of children. Occasionally, a court would cite, in support of a finding that joint custody was in a child's best interests in a particular case, the fact that joint custody orders respect both parents' rights.[567] Courts never treated those rights as determinative or controlling on the issue of custody, though. The same court that approved a fit couple's joint custody agreement one day might disapprove another equally fit couple's joint custody agreement the next.

When a judge acknowledged parents' rights in the course of ordering a particular custody arrangement, other factors independently supporting a finding that the arrangement was in the child's best interests were also present. In other words, the occasional judicial acknowledgement of parental rights was *obiter dictum*. Judges have always regarded parental rights as subordinate to the judicial *parens patriae* power to determine what is in a

---

[567] *See, e.g.*, Mullen v. Mullen, 49 S.E.2d 349 (Va. 1948) (noting that a school/summer division of custody had the advantage of giving recognition to both parents' rights.)

child's best interests. Irrespective of the desire of two fit parents to share custody of their children, for example, a court would not issue a joint custody order if they were highly oppugnant or unable to cooperate, as judges believed that exposure to parental conflict was not in a child's best interests.[568] Mutual parental desire for joint custody could be a factor tending to support an award of joint custody, but it was not determinative.[569] The court's independent determination of what was in a child's best interests was controlling.

The "constitutionalization" of parental rights

In 1923, the United States Supreme Court held that a state law prohibiting parents from teaching their children foreign languages unconstitutionally infringed the right of parents to direct the education of their children, which is an aspect of the right of legal custody. The decision, *Meyer v. Nebraska*,[570] imbued parental custody rights with constitutional protection as "liberty" interests within the meaning of the Due Process Clause of the Fourteenth Amendment. A line of cases subsequent to *Meyer* affirmed that parental rights, including the right to the care, custody and companionship of one's children, are not only protected "liberty" interests; they are fundamental rights of which a parent may be divested only if doing so is necessary for the achievement of a compelling state interest.[571]

Third-party custody

Twentieth century courts generally recognized that the right of a parent to custody of his or her child was superior to the right of any other person. The right was not absolute, however, as the best interest of the child was still the paramount consideration. Nevertheless, most courts applied a rule that in contests between a parent and a non-parent, the parent was presumptively entitled to custody unless shown to be unfit.[572]

---

[568] *See, e.g.*, Bliss v. Ach, 446 N.Y.S.2d 305 (App. Div. 1982); Dodd v. Dodd, 403 N.Y.S.2d 401 (Sup. Ct. 1978)

[569] *See, e.g.*, Bronner v. Bronner, 278 S.W.2d 530 (Tex. Ct. App. 1954)

[570] 262 U.S. 390 (1923)

[571] Parham v. J.R., 442 U.S. 584 (1979); Wisconsin v. Yoder, 406 U.S. 205 (1972); Stanley v. Illinois, 405 U.S. 645 (1972); Pierce v. Society of Sisters, 268 U.S. 510 (1925).

[572] See, e.g., Stubblefield v. State, 106 S.W.2d 558 (Tenn. 1937)

This was because courts presumed that parents act in their children's best interests.[573] The one major exception to this rule was that a third party might be awarded custody of the child of an otherwise fit parent if the parent had permitted the child to be raised in the home of the third party for a number of years.[574]

Significant U.S. Supreme Court decisions

Meyer v. Nebraska[575] - invalidated a state law that prohibited parents from teaching their children foreign languages, because it interfered with the right of parents to direct the education of their children. "The Fourteenth Amendment guarantees the right of the individual ... to establish a home and bring up children...."

Pierce v. Society of Sisters[576] - struck down a law that required children to attend public school, because it "unreasonably interferes with the liberty of parents and guardians to direct the upbringing and education of children." States may not restrict a parent's educational choices to public school instruction. "The child is not the mere creature of the state; those who nurture him and direct his destiny have the right and the high duty, to recognize and prepare him for additional obligations."

Prince v. Massachusetts[577] - held that parental rights are not absolute; the state has a legitimate interest in protecting children from harm, and may limit parental rights to further that interest. The parent in that case was a Jehovah's Witness who had been cited for violating the state's child labor laws in the course of involving her children in religious proselytizing. The Court found no constitutional violation.

Wisconsin v. Yoder[578] - vindicated the right of Amish parents to homeschool their high school age children. A state may infringe upon parental rights only when doing so is necessary to serve a compelling state interest.

---

[573] Parham v. J.R., 442 U.S. 584, 604 (1979)

[574] *See, e.g.,* Wood v. Wood, 77 A. 91 (N.J. Eq. 1910) (denying custody to mother of child who had been in the care of, and raised by, a third party for several years.)

[575] 262 U.S. 390 (1923).

[576] 268 U.S. 510 (1925).

[577] 321 U.S. 158 (1944).

[578] 406 U.S. 205 (1972).

Parham v. J.R.[579] – invalidated a state statute authorizing mental health services to be provided to children against the parents' wishes. "The law's concept of the family rests on a presumption that parents possess what a child lacks in maturity, experience, and capacity for judgment required for making life's difficult choices. More important, historically it has been recognized that natural bonds of affection lead parents to act in the best interests of their children.... The fact that a child may balk at hospitalization or complain about a parental refusal to provide cosmetic surgery does not diminish the parent's authority to decide what is best for the child."

Santosky v. Kramer[580] - held that a state may not terminate parental rights using a "preponderance of the evidence" standard. Instead, they must apply the "clear and convincing evidence" standard. "The fundamental liberty interest of natural parents in the care, custody, and management of their child does not evaporate simply because they have not been model parents or have lost temporary custody of their child to the state.... When the state moves to destroy weakened familial bonds, it must provide the parents with fundamentally fair procedures."

Lehr v. Robertson[581] - limited constitutional protection of the natural rights of parents primarily to mothers, holding that they extend to only those unwed fathers who have established significant custodial, personal, or financial relationships with their children.

Troxel v. Granville[582] - invalidated a statute that authorized courts to grant visitation rights to grandparents over the custodial parent's objection. Declaring that "the Due Process Clause of the Fourteenth Amendment protects the fundamental right of parents to make decisions concerning the care, custody, and control of their children," the Court held that some consideration must be given to parents' rights; third-party visitation rights cannot be granted solely on the basis of a judicial determination that they are in a child's best interests.

---

[579] 442 US 584 (1979).
[580] 455 US 745, 753 (1982).
[581] 463 US 248 (1983).
[582] 530 U.S. 57 (2000).

32. GAY, LESBIAN & TRANSGENDERED PARENTS

> I can bear [all else except that] ... my two children are taken from me by legal procedure. That is, and always will remain to me a source of infinite distress, or infinite pain.... The disgrace of prison is as nothing compared with it.[583]

Nineteenth century poet and playwright Oscar Wilde wrote those words while serving time in prison for sodomy. Although judicial attitudes are changing, historically courts have not favored awards of custody to non-heterosexual individuals.[584]

Reasons for judicial hostility varied, but it is possible to identify five broad categories of explanations: (1) bad moral example; (2) risk of child sexual abuse (founded on a belief that non-heterosexuals are sociopathic sexual deviants); (3) deficient parenting (because unwilling to place child's needs ahead of parent's sexual needs); (4) gender identity confusion for the child; (5) social stigma causing emotional or psychological harm to child.

---

[583] OSCAR WILDE, DE PROFUNDIS 34 (R. Ross ed., 1909)
[584] Elizabeth Trainor, Annotation, *Initial Award or Denial of child Custody to Homosexual or Lesbian Parent*, 62 A.L.R.5th 591, 601 (1998)

Moral unfitness

In colonial and nineteenth century America, non-procreative sex of any kind was considered immoral, and punished criminally. Virtually any kind of sexual activity other than sexual intercourse between a husband and wife for the purpose of procreation was classified as a crime against morals and decency. Thus, sodomy was broadly defined to include anal sex whether it was between a man and a woman, or between a man and a man. The idea, basically, was that sexual pleasure was inherently sinful; it was tolerated only for the limited purpose of producing offspring.

Sodomy and the "crime against nature"

Prohibitions against sodomy have taken different forms in different places over the years, but they all have their roots in religious teachings. In the United States, they derive from the Christian Bible.

Biblical prohibitions have been the subject of differing interpretations over the centuries. Eleventh century medieval Christian theologians employed it to refer to a wide range of non-procreative sexual practices. Later theologians sometimes used it interchangeably with, or confused it with, "unnatural acts," although the latter phrase derives from *Romans I*, and is broader in scope than "sodomy." For example, bestiality may or may not be included within a definition of sodomy, but it always comes within the definition of an "unnatural act." On the other hand, even vaginal sexual intercourse between a married man and woman could be an "unnatural act" if performed in an unusual position, or with contraceptive intent.[585]

Theologians also were not in agreement about whether it was possible for a woman to commit sodomy. Many took the position that only a man could be guilty of sodomy. Some, however, contended that since the definition of sodomy was any non-procreative sexual activity, a woman, too, could be guilty of it.[586]

The English Parliament transformed the religious proscription into a secular one by creating the crime of "buggery," which was made a capital

---

[585] MARK D. JORDAN, THE INVENTION OF SODOMY IN CHRISTIAN THEOLOGY 46, 144-45 (1997)

[586] MARK D. JORDAN, THE SILENCE OF SODOM 62-71 (2000)

offense in 1533. Buggery was defined as sexual intercourse between a human and an animal (bestiality), or anal intercourse between a man and a woman, or between a man and a man.[587]

Colonial American statutes carried forward the English prohibition, sometimes calling it sodomy, sometimes calling it buggery, and sometimes referencing "the crime against nature."[588]

In colonial America, only the male participant in a non-procreative sex act could be punished criminally. Depending on the circumstances, lesbian sexual activity might have been punishable as "lewd and lascivious behavior," but it was not punishable as sodomy, buggery, or a "crime against nature," which were far more serious offenses, sometimes punishable by death. The only exception was New Haven, where "women lying with women" was prohibited by law for ten years. In all other colonies, the laws targeted only male non-procreative sexual gratification.[589]

Sodomy, buggery, and/or "the crime against nature" remained serious criminal offenses throughout the nineteenth century and the first half of the twentieth century. Many states added oral sex to the list of proscribed sexual activity during this time.

In the twentieth century, sexual regulation increasingly focused less on non-procreative heterosexual activity, and more on homosexual activity in particular. Numerous laws discriminating against non-heterosexual individuals were enacted at both the state and the federal level (e.g., exclusions from federal employment and military service; exclusions from employment as teachers; disqualification from adoptive parenting, etc.)

---

[587] William Eskridge, Jr., *Law and the Construction of the Closet: American Regulation of Same-Sex Intimacy*, 1880-1946, 82 IOWA L. REV. 1007, 1012 (1997); Ed Cohen, *Legislating the Norm: From Sodomy to Gross Indecency*, 88 S. ATLANTIC Q. 181, 185 (1989).

[588] Puritanical New England colonies enacted prohibitions that went far beyond those that Parliament had enacted. For example, in 1646 a New Haven man was hanged for engaging in masturbation. *See* John Murrin, *"Things Fearful to Name": Bestiality in Early America*, in AMERICAN SEXUAL HISTORIES 17 (Elizabeth Reis ed., 2001); *see also* Robert F. Oaks, *"Things Fearful to Name": Sodomy and Buggery in Seventeenth-century New England*, 12 J. SOC. HIST. 268 (1978); Jonathan Ned Katz, *The Age of Sodomitical Sin, 1607-1740*, in GAY/LESBIAN ALMANAC 23 (1983).

[589] Murrin, *supra* note 588 at 15; Katz, *supra* note 588 at 29-30.

Consistent with this history, courts originally held, as a matter of law, that anything other than a heterosexual sexual orientation rendered a person unfit to parent, or at least raised a presumption of unfitness to parent.[590] Although most courts no longer apply a per se rule that every non-heterosexual person is unfit to parent, a few courts continue to consider it evidence of "lack of moral example" and treat it as a negative factor in their best interest analyses on that basis.[591]

Impact of the sexual liberalization and no-fault movements

Aversion to homosexual practices survived the sexual liberalization and no-fault movements of the 1960's and 1970's, notwithstanding legislative efforts to eliminate moral judgments from the custody decision-making process. Evidence of this can be found not only in the reports of judicial decisions during this time, but also in the approach that states took to the liberalization of their sexual regulations. For example, during the last quarter of the century, when many states were either legalizing or decriminalizing sexual activity between consenting adults, prohibitions against non-heterosexual activity often were left intact. Moreover, some state legislatures even added new crimes specifically singling out same-sex activity for proscriptive regulation.

In the context of custody law, aversion to homosexual practices clearly was of a higher order than the aversion to what were considered immoral heterosexual practices (fornication and adultery, for example.) Sexual orientation continued to be a significant consideration in custody cases long after marital infidelity ceased to be.[592] Instead of resting their decisions on moral grounds, though, most courts began explaining denials of custody to

---

[590] *See, e.g., Ex Parte* H.H., 830 So. 21 (Ala. 2002) (Moore, C.J., concurring) (arguing that gay and lesbian parents should be deemed presumptively unfit to have custody of children); Roe v. Roe, 324 S.E.2d 671 (Va. 1985) (failing to conceal the fact that one shares his bed with a same-sex partner amounts to "flaunting" one's immorality, rendering one unfit to parent as a matter of law.) To these courts, proof of an adverse effect on the child is unnecessary, as it is believed to be inevitable that a parent's involvement in homosexual activity will have an adverse effect on the child in every case.

[591] *c.f.* Tucker v. Tucker, 910 P.2d 1209 (Utah 1996) (describing it as immoral because it involves cohabitation with a person other than one's spouse while still married)

[592] *See, e.g.*, Pascarella v. Pascarella, 512 A.2d 715 (Pa. Super. Ct. 1986)

non-heterosexual persons in other ways.[593]

Other rationales for denying custody to gays, lesbians, and bisexuals

RISK OF DIRECT HARM

Child sexual abuse

Until 1973, homosexuality was listed as a sexual disorder in the American Psychiatric Association's *Diagnostic and Statistical Manual.* Gay, lesbian, bisexual, and transgendered persons were believed to be suffering from a mental illness or defect that caused them to be sexual "deviants."[594] Especially during the first two-thirds of the twentieth century, it was widely believed that non-heterosexual individuals preferred children as sexual partners. People associated homosexuality with pedophilia.[595] That was why non-heterosexuals generally were not permitted to be teachers, child-care workers, Boy Scout leaders, and so on.

Some judges, when refusing to award custody to a non-heterosexual parent, did not provide much explanation other than a conclusory assertion

---

[593] *But cf.* M.J.P. v. J.G.P., 640 P.2d 966, 969 (Okla. 1982) (holding that an award of custody to a lesbian parent was contrary to the child's best interests because it would result in the child believing there is nothing morally wrong with lesbianism.)

[594] *See* George Chauncey, *From Sexual Inversion to Homosexuality: Medicine and the Changing Conceptualization of Female Deviance,* SALMAGUNDI 114 (1982-1983); Siobhan Somerville, *Scientific Racism and the Invention of the Homosexual Body, in* QUEER STUDIES 241 (Beemyn & Eliason eds., 1996); JENNIFER TERRY, AN AMERICAN OBSESSION: SCIENCE, MEDICINE, AND HOMOSEXUALITY IN MODERN SOCIETY (1999).

[595] A 1970 national survey found that 70% of Americans believed that non-heterosexuals are dangerous "because they try to get sexually involved with children" or will "try to play sexually with children if they cannot get an adult partner." A.D. KLASSEN, C.J. WILLIAMS & E.E. LEVITT, SEX AND MORALITY IN THE U.S.: AN EMPIRICAL ENQUIRY UNDER THE AUSPICES OF THE KINSEY INSTITUTE (1989). As the recent debate over the Boy Scouts' policy of excluding gay men from leadership positions demonstrates, this belief has endured beyond the first half of the twentieth century. *See also* ANITA BRYANT, THE ANITA BRYANT STORY: THE SURVIVAL OF OUR NATION'S FAMILIES AND THE THREAT OF MILITANT HOMOSEXUALITY 114 (1977) (warning that a "deviant-minded [gay] teacher could sexually molest children"); Timothy J. Daley, Family Research Council, *Homosexuality and Child Sexual Abuse* (2002), retrieved from http://www.frc.org/get.cfm?i=IS02E3 on April 16, 2014 (asserting the existence of a "disturbing connection" between "the gay lifestyle" and pedophilia.)

that such a placement would put a child at risk of harm. It is likely that a belief in a connection between homosexuality and pedophilia played a role in these decisions.

AIDS and HIV

In 1981, the Centers for Disease Control published a *Morbidity and Mortality Weekly Report* about five otherwise healthy gay men who had been diagnosed with an infection that normally appears only in individuals with significant immune system damage. Soon, more cases like these were reported, principally in gay men. Eventually, the disease came to be known as acquired immune deficiency syndrome (AIDS). Although it also affected intravenous drug-users, blood transfusion recipients, and sometime s heterosexual women and men, gay men were the principal victims. The new association between homosexuality and terminal illness revitalized antipathy toward gay men. The wives and ex-wives of gay fathers argued that a parent with AIDS or HIV posed too great a health risk to be permitted to have custody or contact with children.

Most courts that have considered this argument have rejected it because AIDS and HIV can only be transmitted through the exchange of bodily fluids (blood or semen), not casual household contact.[596]

Psychological or emotional harm

Some courts have assumed that psychological harm is "inevitable," or have established a presumption that an openly homosexual parent has an adverse psychological or emotional effect on children.[597] The trend, however, is to require actual proof of harm rather than assuming it.

---

[596] Steven L. v. Dawn L., 561 N.Y.S.2d 322 (Fam. Ct. 1990); Doe v. Roe, 526 N.Y.S.2d 718 (Sup. Ct. 1988); Conkel v. Conkel, 509 N.E.2d 983 (Ohio Ct. App. 1987); *cf.* FLA. STAT. § 61.13 (2011) (prohibiting courts from denying a party custody solely because of HIV infection.) Of course, it may be still be relevant if the disease impairs a party's physical health in a way that interferes with his ability to care for children. H.J.B. v. P.W., 628 So. 2d 753 (Ala. Civ. App. 1993).

[597] *See, e.g.*, Pascarella v. Pascarella, 512 A.2d 715 (Pa. Super. Ct. 1986) (finding it "inconceivable" that a child could be exposed to a parent's same-sex relationship and not suffer emotional disturbance); Bottoms v. Bottoms, 457 S.E.2d 102 (Va. 1995) (declaring that harm to child is inevitable)

DEFICIENT PARENTING

Perceiving sexual orientation as a choice, some courts have treated a parent's unwillingness to renounce his sexual preference as evidence that the parent places his own interests ahead of those of his children. Of course, if the parent's activities or relationships actually interfere with her parenting in some way – e.g., where a parent devotes more time and attention to her partner, and/or the gay community, than to her child -- that, too, may be cited as a reason for denying her custody.[598]

STIGMA

Some courts have denied custody to non-heterosexual parents on the grounds that social prejudice against openly gay and lesbian couples may be psychologically or emotionally harmful to the children in their care.[599] The fact that a child is subjected to ridicule or harassment by his peers due to the parent's sexual orientation may suffice to establish the necessary nexus between the parent's sexual orientation and a negative impact on the child's emotional well-being. There have been cases where courts have denied custody based on a parent's failure to dispel rumors about her sexual orientation, where the rumors have made the child feel bad.[600]

Other courts, consistent with the rationale of *Palmore v. Sidoti*,[601] have declined to treat community hostility toward non-heterosexuals as a permissible basis for denying custody to a non-heterosexual parent.[602]

---

[598] *See* Bark v. Bark, 479 So. 2d 42 (Ala. Civ. App. 1985); Hall v. Hall, 291 N.W.2d 143 (Mich. Ct. App. 1980)

[599] *See, e.g.*, S.E.G. v. R.A.G., 735 S.W.2d 164 (Mo. Ct. App. 1987); Jacobson v. Jacobson, 314 N.W.2d 78 (N.D. 1981) (denying custody to mother cohabiting with her lesbian lover, on the basis that the child could suffer the "slings and arrows" of a disapproving society.)

[600] *See, e.g.*, Bowen v. Bowen, 688 So. 2d 1378 (Miss. 1997)

[601] 466 U.S. 429 (1984). In that case, the United States Supreme Court ruled that a judicial desire to protect a child from a community's race-based hostility and prejudice cannot be made the basis for a custody decision.

[602] *See, e.g.*, S.N.E. v. R.L.B., 699 P.2d 875, 879 (Alaska 1985); Jacoby v. Jacoby, 763 So. 2d 410 (Fla. Dist. Ct. App. 2000) (holding that the perceived bias of the community against non-heterosexuals is not a proper basis for a finding of negative impact; also, the mere possibility that conflict between religious teachings and a parent's sexual preferences may confuse a child is not sufficient unless there is

S<small>EXUAL</small> I<small>DENTITY</small> C<small>ONFUSION</small>

See the discussion of transgendered parents, infra.

Presumptions and burden of proof

Courts have approached the question of non-heterosexual parents' rights in one of three ways:[603] (1) a per se rule that anyone who is not heterosexual is unfit to parent, as a matter of law;[604] (2) a rebuttable presumption that a child will be harmed in some way by placement in the custody of a non-heterosexual parent;[605] (3) a "nexus" rule, under which harm is not presumed to flow merely from a parent's sexual orientation itself, but that custody or visitation rights may be denied or restricted if it is shown that a parent's sexual orientation has, or is likely to have, an actual adverse impact on the child.[606]

As societal acceptance of gay, lesbian, bisexual and transgendered persons has grown, there has been a general movement away from the per se rule.[607] Today, most courts apply the "nexus" rule.[608] In most states, the

---

evidence of actual harm to the child); Inscoe v. Inscoe, 700 N.E.2d 70 (Ohio Ct. App. 1997).

[603] *See* Felicia Meyers, Note, *Gay Custody and Adoption: An Unequal Application of the Law*, 14 W<small>HITTIER</small> L. R<small>EV</small>. 839, 840-43 (1993)

[604] *Id.* at 840; *see, e.g.*, Jacobson v. Jacobson, 314 N.W.2d 78, 82 (N.D. 1981) (denying a lesbian mother custody of her child despite the trial court's finding that both parents were fit.) A court applying the per se rule may also restrict the noncustodial parent's visitation rights for the same reason. Joseph R. Price, Comment, Bottoms III: *Visitation Restrictions and Sexual Orientation*, 5 W<small>M</small>. & M<small>ARY</small> B<small>ILL</small> R<small>TS</small>. J. 643, 649-50 (1997)

[605] *See, e.g.*, S.E.G. v. R.A.G., 735 S.W.2d 164, 166 (Mo. Ct. App. 1987) (presuming harm from peer teasing and social ostracism likely to occur); *see generally* Katja M. Eichinger-Swainston, Note, Fox v. Fox: *Redefining the Best Interest of the Child Standard for Lesbian Mothers and Their Families*, 32 T<small>ULSA</small> L.J. 57, 58 (1996)

[606] *See, e.g.*, Mardie v. Mardie, 680 So. 2d 538, 540 (Fla. Dist. Ct. App. 1996); Bezio v. Patenaude, 410 N.E.2d 1207, 1216 (Mass. 1980); Eichinger-Swainston, *supra* note 605 at 59; Trainor, *supra* note 584 at 601 (1998)

[607] Heidi C. Doerhoff, Note, *Assessing the Best Interests of the Child: Missouri Declares that a Homosexual Parent is Not Ipso Facto Unfit for Custody* J.A.D. v. F.J.D., 64 M<small>O</small>. L. R<small>EV</small>. 949 (1999)

[608] *See, e.g.*, O<small>R</small>. R<small>EV</small>. S<small>TAT</small>. § 107.137 (2011) (authorizing courts to consider marital status, social environment and lifestyle only if shown to be emotionally or physically damaging to the child); *Ex parte* J.M.F., 730 So. 2d 1190 (Ala. 1998); Packard v. Packard, 697 So. 2d 1292 (Fla. Dist. Ct. App. 1997); Pryor v. Pryor, 709

fact that a parent is gay, lesbian, bisexual or transgendered is not sufficient, by itself, to disqualify him or her from custody. The party seeking to disqualify a person on that basis must produce evidence to show that the person's sexual orientation has or is likely to have an actual adverse impact on the child.

Evidence of adverse impact

It may be expected that in a state that applies the "nexus" rule, a closeted non-heterosexual parent (one who keeps his sexual orientation concealed, at least from the child) should be on roughly equal footing with a heterosexual parent.[609] It is difficult to imagine how a person's sexual orientation could have an impact on a child if she does not know about it. Outward expressions of affection toward a same-sex partner in a child's presence, on the other hand, are often – though not always -- deemed to be harmful to a child.[610] Some judges apply a double standard in this respect, assuming damage to a child from witnessing a same-sex couple's hugs, kisses or other displays of affection but not when a heterosexual couple engages in these behaviors in a child's presence.

There are several other ways in which a nexus between a parent's sexual orientation and a negative impact on the child has been proven.

N.E.2d 374 (Ind. Ct. App. 1999) (holding that sexual orientation, standing alone, is not a sufficient basis for denying custody); *In re* Marriage of Teepe, 271 N.W.2d 740 (Iowa 1978); Paul C. v. Tracy C., 622 N.Y.S.2d 159 (App. Div. 1994); Di Stefano v. Di Stefano, 380 N.Y.S.2d 394 (App. Div. 1976); Mohrman v. Mohrman, 565 N.E.2d 1283 (Ohio Ct. App. 1989); Constant A. v. Paul C.A., 496 A.2d 1 (Pa. Super. Ct. 1985); Massey-Holt v. Holt, 255 S.W.3d 603 (Tenn. Ct. App. 2007); *In re* Marriage of Cabalquinto, 669 P.2d 886 (Wash. 1983), *appeal after remand*, 718 P.2d 7 (Wash. Ct. App. 1986);); M.S.P. v. P.E.P. 358 S.E.2d 442 (W. Va. 1987); *cf.* Feldman v. Feldman, 358 N.Y.S.2d 507 (App. Div. 1974) (holding that sexual deviation and aberrant sexual practices do not necessarily make a parent unfit to have the custody of children.)

[609] *See* Hodson v. Moore, 464 N.W.2d 699 (Iowa Ct. App. 1990) (holding that custody will be awarded to a lesbian mother if she is discreet and does not engage in any inappropriate behavior in the presence of the children)

[610] *See, e.g.*, Lundin v. Lundin, 563 So. 2d 1273 (La. Ct. App. 1990); *see generally* N. Maxwell & R. Donner, *The Psychological Consequences of Judicially Imposed Closets in Child Custody and Visitation Disputes Involving Gay or Lesbian Parents*, 13 WM & MARY J. WOMEN & L. 305, 307 (2006); *but cf.* Teegarden v. Teegarden, 642 N.E.2d (Ind. Ct. App. 1994) (declining to presume that lesbian displays of affection have an adverse impact on children.)

Evidence that it is a contributing cause to the child's depression, anxiety or other psychological or emotional disorder may suffice.[611] Involving a child in gay community activities,[612] or giving higher priority to a same-sex relationship than to the child,[613] may support a finding of a nexus to harm to the child. Courts are split as to whether witnessing a parent kissing or engaging in other displays of affection with a same-sex partner is harmful to children, but it generally is not difficult to convince a judge that being nude or engaging in sexual activities in a child's presence has a harmful effect on the child. And of course, if a non-heterosexual parent actually engages a child in sexual activity, i.e., if the parent perpetrates child sex abuse, then a court normally will find that the child has been harmed by it, just as courts generally find children are harmed by heterosexual child abuse.

Transgendered persons[614]

There have not been very many reported cases addressing the custody rights of transgendered parents. This is probably because transgendered people historically have been thought to be mentally ill and dangerous to children.[615] It was viewed as a basis not only for denying custody, but also

---

[611] *See, e.g.*, Knotts v. Knotts, 693 N.E.2d 962 (Ind. Ct. App. 1998); *In re* Marriage of Wiarda, 505 N.W.2d 506 (Iowa Ct. App. 1993)

[612] J.B.F. v. J.M.F., 730 So. 2d 1190, 1195-96 (Ala. 1998); Hertzler v. Hertzler, 908 P.2d 946, 951 (Wyo. 1995) (restricting mother's visitation rights because she involved the children in a same-sex commitment ceremony and took them to a gay and lesbian rights parade); *but cf.* Pleasant v. Pleasant, 628 N.E.2d 633, 636-42 (Ill. App. Ct. 1993) (holding that it is error to restrict a mother's visitation rights for taking her son to a gay pride parade, where there was no evidence that he had been harmed by the parade)

[613] *See* Charpentier v. Charpentier, 536 A.2d 948, 950 (Conn. 1988) (affirming custody award to father, where the evidence showed that the children felt neglected by their mother because of her new same-sex relationship); Hall v. Hall, 291 N.W.2d 143, 144 (Mich. Ct. App. 1980) (affirming custody award to the father on the basis of a belief that the mother would choose her lesbian relationship over her children).

[614] Transgendered people are "individuals whose gendered self-presentation (evidenced through dress, mannerisms, and even physiology) does not correspond to the behaviors habitually associated with the members of their biological sex." VIVIANE K. NAMASTE, INVISIBLE LIVES: THE ERASURE OF TRANSSEXUAL AND TRANSGENDERED PEOPLE 1 (2000). As used herein, the term includes cross-dressers as well as pre-op and post-op transsexuals.

[615] The DSM-IV included "gender identity disorder" as a mental disorder. AMERICAN PSYCHIATRIC ASSOCIATION, DIAGNOSTIC AND STATISTICAL MANUAL

for restricting visitation; to some courts, it was a reason to terminate parental rights altogether.[616]

Some courts continue to assume that any contact between a child and a transgendered parent is harmful to the child.[617] The modern trend, though, seems to be to apply the same rule that is applied in the case of gay and lesbian parents, so that a parent's transgendered status operates as a bar to custody only if there is a nexus to some provable harm or danger to the child's emotional well-being or development, or to an adverse affect on the parent-child relationship.[618]

In one highly-publicized case, a Florida court approved a mediated agreement placing a child in the custody of Michael Kantaras, a female-to-male transsexual, largely because no showing of a nexus between the parent's transsexuality and harm to the child had been made.[619]

OF MENTAL DISORDERS, DMS-IV-TR (4th ed. 2000). The most recent edition uses the phrase, "gender dysphoria." Research does not support the notion that transgendered parents are inherently dangerous to children, however. *See* R. Green, *Sexual Identity of 37 Children Raised by Transsexual or Homosexual Parents*, 135 AM. J. OF PSYCHIATRY 692 (June 1978) ("Children being raised by transsexual or homosexual parents do not differ appreciably from children raised in more conventional family settings.")

[616] *See, e.g.,* Daly v. Daly, 715 P.2d 56 (Nev. 1986); Cisek v. Cisek, No. 80 C.A. 113, 1982 Ohio Ct. App. LEXIS 13335 at *3 (Ohio Ct. App. July 20, 1982); *cf. In Re Darnell*, 619 P.2d 1349 (Or. Ct. App. 1980) (terminating a mother's parental rights on the basis of her refusal to discontinue relationship with a transsexual); *see generally* Phyllis Randolph Frye, *Facing Discrimination, Organizing for Freedom: The Transgender Community, in* CREATING CHANGE: SEXUALITY, PUBLIC POLICY, AND CIVIL RIGHTS 451, 454 (John D'Emilio et al. eds., 2000).

[617] *See, e.g.,* J.L.S. v. D.D.S., 943 S.W.2d 766, 775 (Mo. Ct. App. 1997) (reversing an order that had awarded visitation rights to a transgender parent, on the grounds that there was not an adequate showing that such contact was in the child's best interest.)

[618] *See* Julie Shapiro, *Custody and Conduct: How the Law Fails Lesbian and Gay Parents and Their Children*, 71 IND. L.J. 623, 633 (1996). A majority of courts today follow the "nexus" test rather than the per-se rule. *Id.* at 635; *see, e.g.,* Christian v. Randall, 516 P.2d 132 (Colo. Ct. App. 1973).

[619] *Judge Gives Transsexual Father Custody of Children in Florida*, N.Y. TIMES, February 22, 2003. Courts generally seem to find a potential for harm to children more readily when the case involves a male-to-female transgendered person than when it involves a female-to-male transgendered person. *Compare* Christian v. Randall, 516 P.2d 132 (Colo. Ct. App. 1973) (granting custody of a child to female-to-male transsexual) *with* Daly v. Daly, 715 P.2d 56 (Nev. 1986) (terminating parental rights

While the trend seems to be toward greater acceptance of transgendered persons, courts can be expected to proceed with caution in this area. There is a concern that contact with a transgendered parent may negatively affect a child's understanding of sexuality, or his or her own gender identity. Courts may view a child's difficulty understanding his parent's transsexuality as an emotional or psychological danger to the child.[620]

In *Daly v. Daly*[621] the Nevada Supreme Court affirmed the termination of a male-to-female transsexual's parental rights on the basis that he was an embarrassment to his daughter.

Of course, if the other parent is unfit, or if other "best interest" factors very strongly favor the transgendered parent, a court might assign less weight to the child's discomfort or embarrassment, particularly if the other parent has fostered and encouraged the child's discomfort.[622]

If a transgendered person can keep his or her gender identity issues and practices hidden from the child, then they should not be a bar to custody, at least not in a state where courts apply a "nexus" test.[623] It is conceivable that a court may be persuaded to grant custody to a transsexual if the child has no difficulty dealing with it and if the parent's transsexuality does not appear likely to create issues for the child in the future.[624] The fact

---

altogether on the basis of the parent's male-to-female transsexuality) *and* Cisek v. Cisek, No. 80 C.A. 113, 1982 Ohio Ct. App. LEXIS 13335 (Ohio Ct. App. July 20, 1982) (terminating all visitation with the father after his sex-change operation, on the grounds that a child would have difficulty adjusting to the change.)

[620] *See* Cisek v. Cisek, No. 80 C.A. 113, 1982 Ohio Ct. App. LEXIS 13335 (Ohio Ct. App. July 20, 1982); Kari J. Carter, Note, *The Best Interest Test and Child Custody: Why Transgender Should Not Be a Factor in Custody Determinations*, 16 HEALTH MATRIX 209, 221 (2006); David Freedman et al., *Children and Adolescents with Transsexual Parents Referred to a Specialist Gender Identity Development Service: A Brief Report of Key Developmental Features*, 7 CLINICAL CHILD PSYCHOL. & PSYCHIATRY 423, 424 (2002)

[621] 715 P.2d 56 (Nev. 1986). The court cited the father's sexual reassignment surgery as evidence that he was a "selfish person whose own needs, desires and wishes were paramount and were indulged without regard to their impact on [his] daughter, Mary." *Id.* at 59.

[622] *See, e.g., In re* V.H., 412 N.W.2d 389 (Minn. Ct. App. 1987)

[623] *Id.; see also* P.L.W. v V.T.R.W., 890 S.W.2d 688 (Mo. Ct. App. 1994); D.F.D. v. D.G.D., 862 P.2d 368, 376-77 (Mont. 1993)

[624] *See In re* T.J., No. C2-87-1786, 1988 WL 8302 at *3-4 (Minn. Ct. App. Feb. 9, 1988) (awarding custody to a male-to-female transsexual)

that a transgendered person does not act on his gender-identity proclivities in the presence of his children (i.e., remains closeted, and appears likely to remain closeted in the future when he is around his children) may be important to a court. A court may even regard it as an essential pre-condition to an award of custody, at least when the custody of the children of a male-to-female transgendered person is at issue.[625]

A growing number of jurisdictions have enacted laws intended to promote greater acceptance of transgendered persons. In 1994, San Francisco enacted an ordinance prohibiting discrimination against transgendered persons.[626] Since then, several other jurisdictions have followed suit.[627] Consistent with the rationale in *Palmore v. Sidott*[628] a court in a state where such laws have been enacted may be expected to require a greater showing of harm to preclude an award of custody to a transgendered parent than the harm stemming from the community's, the court's or the child's own prejudices against transgendered persons alone.

Constitutional protections

Although sexual orientation is not yet treated as a suspect classification for purposes of Fourteenth Amendment analysis, this does not mean that states are free to discriminate against non-heterosexual persons. In *Lawrence v. Texas*,[629] the U.S. Supreme Court invalidated state prohibitions against homosexual practices (specifically, Texas's criminal sodomy law) on the basis that consensual sexual conduct is a liberty interest protected by Fourteenth Amendment substantive due process.

---

[625] *Id.*; *see also In re* V.H., 412 N.W.2d 389, 393 (Minn. Ct. App. 1987).

[626] San Francisco, Cal., Ordinance 433-94 (December 30, 1994); *see also* SANTA CRUZ, CAL., MUNICIPAL CODE §9.83.010 to .120 (1992)

[627] *See, e.g.*, CAL. CIV. CODE § 51 (2011); MINN. STAT. §§ 363A.03, .12 (2012); N.M. STAT. § 28-1-2(Q) (2011); R.I. GEN. LAWS §§ 11-24-2, -24-2.3 (2011) (hotels and public places); *see also* MO. REV. STAT. § 557.035 (2011) (hate crimes.) It should be noted that few, if any, of these laws explicitly apply to child custody determinations, but they do reflect a growing cultural trend toward acceptance of transgendered persons.

[628] 466 U.S. 429 (1984).

[629] 539 U.S. 558 (2003).

In *Romer v. Evans*[630] the U.S. Supreme Court held that discrimination on the basis of sexual orientation is not permitted if it is not reasonably related to a legitimate state interest; and abhorrence of homosexuality, standing alone, does not qualify as a legitimate state interest. Of course, the state, in its role as parens patriae, has a legitimate interest in protecting children from harm. But a court's denial of custody to a non-heterosexual person without requiring any proof of actual harm or danger to children cannot be said to be reasonably related to that interest. Accordingly, the per se rule appears to be constitutionally suspect.[631]

Of course, neither these Supreme Court precedents nor any legislative enactments preclude courts from taking sexual orientation into consideration in child custody cases if some nexus to a specific danger of harm to the child's interests (such as emotional difficulties adjusting to the parent's sexuality) is demonstrated. They do, however, cast serious doubt on the continuing validity of cases treating a parent's sexual orientation as a reason, in itself, to deny the parent custody of children.

---

[630] 517 U.S. 620, 634 (1996)

[631] *See, e.g.*, Moses v. King, 637 S.E.2d 97, 98 (Ga. Ct. App. 2006) (holding that a mother's cohabitation with her lesbian partner is not a proper basis for depriving her of custody, in the absence of proof that the child was harmed or exposed to inappropriate conduct); McGriff v. McGriff, 99 P.3d 111 (Idaho 2004) (citing *Lawrence v. Texas* in support of the proposition that sexual orientation, standing by itself, does not disqualify a parent from having custody of children); A.O.V. v. J.R.V., Nos. 0219-06-4, 0220-06-4, 2007 WL 581871 at *11 (Va. Ct. App. Feb. 27, 2007) (same); *see also* Trainor, *supra* note 584 (Supp. 2011) at 601 and cases cited therein (refusing to presume harm from the mere possibility of confusion about sexuality.)

33. CHILD PROTECTION AND FOSTER CARE

Most custody cases involve a contest between individuals. Usually, those individuals are the child's parents. In some cases, the contest is between a parent and a non-parent (e.g., a relative), or between two non-parents. There is a smaller but growing category of cases, however, in which the contest is between the state and the child's parents. These are the cases in which the state intervenes to protect a child from abuse, neglect or endangerment.

Criminal prosecution of child abuse in early America

From the beginning of the country to the present-day, the state has always taken action, in one way or another, to try to protect children from harm. The first efforts at this were through the criminal law. Assault and battery have been crimes since colonial times, and it has always been as much a crime to assault a child as it is to assault an adult. In colonial times, as now, a person who struck, or threatened to strike, or who physically injured or threatened to physically injure, a child, could be convicted of a crime and sentenced accordingly.

The common law gave parents a special defense that was not available to non-parents – a privilege to use corporal punishment to discipline a child. A parent could spank a child without fear of being prosecuted criminally.

The privilege was a limited one, though. Parents were not entitled to strike or beat their children for a purpose other than discipline or guidance. They did not have a common law privilege to subject their children to excessive discipline.

The privilege extended only to a parent's own child. People were not legally permitted to assault other people's children.

Child abuse was punished by the criminal law in the same way crimes against adults were. For example, just as a person could be punished criminally for unlawfully restraining another person's freedom of movement (the crime of false imprisonment), so a parent could be punished criminally for unreasonably confining a child, if the confinement was either an unreasonably excessive form of discipline, or done for a purpose other than discipline. Thus, in 1869 the Illinois Supreme Court ruled that a father could be prosecuted criminally for confining his son in a cold cellar in the middle of winter.[632]

Removal of children from their homes

One of the first laws enacted in the American colonies was an educational neglect statute. Enacted in the Massachusetts Bay Colony in 1642, it authorized courts to remove children from parents who failed to educate them.[633]

Child abuse was also grounds for removing a child from a home in colonial times. In 1735, for example, a Georgia court removed a girl from her home because she had been sexually abused.[634]

---

[632] Fletcher v. People, 52 Il. 395 (1869).
[633] ANCIENT CHARTERS AND LAWS OF MASSACHUSETTS BAY, Ch. XXIL (1642)
[634] Buckingham, *supra* note 270.

In the nineteenth century, several states enacted laws authorizing courts to intervene in a family if a child was orphaned; or when a parent abused or neglected a child; or when a parent's character or conduct endangered a child's health, safety or morals. An 1866 Massachusetts statute, for example, authorized courts to intervene when "by reason of orphanage or of the neglect, crime, drunkenness or other vice of parents," a child was "growing up without education or salutary control, and in circumstances exposing said child to an idle and dissolute life."[635]

Statutory authorization for judicial intervention in families for the protection of children was not really necessary. Judges regarded themselves as possessing inherent power to protect all children within the jurisdiction of the court, with or without permission from the legislature. The chancery courts of England had established this power (called *parens patriae* authority) many years earlier, and American judges followed suit.

Parens patriae is Latin for "parent of the country." It refers to the role of the sovereign (the government) as guardian of such of its citizens as are unable to take care of themselves, including children and severely disabled persons.[636] As agents of the sovereign, courts have implicit authority to ensure that the children within their jurisdiction are properly cared for and protected. The *parens patriae* power of the sovereign, acting through its legislature and courts, is the source of all child protection legislation and judicially issued child protection orders today.[637]

Societies for the prevention of cruelty to children

Although early American courts had authority to intervene in families to protect children from harm, they did not exercise the power very often. This was due, in part, to the fact that law enforcement officers generally declined to become involved in family problems; and private child-helping

---

[635] An Act Concerning the Care and Education of Neglected Children, 1866 Mass. Acts ch. 283

[636] BLACK'S LAW DICTIONARY 510 (2d Pocket Ed., 2001); *see also* 3 W. BLACKSTONE, COMMENTARIES *47 (describing it as deriving from the king's royal prerogative as the "general guardian of all infants, idiots, and lunatics"); *see generally* Jack Ratliff, *Parens Patriae: An Overview*, 74 TUL. L. REV. 1847, 1850-51 (2000)

[637] JOSEPH STORY, COMMENTARIES ON EQUITY JURISPRUDENCE AS ADMINISTERED IN ENGLAND AND AMERICA § 1341 (13th ed. 1886).

charities did not have the legal authority to do so. Moreover, no specific department of the government was tasked with responsibility for investigating reports of child abuse, neglect or endangerment; and juvenile courts did not exist yet.

The problem came to the fore in 1874, when religious missionary Etta Wheeler learned about a ward named Mary Ellen Wilson who was routinely being beaten and neglected by her guardians. Ms. Wheeler contacted law enforcement. They refused to become involved in the situation. The private charities she contacted also refused to intervene. Finally, she turned to the founder of the American Society for the Prevention of Cruelty to Animals (ASPCA), Henry Bergh, for help. Mr. Bergh's legal counsel succeeded in petitioning a court for the removal of the child from the home.

The experience sensitized Mr. Bergh to the need for an organization with responsibility for protecting children. To that end, he established a charitable organization that would devote itself entirely to the project of protecting children from harm. Founded in 1875, the New York Society for the Prevention of Cruelty to Children (NYSPCC) was the first child protection organization in the world. By 1922, around 300 child protection societies had been created, each located in different regions of the country.[638]

Juvenile courts

The first juvenile court was established in 1899, in Chicago, Illinois. By 1919, all but three states had them, and eventually every state did.[639] The jurisdiction of these courts extended to both juvenile delinquency and child protection.

Child protection agencies

Child protection functions originally were performed by charitable organizations; specifically, the NYSPCC and others patterned after it. Due to their limited resources, however, these organizations could only help a small number of children. A tax-funded government agency has the capacity to reach a much greater number of children, and can provide a

---

[638] John E.B. Myers, *A Short History of Child Protection in America*, 42 FAM. L.Q. 450, 452 (2008-2009)

[639] *Id.*

wider array of services to them. As the role of government in social services increased during the first few decades of the twentieth century, support for the idea of delegating responsibility for child protection to government grew.[640] When charitable donations started drying up during the Great Depression, socialization of child protection became the only realistic alternative.

Groundwork for the socialization of child protection had already been laid prior to the Great Depression. In 1912, Congress had made a significant first step into the field of child welfare by creating a Children's Bureau. Between 1921 and 1929, the Sheppard-Towner Act had funded health services for babies and their mothers. Then, in 1935, as part of President Franklin Roosevelt's New Deal, the Social Security Act was passed. This Act created a number of social "safety net" programs and services, such as Aid to Dependent Children. It also directed the Children's Bureau "to cooperate with state public-welfare agencies in establishing, extending, and strengthening ... [services] for the protection and care of homeless, dependent, and neglected children, and children in danger of becoming delinquent."[641]

Between 1935 and 1965, responsibility for child protection increasingly shifted from charitable organizations to government agencies. By 1956, nongovernmental child protection societies had declined from 300 to 84.[642]

In 1962, C. Henry Kempe published an influential article in the *Journal of the American Medical Association* calling attention to the problem of child abuse.[643] That same year, Congress amended the Social Security Act to make it clear that "child welfare services" included child protective services, and required states to make these services available statewide, giving them until July 1, 1975 to do so.[644] By 1967, nearly all states had laws placing

---

[640] *See, e.g.,* Douglas P. Falconer, *Child and- Youth Protection, in* 3 SOC. WORK Y.B. 63, 65 (Fred **S.** Hall ed., 1935)

[641] Social Security Act of 1935, § 521, 49 Stat. 620, 633.

[642] VINCENT DE FRANCIS, CHILD PROTECTIVE SERVICES IN THE UNITED STATES: REPORTING A NATIONWIDE SURVEY (1956).

[643] C. Henry Kempe et al., *The Battered-Child Syndrome,* 181 J. AM. MED. ASS'N 17 (1962).

[644] Public Welfare Amendments of 1962, Pub. L. No. 87-543, § 528, 76 Stat. 172, 172; *cf.* VINCENT DE FRANCIS, AM. HUMAN ASS'N, CHILD PROTECTIVE SERVICES: A NATIONAL SURVEY 4 (1967)

responsibility for child protection in a government agency, and the number of nongovernmental child protection societies had dwindled to ten.[645]

Mandatory child abuse reporting laws

Concomitant with the transfer of responsibility for child protection to government agencies, measures were developed to ensure that incidents of child abuse would be brought to the attention of these agencies. The Children's Bureau recommended that states enact legislation requiring doctors to report suspicions of abuse to police or a child welfare agency. By 1967, all states had enacted mandatory reporting laws of this kind. Most states eventually extended the reporting requirement to apply to virtually all health care providers and to professionals in other fields as well, such as teachers and child-care workers.

Foster care

Throughout most of the nineteenth century, children who could not live with their parents (or another legal custodian) for any reason were institutionalized. Specifically, they were housed in orphanages and poorhouses. During the latter half of the century, reformers began advocating for the placement of abused, neglected and abandoned children in the homes of families rather than in institutions. Eventually, their efforts were successful. In the twentieth century, the foster care system (placing children in individual homes rather than in institutions) became the preferred method of dealing with children who were removed from their homes due to abuse, neglect, abandonment, or endangerment.

Child Abuse Prevention and Treatment Act of 1974

Enacted in 1974, the federal Child Abuse Prevention and Treatment Act (CAPTA)[646] sought to improve state efforts to prevent child abuse and to help victims of child abuse. It provided funding for research and training programs to improve child abuse investigations, reporting and treatment; and for regional multidisciplinary centers and other child-abuse-related programs. Administrative responsibility for CAPTA was assigned to a new agency established by the Act for that purpose, the National Center on

---

[645] *Id.*
[646] Pub. L. No. 93-247, 88 Stat. 4 (1974)

Child Abuse and Neglect (NCCAN.) CAPTA-funded research has had a significant influence on the operation, methods and strategies employed by state and local child protection agencies.

Adoption Assistance and Child Welfare Act of 1980 (AACWA)

The growth of child protection agencies, together with mandated reporting and increased awareness of child abuse, resulted in large numbers of children being removed from their homes and placed in foster care. To prevent states from being overzealous in their disruption of families Congress, in 1980, enacted the Adoption Assistance and Child Welfare Act (AACWA).[647] This legislation required states to make "reasonable efforts" to keep children together with their parents, wherever possible. In cases where removal was necessary, it required states to make reasonable efforts to reunite children with their families. These efforts needed to be reflected in a permanency plan, which states were required to formulate in every case in which a child was removed from his home and placed in a foster home. The plan needed to detail the steps that would be taken to return the child to his home or move toward termination of parental rights. In cases where a child could not be returned to his home, the AACWA provided financial incentives for adoption. It also provided financial incentives for people who adopted children with special needs.

Adoption and Safe Families Act of 1997

The family preservation policy embodied in the AACWA came under fire in the 1990's. Critics charged that undue emphasis on keeping biological families together put abused and neglected children at risk. In *The Book of David: How Preserving Families Can Cost Children's Lives*[648] sociologist Richard J. Gelles wrote:

> It is time to abandon the myth that "the best foster family is not as good as a marginal biological family." The ability to make a baby does not ensure that a couple have, or ever will have, the ability to be adequate parents. The policy of family reunification and family

---

[647] Pub. L. No. 96-272, 94 Stat. 500 (1980).
[648] RICHARD J. GELLES, THE BOOK OF DAVID: HOW PRESERVING FAMILIES CAN COST CHILDREN'S LIVES (1996)

preservation fails because it assumes that *all* biological parents can become fit and acceptable parents if only appropriate and sufficient support is provided.[649]

Gelles and others argued that the family preservation policy of the AACWA resulted in children being left in dangerous homes. Congress agreed, and in 1997 enacted the Adoption and Safe Families Act (ASFA).[650]

While retaining a general policy in favor of family preservation, ASFA added measures intended to ensure that children's safety would be given top priority. One such measure was to establish limited time frames for states to either return children to their parents or terminate parental rights and free them for adoption. ASFA authorized states to dispense with family reunification efforts altogether for children who were victims of sexual abuse or chronic physical abuse. States were authorized to take immediate steps to terminate parental rights so these children could be freed up for adoption without delay.

Today, questions are being raised about whether the State has extended its reach too far into the family. Parents' rights organizations are expressing a concern that federally funded adoption assistance programs and grants incentivize states to enact child protection laws and procedures that too readily sever biological relationships in order to expedite adoptions.

---

[649] *Id.* at 149-50.
[650] Pub. L. No. 105-89, 111 Stat. 2115 (1997).

34. WELFARE AND CHILD SUPPORT

No history of modern custody law would be complete without a discussion of the impact of welfare and child support enforcement programs and laws on state custody standards and practice.

At one time, the child support obligation had a direct impact on child custody. Judges historically considered a father's nonsupport of his children to be grounds for finding him unfit to have custody of them. Some courts continue to treat a father' nonsupport of his child as grounds for a finding of parental unfitness, if it is for such an extended period of time, and for such unjustified reasons, as to amount to child abandonment. Today, though, the child support obligation and its enforcement arguably have a much more pervasive, albeit indirect, impact on the substantive law of custody than this.

To understand how child support laws impact custody law and practice it is necessary to have some familiarity with the origins and nature of governmental involvement in the enforcement of private support obligations.

Common law origins

The parental obligation of support

American courts have always possessed power to order a noncustodial parent to provide financial support to his children. The power derives from the inherent *parens patriae* authority of a court of equity, as agent of the sovereign, to ensure that children within its jurisdiction are adequately cared for and protected. From the beginning, courts have recognized that parents have a legally enforceable obligation to support their children.[651]

Throughout most of American history, a court's exercise of the power has been limited in application, either by statute or by judicial precedent, to noncustodial fathers. It was not until the end of the twentieth century that courts began imposing child support obligations on noncustodial mothers, too. Today, most states have laws requiring courts to address child support in every child custody order, whether custody is awarded to a woman or to a man.

Recoupment of necessaries furnished by the state

The English Poor Law of 1601[652] authorized local parishes to recover from the father any funds the community spent caring for an unwed mother and her children, in cases where the father was not providing adequate care for the children himself. This law provided a means by which a town could recoup the expenses it had incurred for the support of a single mother and her children. It did not provide a means by which a parent or a third party could seek a contribution to child support expenses.

The Poor Law was carried over to the American colonies in the 1600's and became part of American law, both common and statutory.[653]

---

[651] *See, e.g.*, Stanton v. Willson, 3 Day 37 (Conn. 1808) ("Parents are bound by law to maintain, protect, and educate their legitimate children during their infancy or nonage. This duty rests on the father....")

[652] 43 Eliz. c. 2 (Eng. 1601).

[653] TAPPING REEVE, THE LAW OF BARON AND FEMME 414 (1862); JAMES SCHOULER, A TREATISE ON THE LAW OF THE DOMESTIC RELATIONS 320 (1870).

Reimbursement of necessaries furnished by a third party

Although English common law was not as beneficent, American common law has long recognized the right of a third party to sue a father for reimbursement of "necessaries" (support) the third party has furnished to his wife or his children.[654] The legal rationale for this cause of action is implied contract.

> A parent is under a natural obligation to furnish necessaries for his infant children; and if the parent neglects that duty, any other person who supplies such necessaries is deemed to have conferred a benefit on the delinquent parent, for which the law raises an implied promise to pay on the part of the parent.[655]

The obligation was limited to *necessities*. A third party had no valid claim to reimbursement of money or property given to a child whose parents were adequately attending to their children's needs without the third party's help.[656]

Enforcement of child support by charitable humane societies

During the latter half of the nineteenth century, single, separated and divorced mothers often turned to charitable relief organizations for financial assistance. In the 1870's and 1880's, they became a significant burden on these organizations' funds.[657] To recoup their costs, these organizations utilized the laws establishing a third party's right of action against a father for necessaries furnished to his wife or children.

---

[654] See, e.g., Eitel v. Walter, 2 Bradf. 287, 289 (N.Y. Sur. Ct. 1853) in which the judge, after acknowledging the existence of English precedent to the contrary, wrote, "I think a more humane doctrine prevails here, and that the father is held liable for necessaries, or, in other words, the law will imply a contract on his part, if he refuses or neglects to perform his natural duty to his offspring."

[655] Van Valkinburgh v. Watkins, 13 Johns 480 (N.Y. 1816); *see also* Tomkins v. Tomkins, 11 N.J. Eq. 512 (Ch. 1858)

[656] Van Valkinburgh v. Watkins, 13 Johns 480 (N.Y. 1816)

[657] *See Foundlings and Deserted Children, in* PROCEEDINGS OF THE EIGHTH ANNUAL CONFERENCE OF CHARITIES AND CORRECTION 282, 282-84 (1881) (statement of Susan I. Lesley, Phil. Soc'y for Organizing Charity).

These relief organizations also helped women establish support orders. In many cases, they collected support money from fathers on behalf of the mothers who sought their help, and acted as disbursing agents of the funds collected. And they successfully lobbied for stronger desertion and criminal nonsupport laws.[658]

From private obligation to civic duty

The judicial power to issue child support orders derived from the judicially established *parens patriae* policy of ensuring adequate care and support for children. Conceptually, a child support order represented a court's discharge of its own obligation to the sovereign by means of enforcing a father's obligation to his family. The original purpose of child support orders was to enhance children's welfare by ensuring that their parents took proper care of them.

The essential nature of the child support order underwent a significant change in the nineteenth century. With the sanctification of motherhood (stay-at-home mothering) attendant to the intensification of the division of social roles by sex wrought by the Industrial Revolution came a growing concern among judges that single, divorced and separated women and their children would become a financial burden upon the community (the state). Unless the father or ex-husband provided for them economically, a mother and her children could become dependent either on the state or on the limited resources of charitable relief organizations for their support. As a result, late nineteenth century judges increasingly cited a public policy in favor of preventing women and children from becoming financial burdens upon the state as the basis for their support orders. For this reason, courts began to describe a father's child support obligation as being something more than a merely private obligation between parents; now it was also a "duty to the public."[659]

---

[658] *See, e.g.*, MASSACHUSETTS SOC'Y FOR THE PREVENTION OF CRUELTY TO CHILDREN, SECOND ANNUAL REPORT 15-17 (1882); *see also* Martha May, *The "Problem of Duty": Family Desertion in the Progressive Era*, 62 SOC. SERV. REV. 40, 43-44 (1988)

[659] Steele v. People, 88 Ill. App. 186, 187 (App. Ct. 1899); *see also* Courtright v. Courtright, 40 Mich. 633, 635 (1879) (stating that a father has a duty to his children and "as against the public" to support his children after a divorce); Bowen v. State, 46 N.E. 708,709 (Ohio 1897) (describing a father's child support obligation as "a

Criminal nonsupport

The concept of child support as a civic obligation, as distinguished from a purely private one, was reflected in the criminal nonsupport statutes that were enacted in the nineteenth century. These statutes made it a crime for a father or husband to fail to support his wife or children financially. They were enacted primarily for the purpose of preserving public funds, the intended effect being to deter fathers and husbands from allowing women and children to become dependent on government largesse or charitable relief aid for their support.

Nonsupport was a serious offense. The penalty, in some states, was imprisonment and hard labor.[660] In most states, the penalty was a fine, imprisonment, or both.[661]

Courts originally construed criminal nonsupport statutes in a manner consistent with their purpose. Thus, in *State v. Rice*[662] the Indiana Supreme Court ruled that an absent husband could not be prosecuted for nonsupport if his wife had adequate financial resources of her own. That is to say, consistent with the intent of these statutes, a father could not be punished merely for failing to contribute money to his children unless they actually went without parental support. It was only those fathers who put their children at risk of becoming dependent on state funds for their support who could be prosecuted under these statutes.

In most states today, a parent may be prosecuted for nonsupport even if the other parent is independently wealthy. In addition, the laws of most states have been gender-neutralized so that -- in theory, at least -- a mother, too, may be prosecuted for criminal nonsupport.

---

duty which he owes to the state, as well as to his children; and he has no more right to allow them to become a public charge than he has to allow them to suffer for want of proper care and sustenance.")

[660] *See, e.g.,* 1884-1885 N.J. Acts ch. 2

[661] *See, e.g.,* IND. REV. STAT. § 2133 (1881). 1882 Mass. Acts ch. 270; 1885; 1883 N.H. Laws ch. 58; Wis. Laws ch. 422.

[662] 5 N.E. 906, 907 (Ind. 1886); *see also* See State v. Watson, 33 A. 943 (N.J. 1896); Williams v. State, 48 S.E. 938 (Ga. 1904) (holding that a conviction for nonsupport may be sustained only if there is evidence that the father left his wife or children in a destitute condition.)

Federal involvement in child support enforcement

Except with respect to interstate issues, the regulation of domestic relations is one of the powers that the Tenth Amendment reserves to the states because it is not a power that the Constitution delegates to the federal government. Congress, however, has used its Taxing and Spending powers to exert a tremendous amount of influence on the content of state child custody and support laws.[663] The following is a brief summary of some of the most significant federal child support legislation.

The Social Security Act of 1935

Title IV of the Social Security Act of 1935[664] provided grants in aid to states that gave aid to dependent children pursuant to a plan that complied with the conditions set out in the Act.

As originally enacted, the Aid to Dependent Children (ADC) program was designed to enable states to dispense welfare payments for needy children who had been deprived of parental support because a parent was deceased or absent from the home. Every state adopted an ADC program plan to take advantage of these grants. Under this program, the federal government reimbursed states for payments of ADC benefits that they made to parents who qualified for the assistance, at "matching" rates inversely related to a state's per capita income.

The original intent of the ADC grant program was to subsidize stay-at-home mothers. By 1961, the program had been extended to subsidize, in addition, households that consisted of an unemployed parent and a caretaker relative. In 1962, it was further extended to include two-parent households in which one of the parents was incapacitated or unemployed. At this point, the name of the program was changed to Aid to Families with Dependent Children (AFDC).

---

[663] For a case upholding the constitutionality of this exercise of the Congressional spending power, see Kansas v. United States, 214 F.3d 1196 (10th Cir.), *cert. denied*, 531 U.S. 1035 (2000).

[664] 49 STAT. 627 (1935), 42 U.S.C. (1935 Supp.) §§ 601-606, now 42 U.S.C. §§ 601-687 (2013)

1950 amendments

The federal government's first step into the support enforcement field occurred in 1950. Public Law 81–734, the Social Security Amendments of 1950, added section 402(a)(11) to the Social Security Act.[665] It required state welfare agencies to notify law enforcement officials whenever ADC benefits were provided for a child who had been abandoned or deserted by a parent. The hope was that more prosecutions of noncustodial fathers for criminal nonsupport would impel absent fathers to take financial responsibility for their children, thereby reducing the dependency of mothers on welfare, and relieving some of the strain on the federal budget.

1965 amendments

Public Law 89–97 authorized a state or local welfare agency to obtain from the federal government information about the address and employment of an absent parent who owed court-ordered child support.

1967 amendments

Public Law 90–248, the Social Security Amendments of 1967, laid the groundwork for a coordinated federal-state child support enforcement system. Among other things, it required each state to establish an agency specifically responsible for establishing paternity orders and collecting child support for children receiving AFDC benefits.

When a state collected child support payments from a noncustodial parent on behalf of a family receiving AFDC benefits, the state would reimburse the federal government for the federal share of AFDC benefits that had been paid to the family, i.e., 50% to 83% of the total benefit payment, depending on state per capita income.[666]

Title IV-D (1975 amendments)

Probably the most historically significant amendments to the Social Security Act were made in Public Law 93–647, the Social Security

---

[665] 42 USC § 602(a)(11)
[666] CARMEN SOLOMON-FEARS, CONGRESSIONAL RESEARCH SERV., CHILD SUPPORT ENFORCEMENT PROGRAM INCENTIVE PAYMENTS: BACKGROUND AND POLICY ISSUES App. A (2013)

Amendments of 1974, creating part D of title IV of the Social Security Act.[667] Signed into law by President Gerald Ford, this legislation created a federal Office of Child Support Enforcement (OCSE). It directed the OCSE to establish a parent locator service; to establish standards for the operation, organization and staffing of state child support offices; to review state plans for compliance with federal program requirements; to audit and evaluate state programs; to certify certain child support cases to federal courts for enforcement; to certify cases to the IRS for support collections; to provide assistance to state programs; to collect and maintain information and records about state operations, expenditures and collections; and to report annually to Congress.

To comply with federal plan requirements, states were required, among other things, to: establish a child support agency; undertake responsibility for establishing paternity judgments and support orders on behalf of people who either receive AFDC benefits or apply for child support enforcement services; collect and distribute child support payments for custodial parents; enter into cooperative agreements with other states and law enforcement agencies for child support enforcement purposes; establish a state parent locator service; cooperate with any other state in locating an absent parent, establishing paternity, and collecting support; and maintain complete records of all collections and disbursements of child support.

In addition, the 1975 amendments required AFDC recipients to assign all of their support rights to the state and to cooperate with the state in establishing paternity and collecting support. This authorized the state (or a county acting as an instrumentality of the state) to commence legal proceedings in its own right to establish and collect child support from the absent parent to reimburse itself, and the federal government, for AFDC payments they had made to the custodial parent.

Since the purpose of collecting child support in AFDC cases was to obtain reimbursement from noncustodial parents for moneys expended by the government on AFDC benefits paid to the custodial parent, only those governmental units that contributed to AFDC benefit payments had an incentive to collect reimbursement from child support collections. Counties

---

[667] 42 U.S.C. §§ 651 *et seq.*).

did not contribute to AFDC benefit payments, so they had no incentive to establish and enforce support orders. To give them an incentive, the 1975 amendments provided for the payment of special bonuses – incentive payments – to each county based on the amount of child support the county collected from a noncustodial parent on behalf of an AFDC recipient.[668] For similar reasons, incentive payments were also provided to states that collected child support for another state. In this situation, too, the amount of the incentive payment was based on the amount of support collected from a noncustodial parent to reimburse amounts paid out as AFDC.[669]

The amount of the incentive was equal to 25% of the amount of child support collected on behalf of the AFDC recipient for the first twelve months, and 10% thereafter. Incentive payments were paid out of the federal share of the child support recovered on behalf of AFDC families.[670]

1977 amendments

Public Law 95-30 increased the ongoing incentive payment from 10% of AFDC collections to 15%.

Public Law 95–142, the Medicare-Medicaid Antifraud and Abuse Amendments of 1977, established a medical support enforcement program component. This law also added incentives to local governments that undertook child support collections for states, and for states that collected child support on behalf of other states.

1980 amendments

Public Law 96–265, the Social Security Disability Amendments of 1980, provided federal matching funds up to 90% for developing, implementing, and improving automated information systems; and provided matching funds for child support enforcement duties performed by court personnel. IRS arrearage collection programs were extended to both AFDC and non-AFDC families, and state and local child support agencies were given access to Social Security Administration records.

---

[668] 42 U.S.C. § 658(a) (1977); SOLOMON-FEARS, *supra* note 666.
[669] SOLOMON-FEARS, *supra* note 666.
[670] *Id.*

The Adoption Assistance and Child Welfare Act of 1980

The Adoption Assistance and Child Welfare Act of 1980 (Public Law 96-272) provided some federal financial incentives for non-AFDC collection services.

Omnibus Budget Reconciliation Act of 1981

The Omnibus Budget Reconciliation Act (Public Law 97–35) authorized the IRS to withhold federal income tax refunds for payment of delinquent child support; required child support agencies to assume responsibility for collecting spousal support for AFDC recipients; made support obligations that had been assigned to the state non-dischargeable in bankruptcy; and made withholding applicable to unemployment benefits.

Tax Equity and Fiscal Responsibility Act of 1982

Public Law 97–248, the Tax Equity and Fiscal Responsibility Act of 1982, reduced the amount of incentive payments to states from 15% to 12% of child support collections made on behalf of AFDC families. It also authorized states to collect spousal support in certain non-AFDC cases.

Child Support Enforcement Amendments of 1984

Public Law 98–378, the Child Support Enforcement Amendments of 1984, required states to enact legislation to improve support enforcement, including: (1) mandatory income withholding; (2) expedited procedures for establishing and enforcing support orders; (3) interception of state income tax refunds; (4) liens against property; and (5) reporting child support arrears to consumer credit reporting agencies.

Federal matching funds were reduced to 66%, but new matching funds at 90% were made available for the development and installation of computerized systems to facilitate income withholding and other new requirements the amendments established.

State incentive payments for support collections were extended to apply to non-AFDC cases as well as AFDC cases. They were set at 6% in both AFDC and non-AFDC cases, or up to 10% for cost-effective states. State incentive payments were required to be passed through to local child support agencies. Incentives were paid out of the federal share of the child support collected from noncustodial parents on behalf of AFDC recipients.[671]

Penalties for noncompliance ranging from 1% to 5% of the federal share of a state's AFDC funds were established.

New provisions for the interstate enforcement of child support orders were added. For example, in interstate collection cases, incentive payments would be made to both states, not just to the state that collected the support on behalf of the other state.[672]

Mechanisms for the enforcement of support (e.g., federal income tax interception) were required to be made available in both AFDC and non-AFDC cases.

The rationale for extending child support enforcement program funding and resources to non-welfare cases was said to be that fewer families would need welfare if more noncustodial parents satisfied their support obligations.[673] On the other hand, program eligibility was extended even to custodial parents whose income levels are already so high that they would be ineligible for welfare with or without child support payments.

The law made a variety of additional changes. For example, it required states to collect both spousal and child support where both have been ordered in a case; to formulate guidelines for determining the amount of child support; to charge non-AFDC families a fee for services; and to establish medical support orders in addition to basic child support.

The Tax Reform Act of 1984

Public Law 98–369, the Tax Reform Act of 1984, altered rules relating to the deductibility of alimony, and required the income tax dependency exemption for a child of divorced or separated parents to be allocated to the custodial parent unless she signs a written declaration that she will not claim the exemption.

---

[671] *Id.*

[672] *Id.*

[673] *Id.* at CRS-24.

The Omnibus Budget Reconciliation Act of 1986

Public Law 99–509, the Omnibus Budget Reconciliation Act of 1986, prohibited the retroactive modification of child support.

The Omnibus Budget Reconciliation Act of 1987

Public Law 100–203, the Omnibus Budget Reconciliation Act of 1987, required states to extend child support enforcement services to Medicaid recipients as well as AFDC recipients.

The Family Support Act of 1988

The Family Support Act of 1988 (Public Law 100–485) called for a number of changes. First, it required states to enact mandatory child support guidelines.

Second, it required states to make a specified level of paternity determinations in proportion to the number of children in the state who were born out of wedlock and receiving AFDC benefits or IV-D support services. States were required to order all parties in a contested paternity case to take a genetic test upon any party's request.

Next, it required every state to have a statewide automated tracking and monitoring system in place by 1995. Federal matching funds at 90% were awarded for this.

Wage withholding was made mandatory in all cases (IV-D or non-IV-D), unless the parties had a written agreement otherwise, or the court found good cause not to order it. Wage withholding was also made mandatory in all cases in which there was an arrearage.

Next, it required states to require parents to furnish their Social Security numbers to the state when a birth certificate is issued, for child support collection purposes.

Finally, a federal Commission on Interstate Child Support was established. The Commission ultimately would recommend the adoption of a new performance-based incentive system.[674]

---

[674] *Id.*

The Child Support Recovery Act of 1992

Public Law 102–521, the Child Support Recovery Act of 1992, made it a federal crime, under certain circumstances, to willfully fail to pay child support for a child who resides in another state.

The Omnibus Budget Reconciliation Act of 1993

Public Law 103–66, the Omnibus Budget Reconciliation Act of 1993, required states to adopt procedures by which parents may voluntarily acknowledge paternity of a child. It also required states to enact legislation designed to ensure that health insurers and employers comply with medical support orders.

The Full Faith and Credit for Child Support Orders Act of 1994

Public Law 103–383, the Full Faith and Credit for Child Support Orders Act, required states to enforce support orders issued in other states, and it set out certain jurisdictional rules.

The Bankruptcy Reform Act of 1994

Public Law 103–394, the Bankruptcy Reform Act of 1994, created an exception to the Bankruptcy Code's automatic stay provision so that a paternity, child support or alimony case could proceed despite the filing of a bankruptcy petition. It also made child support and alimony priority claims in bankruptcy.

The Personal Responsibility and Work Opportunity Act of 1996 (PRWOA)

Public Law 104–193, the Personal Responsibility and Work Opportunity Reconciliation Act (the "welfare reform law") made some major reforms to child support enforcement programs.

Among many other things, the Act replaced the AFDC program with the Temporary Assistance to Needy Families (TANF) program; required employers and labor unions to provide detailed information about new hires to a state directory of new hires; strengthened income withholding regulations; authorized access to the federal parent locator service to obtain information for the enforcement of custody and visitation orders;

established a federal registry of child support orders; required collection of Social Security numbers in a wide variety of circumstances; required states to adopt the Uniform Interstate Family Support Act (UIFSA); provided details for the involvement of the U.S. Department of Health and Human Services in interstate support collections; authorized state IV-D programs to order genetic testing for paternity establishment, and to issue subpoenas without need for a court order; streamlined and provided for mandatory genetic testing in contested paternity cases; required states to encourage voluntary recognitions of paternity; required all support delinquencies to be reported to credit bureaus; required states to have laws providing for the suspension of driver's, professional, occupational, and recreational licenses, and for denial of passports, as child support enforcement mechanisms; authorized states to enforce a child support obligation of a minor child against the parents of the noncustodial parent; and clarified that child support is not dischargeable in bankruptcy.

The Act also called for a new performance-based incentive system to be developed by the Department of Health and Human Services.[675]

The Child Support Performance and Incentive Act of 1998

Public Law 105-200, the Child Support Performance and Incentive Act of 1998, adopted the new performance-based incentive system recommended by the Secretary of the Department of Health and Human Services.[676] It replaced the former incentive payment system with one that calculated incentive payments not only on the basis of success in establishing and collecting child support, but also based on certain additional performance measures, including cost-effectiveness. The Act required states to reinvest incentive payments into the child support enforcement program.[677] Caps were imposed on the aggregate amount of incentive payments that could be made to a state.

---

[675] *Id.*

[676] For the full text of the recommendations, see U.S. DEP'T OF HUM. SERV., CHILD SUPPORT ENFORCEMENT INCENTIVE FUNDING, REPORT TO THE HOUSE OF REPRESENTATIVES COMMITTEE ON WAYS AND MEANS AND THE SENATE COMMITTEE ON FINANCE, Feb. 1997.

[677] SOLOMON-FEARS, *supra* note 666.

Effective October 1, 2001, when the new incentive payment system was fully phased in, incentive payments are no longer paid out of child support collected on behalf of welfare recipients. Instead, the incentive payments are made out of the general treasury.[678]

The Deadbeat Parents Punishment Act of 1998

Public Law 105-187, the Deadbeat Parents Punishment Act of 1998, made it a federal felony to: (1) travel across state lines, or to a foreign country, with the intent to evade a support obligation that is delinquent for more than one year or in an amount in excess of $5,000; or (2) willfully fail to pay child support ordered for a child in another state, where arrears have accumulated for at least two years or in an amount in excess of $10,000.

Deficit Reduction Act of 2005

Public Law 109-171, the Deficit Reduction Act of 2005, discontinued the matching funds the federal government had been paying to states for incentive payments that states were reinvesting into child support programs.[679] The federal government would continue to reimburse each state 66% of all allowable expenditures on child support enforcement activities; and to provide states with certain incentive payments.[680]

Calculation of incentive amounts

The formula for calculating the amount of incentive payment to be made to a state is a bit complex. Basically, it takes into account both the amount of support collected and the state's performance in five areas related to child support enforcement: (1) number of paternity adjudications or establishments; (2) number of child support orders established; (3) success in collecting current payments owed; (4) success in collecting arrearages; and (5) cost-effectiveness (amount collected divided by program costs.) States also must meet data reliability standards to remain eligible. [681]

---

[678] *Id.*

[679] The American Recovery and Reinvestment Act of 2009 (Pub. L. 111-5) temporarily reinstated these for fiscal years 2009 and 2010.

[680] SOLOMON-FEARS, *supra* note 666 at CRS-2.

[681] *Id.* at CRS-6 to 9.

Under the new system, incentive payments are no longer calculated as a percentage of support collected. Rather, states compete against each other for a share of an aggregate amount of incentive payments the federal government appropriates for this purpose each year. The amount each state "wins" depends not only on support collected but also on the performance measures outlined above in comparison to the performance of other states.[682]

Conditioning welfare on the absence of a parent

The Aid to Dependent Children program established by the Social Security Act of 1935 made "needy" children eligible for cash assistance. (More precisely, it made the custodian of a needy child eligible to receive cash assistance on the child's behalf.) A child was defined as "needy" if, among other possible reasons (e.g., the death or disability of a parent), he or she "has been deprived of parental support or care by reason of the ... continued absence from the home ... of a parent."[683]

The requirement that one of the parents be "absent" arguably created an incentive for single mothers to remain unmarried, and helped subsidize a married woman's decision to divorce her husband, provided she was confident she would retain custody of her children, either because she reasonably anticipated that a court would apply a maternal preference or for some other reason. The requirement that a parent be absent from the home also created a disincentive for a divorced or separated mother to reconcile with her husband.

The Personal Responsibility and Work Opportunity Act of 1996 repealed the statute that had conditioned eligibility for welfare benefits on the "continued absence" of a parent from the home. In its place, it substituted a new statutory provision (42 U.S.C. Section 608) that prohibited states from granting aid to a family "unless the family includes (i) a minor child who resides with the custodial parent or other adult caretaker relative of the child; or (ii) a pregnant individual." The following year, Public Law 107-33 (1997) replaced the word "custodial parent" with "family," and added a requirement that states deny assistance to a family if the child does not reside in the home of the family for forty-five

---

[682] *Id.*
[683] 42 U.S.C. § 606(a) (1964 ed., Supp. II),

consecutive days. States were given the option of specifying a different period of time, so long as the period selected was between thirty and 180 days. This condition effectively created a disincentive for welfare recipients to agree to alternating custody arrangements, or to joint custody arrangements that called for a school/summer split of time.

Impact of federal child support enforcement incentives

Federal budgetary concerns were the impetus for federal involvement in child support enforcement. With the advent of no-fault divorce in the 1970's, and the destigmatization of birthing children out of wedlock, an increasingly large number of women became eligible for AFDC benefits. The increased strain on the federal budget prompted Congress to enter the child support enforcement field, the hope being that responsibility for supporting these women could be shifted from the federal government to the men who fathered the children.

Incentive payments, matching funds, and block grants to states are the basic mechanisms by which Congress specifies and controls the content of state divorce, paternity and other family laws. A state is free to refuse to enact the laws Congress has outlined for it, but if it does then it forfeits a significant share of the federal money that Congress has made available to states, and to individuals within the states, that do comply with the Congressional program.

To date, no state has refused to comply with the conditions Congress has specified. States find the federal funds quite attractive. For example, 74% of the state of Minnesota's total child support enforcement funding comes from the federal government. Federal Financial Participation (FFP), which is provided at a flat rate of 66% of state and county spending, accounts for most of that. The rest comes from federal financial incentives paid to the state and distributed to counties for the establishment of paternity, and for support establishment and collections.[684] This is in addition to federal financing of up to 90% of certain child support collection-related program costs.

---

[684] MINNESOTA HOUSE OF REPRESENTATIVES RESEARCH DEP'T, INFORMATION BRIEF: MINNESOTA'S CHILD SUPPORT LAWS 2 (2011)

Federal funds also benefit states indirectly, in the sense that bringing more federal money into a state can help stimulate the local economy; and ensuring people's eligibility for federal welfare benefits relieves a state of some of its share of responsibility for supporting dependent mothers and children (and now, sometimes, fathers) residing within the state.

According to a 1998 House Ways and Means Committee report,[685] states were earning a "profit" from federally-incentivized child support programs. This statement made some sense at the time it was made, since the federal government, at that time, was paying each complying state a bonus of at least 6% of all child support the state collected, in both welfare-reimbursement and non-welfare-reimbursement cases.[686] Today, the incentive payment is no longer calculated as a percentage of the amount collected, and instead involves a limited aggregate fund to be divvied up among the states according to their relative performances, and incentive payments that are received must be reinvested in the child support enforcement program. Moreover, the child support that is collected is either used to reimburse the government for its TANF outlays, or distributed to the parent to whom the support is owed. Accordingly, it may not be quite as accurate today as it once was to characterize federal support enforcement incentives as "profit" to states. Nevertheless, it is still possible to argue, as political scientist Stephen Baskerville has, that the system gives states an incentive to "turn as many parents as possible into payers by providing financial incentives to mothers to divorce"[687] – at least in the sense that any federal funds received help offset state outlays.

While there may be disagreement about whether states really make a "profit" on child support collections or not, the profitability of the child support guidelines for custodial parents has been clear. According to an analysis conducted by economist Robert Willis, less than one-third of child support payments are actually used for children; the remainder is profit for

---

[685] HOUSE WAYS & MEANS COMM., 105TH CONG., 2D SESS., 1998 GREENBOOK 596 (Comm. Print 1998)

[686] William Akins, *Why Georgia's Child Support Guidelines Are Unconstitutional*, 6 GA. BAR J. 9-10 (2000) (arguing that calculating federal payments as a percentage of support collected creates an "incentive to establish support obligations as high as possible without regard to appropriateness or amount.")

[687] STEPHEN BASKERVILLE, TAKEN INTO CUSTODY: THE WAR AGAINST FATHERS, MARRIAGE, AND THE FAMILY 122 (2007)

the custodial parent.[688] To the extent this remains the case in a particular state, it creates a significant financial incentive for a single mother to refrain from marrying, and for a married mother to divorce, at least if she is confident a court will grant her sole custody of the children.[689]

No federal welfare or incentive program requires states, as a condition of eligibility for federal funds, to successfully encourage unwed couples to enter into marriage for the benefit of their children. States, in their discretion, may spend some of their TANF block grants on "non-cash service" programs aimed at preventing out-of-wedlock pregnancies (e.g., abstinence education), but federal law does not mention encouraging marriage as a means of preventing births out of wedlock. Nor does the federal government reward any state for successfully bringing about a divorcing couple's reconciliation. States receive payments for establishing paternity and divorce support orders, not marriages.

Until 1997, federal law (specifically, 42 U.S.C. Section 651) authorized federal appropriations to states for the enforcement of the support obligations of "absent" parents. The Personal Responsibility and Work Opportunity Act of 1996 substituted the word "noncustodial" in place of "absent." Since neither of two joint custodians is a "noncustodial" parent, this arguably created a financial incentive for states to apply a preference for sole custody awards in preference to joint custody, given that the amount of a state's incentive payment was directly related to the amount of support established and collected from noncustodial parents. This particular incentive, however, was weakened considerably, if it even continues to exist at all, by the phase-in of the new performance-based incentive system.

It is likely, however, that state child support guidelines (the use of which is also a condition of receiving federal funds) continue to have a

---

[688] Robert J. Willis, *Child Support and the Problem of Economic Incentives, in* THE LAW AND ECONOMICS OF CHILD SUPPORT PAYMENTS 31, 42 (William S. Comanor ed., 2004)

[689] *See* Robert A. McNeely & Cynthia A. McNeely, *Hopelessly Defective: An Examination of the Assumptions Underlying Current Child Support Guidelines, in* THE LAW AND ECONOMICS OF CHILD SUPPORT PAYMENTS 170 (William S. Comanor ed., 2004); *see also* LOWELL GALLAWAY & RICHARD VEDDER, POVERTY, INCOME DISTRIBUTION, THE FAMILY AND PUBLIC POLICY 84-89 (1986); Saul Hoffman & Greg Duncan, *The Effects of Incomes, Wages, and AFDC Benefits on Marital Disruption,* 30 J. HUM. RESOURCES 19-41 (1995)

negative impact on a state's policies concerning joint physical custody. Child support guideline formulae and amounts vary from state to state, but a common feature among them is that they generally call for higher amounts when sole physical custody is awarded than when joint physical custody is. The legal rationale for this is that a sole custodian is said to be responsible for a greater share of the child-related expenses than a noncustodial parent is. (This rationale makes sense if joint physical custody is conceived of as being quantitatively, rather than qualitatively different from visitation. A parent who has the child five days out of the week will need to spend more on the child than a parent who has the child for only two days every other week.) Judges seeking to ensure abundant financial resources for a mother therefore have an incentive to favor sole custody and to disfavor joint custody.

In short, although child support no longer factors into child custody determinations as directly as it once did, child support laws arguably have a considerable impact, albeit an indirect one, on custody outcomes.

35. VISITATION

The nineteenth century rule governing visitation, i.e., that courts have broad discretion to award such visitation to a parent as the court determines is in the best interests of the child, remained unchanged throughout the twentieth century. Near the end of the century, though, the visitation rights of parents were strengthened and, to varying degrees in different states, extended to other people.

Parental visitation rights

Following the United States Supreme Court's recognition of parental rights as fundamental rights protected by the federal constitution, legislatures and courts began limiting the circumstances under which courts could deny or restrict the visitation rights of noncustodial parents.

Early twentieth century courts had refused visitation rights to putative fathers on the basis that seeing their fathers would remind these children of their "illegitimacy." Of even greater concern to early twentieth century courts was that the development of a bond between a father and his child born out of wedlock might make the future adoption of the child by a stepparent or an adoptive couple more difficult. Since the United States

Supreme Court's decision in *Stanley v. Illinois*, however, expressions of these kinds of concerns have all but disappeared from the published reports of judicial decisions. Today, visitation with a father (or a mother, if the father has custody) is presumed to be in every child's best interests, whether the child has been born to an unmarried couple or to a married one.

By the end of the century, visitation had come to be viewed as a noncustodial parent's right.[690] It was not enforceable in the absence of a court order granting it, but a court could not deny a parent's request for a visitation order in the absence of a showing that contact with the noncustodial parent was not in the child's best interests.

The kind of showing required to defeat a parent's right to visitation varied from state to state. In some states, a positive showing of some specific danger of harm to the child was necessary. In other states, the custodial parent needed only to demonstrate that visitation was not in the child's best interest. In either case, the party opposing visitation bore the burden of proof as to why visitation should not be granted, or why it should be restricted.

"Reasonable visitation"

Twentieth century visitation orders often provided simply for "reasonable" visitation, leaving it to the parties to work out the details between themselves. When called upon to decide what kind of visitation was reasonable, courts tended to define it as consisting of alternate weekends and alternating holidays. In every case, though, judicial discretion remained broad enough to order visitation in greater or lesser amounts, and on different days and times.

From visitor to co-parent

Judges in the nineteenth century commonly used the term *access* to describe a noncustodial parent's right to spend time with his child. The term was broad enough to include any kind of contact with the child, whether it occurred in the custodial parent's home or elsewhere. By the early twentieth century, courts were using the term *visitation* to describe a particular kind of access, namely, the act of coming to a person's residence

---

[690] Frechette, *supra* note 546 at 887, 890

and spending time with a person there. In a 1954 case, *York v. York*, [691] the Iowa Supreme Court drew a distinction between the right to visit with a child in the custodial parent's home and the right to take the child out of the home. The former was called *visitation*; the latter was called *temporary custody*.

For these reasons, it is not unusual to find court orders in the late nineteenth and early twentieth centuries specifying the times when the noncustodial parent would be permitted "to visit" the child, and whether and when a child would be permitted "to visit" the noncustodial parent.[692]

In addition to granting a noncustodial parent a right of access to a child, courts found it necessary to specify in their visitation orders whether the noncustodial parent would be permitted to take the child from the custodial parent's home or not.[693]

Eventually, courts in every state came to use the term *visitation* to refer to any period of time the noncustodial parent spent with his child, whether the time was to be spent in the custodial parent's home or elsewhere.

As the century came to a close, disenchantment with the term "visitation" grew. Noncustodial parents objected to the term because it seemed to relegate them to the role of a mere visitor in their children's lives, rather than a parent. Today, several states employ the term "parenting time" instead of "visitation" when referring to the time a parent spends with his or her children.

---

[691] 67 N.W.2d 28 (Iowa 1954)

[692] *See, e.g.*, State *ex rel.* Flint v. Flint, 65 N.W. 272 (Minn. 1895)

[693] *See, e.g.*, State *ex rel.* Boxell v. Boxell, 80 N.W. 1133 (Minn. 1899) (affirming order granting the noncustodial father the right to visit with his child, with the understanding that it would occur in the custodial mother's home); State *ex rel.* McDonough v. O'Malley, 80 N.W. 1133 (Minn. 1899) (affirming lower court's denial to the father of the right to take his child out of the custodial mother's home during visitations); *cf.* Cormier v. Cormier, 193 La. 158, 190 So. 365 (1939) (approving an order permitting the noncustodial parent to visit the child once a week at the mother's home and, in addition, to take the child to his own home for eight hours once a month); State *ex rel.* Flint v. Flint, 65 N.W. 272 (Minn. 1895) (affirming award to a noncustodial father of the right to take his child to his home on Sunday afternoons, in addition to visiting the child in the mother's home during the week.)

Third-party visitation rights

Following the enactment of no-fault divorce legislation in the 1970's, the divorce rate in the United States increased greatly. Since courts ordered sole custody in the vast majority of cases, significantly more children began experiencing disruptions of their relationships with extended family on the noncustodial parent's side. The common law, however, defined visitation as a parental right. A court lacked authority to grant the right to a non-parent.[694] Responding to this problem, state legislatures enacted statutes giving grandparents standing to request court-ordered visitation rights with respect to the children of divorced or divorcing parents. The first grandparent visitation statute was enacted in New York in 1966. By 1986, every state had enacted one.[695]

Some states extended the right to other relatives in addition to grandparents. A few states extended it to non-relatives, too, and to both divorce and non-divorce cases.

The question of the constitutionality of these statutes came before the United States Supreme Court in *Troxel v. Granville*.[696] A Washington statute had authorized courts to grant third-party visitation rights solely on the basis of a "best interests of the child" test. The Court held that this kind of statute unconstitutionally infringes upon the right of parents to direct the upbringing of their children.

The Court did not declare all third-party visitation statutes unconstitutional, just those that place non-parents on a par with parents.

To comply with the constitutional requirements outlined in *Troxel*, some states have amended their third-party visitation statutes to require courts to give at least some special consideration to a custodial parent's rights.

---

[694] 2 J. ATKINSON, MODERN CHILD CUSTODY PRACTICE § 8.10 (1986); MARTIN GUGGENHEIM, ALEXANDRA DYLAN LOWE & DIANE CURTIS, THE RIGHTS OF FAMILIES 19 (1996); 1 D. KRAMER, LEGAL RIGHTS OF CHILDREN 124, 136 (2d ed. 1994)

[695] Ch. 631, 1966 N.Y. Laws 766 (McKinney); Troxel v. Granville, 530 U.S. 57, 74 n. * (2000) (listing the statutes.) The District of Columbia did not enact a grandparent visitation statute.

[696] 530 U.S. 57 (2000).

36. JOINT CUSTODY

Joint custody frequently is characterized as a new development in the law, said to have first surfaced in California in 1979.[697] In reality, it had been a part of the law of custody in the late nineteenth century, and awards of joint physical custody were not uncommon in the early twentieth century. During that period, joint physical custody (then called "divided custody" or "alternating custody") was granted "almost as a matter of course" if the parents requested it.[698]

Historically, courts did not distinguish between physical and legal custody. Alternating custody meant alternating periods of legal and physical custody. Today, most courts recognize a distinction between legal and physical custody, treating them as separate and divisible rights.

For purposes of physical custody, alternating custody and joint custody are the same thing: the child sometimes lives in one home;

---

[697] *See, e.g.,* David D. Meyer, *The Constitutional Rights of Noncustodial Parents,* 35 HOFSTRA L. REV. 1461, 1470 (2006) (describing joint custody as "the next major development in child custody law" after the 1970's.)

[698] M.L. Cross, Annotation, *"Split," "divided," or "alternate" custody of children,* 92 A.L.R.2d 695, 698 (1963).

sometimes he lives in the other. In the context of legal custody, however, they do not mean the same thing. Joint legal custodians must make major decisions together. They do not have sole decision-making authority at any time. Alternating legal custodians take turns exercising decision-making authority.

Nineteenth century courts had never really addressed the subject of joint custody in earnest. Instead, most of them seemed to have simply assumed that they only had the power to award custody to one or the other party unless both parties had specifically asked for joint custody. Courts seemed to think it necessary to specify an allocation of the children between the parties for the same reason they deemed it necessary to allocate their property between them, namely, to keep the peace. According to the Illinois Supreme Court, "in the event of a separation of the parents, this right [custody] must be conferred upon one of them, otherwise the impulses of their natures would induce them to resort to violence to retain possession of their children."[699] Neither the Illinois Supreme Court nor any other court has ever furnished any factual basis for the assumption that parents share the judicial view of their children as items of property. Nor has any court provided a factual basis for the assumption that parents will resort to violence if they are awarded custody of their children jointly.

One of the earliest, and possibly the first, reported cases to deny joint custody on the basis of a consideration of what is in a child's best interests was *Turner v. Turner.*[700] In that case, decided in 1908, the lower court had ordered the parties to alternate physical custody every three months. The child was one year old. The Mississippi Supreme Court disapproved the arrangement because it conflicted with the tender years doctrine, which mandated placement of very young children in the sole custody of their mothers. Since, in the case before the court, the father had not established that the mother was unfit, the court held that she should have been awarded sole custody.

By the 1930's the maternal preference had become so strong that it would not allow any sharing of the mother's right to custody with the father. By 1963, several appellate courts had opined that joint physical

---

[699] *Miner v. Miner*, 11 Ill. 43, 49 (1849).
[700] 46 So. 413 (Miss. 1908).

custody was contrary to a child's best interests; and that it should never be awarded "except in exceptional circumstances."[701]

Not all judges were hostile to the idea. Some believed joint physical custody arrangements could be in children's best interests so long as the arrangement involved one or the other parent having a majority of the time with the child. These courts reasoned that it is desirable for children to have the love, interest and education that both parents can provide, so children's interests are best served by placing them in the custody of each parent for a significant amount of time during the year.[702]

In those states where joint physical custody was deemed to be contrary to a child's best interests as a matter of law, it was said that "frequent shifting of a child from home to home exposes it to changes of discipline and habits, and may invite lax discipline and disobedience."[703] For this reason, even the parents' mutual desire for joint custody was not enough to overcome the judicial preference for sole custody.[704]

Despite the general judicial hostility toward joint custody, courts did not apply an absolute prohibition against it. It could be, and was, ordered

---

[701] *See, e.g.,* Wilson v. Wilson, 291 P.2d 1113 (Idaho 1955); Mason v. Zolnosky, 103 N.W. 2d 752 (Iowa 1960); McLemore v. McLemore, 346 S.W.2d 722 (Ky. 1961); Wilmot v. Wilmot, 65 So. 2d 321 (La. 1953); McCann v. McCann, 173 A. 167 (Md. 1934) (denouncing joint physical custody as "an evil fruitful in the destruction of discipline, in the creation of distrust, and in the production of mental distress in the child"); McDermott v. McDermott, 255 N.W. 247 (Minn. 1934); Larson v. Larson, 223 N.W. 789 (Minn. 1929); McFadden v. McFadden, 292 P.2d 795 (Or. 1956); Dunn v. Dunn, 217 S.W.2d 124 (Tex. Ct. App. 1949); Cross, *supra* note 698 at 698. Some judges simply assumed that custody needed to be awarded to one or the other parent, just as each item of property the couple owned must be allocated to one or the other party. *See, e.g.,* Weinman, *supra* note 514 at 726 ("The custody of a child cannot, of course, be given to both of the parents....")

[702] *See* Sneed v. Sneed, 26 So. 2d 561 (Ala. 1946); Searle v. Searle, 172 P.2d 837 (Colo. 1946); Stillmunkes v. Stillmunkes, 65 N.W.2d 366 (Iowa 1954); Lambert v. Lambert, 222 S.W.2d 544 (Mo. Ct. App. 1949); Raw v. Raw, 245 P.2d 431 (Or. 1952); Mullen v. Mullen, 49 S.E.2d 349 (Va. 1948); Brock v. Vrock, 212 P. 550 (Wash. 1923); Patrick v. Patrick, 117 N.W.2d 256 (Wis. 1962).

[703] Cross, *supra* note 698 at 698-99; *see also* Bennett v. Bennett, 203 N.W. 26 (Iowa 1925); *accord*: Phillips v. Phillips, 13 So. 2d 922, 923 (Fla. 1943) (citing the Biblical teaching that no one can serve two masters.)

[704] Youngblood v. Youngblood, 252 S.W.2d 21 (Ky. 1952); Kaehler v. Kaehler, 18 N.W.2d 312 (Minn. 1945)

on occasion, provided a showing could be made that "exceptional circumstances" justified it in a particular case.[705] Courts did not often explain what kinds of circumstances qualified as "exceptional," but it is possible to identify a few factors that seemed to be important to some judges.

Joint custody considerations

Age and sex of the child

Judges were loath to make an award of joint physical custody of children of tender years. Young children, especially those under seven years of age, were deemed to need greater stability than older children, and judges assumed that sole custody would provide the needed stability. Consequently, a request for joint custody was more likely to be granted when the child involved was older, particularly if the child herself had requested it.[706]

Consistent with the tender years doctrine, some judges believed that while it was in the best interests of children of tender years to be in the sole custody of their mothers, it was in the best interests of healthy, older male children to have significant contact with their fathers. The reasoning was that healthy male children needed increased contact with their fathers as they grew older, to help prepare them for their station in life as an adult, i.e., military service and work. Accordingly, some courts were not as reluctant to order joint physical custody of healthy older sons as they were to order joint physical custody of daughters, younger sons, or disabled or unhealthy children of any age.[707]

---

[705] Sneed v. Sneed, 26 So. 2d 561 (Ala. 1946); 172 P.2d 837 (Colo. 1946); Stillmunkes v. Stillmunkes, 65 N.W.2d 366 (Iowa 1954); Gallagher v. Gallagher, 212 P.2d 746 (Or. 1949); and cases collected in at Cross, *supra* note 698 at 702-03.

[706] *See, e.g.*, Ward v. Ward, 353 P.2d 895 (Ariz. 1960); Davis v. Davis, 159 S.W.2d 999 (Ky. 1942); Mansfield v. Mansfield, 42 N.W.2d 315 (Minn. 1950); Kaehler v. Kaehler, 18 N.W.2d 312 (Minn. 1945); Ott v. Ott, 245 S.W.2d 982 (Tex. Ct. App. 1952); Cross, *supra* note 698 at 699; *but cf.* Lutker v. Lutker, 230 S.W.2d 177 (Mo. App. 1950) (dividing custody of two-year-old boy); Holman v. Holman, 77 P.2d 329 (Utah 1938) (six-year-old girl)

[707] *See, e.g.*, Lewis v. Lewis, 301 S.W.2d 861 (Mo. Ct. App. 1957); Burtrum v. Burtrum, 210 S.W.2d 364 (Mo. Ct. App. 1948)

Geography

Though not determinative, the fact that the parents resided very close to each other sometimes helped convince a judge that a request for joint custody would not be detrimental to the child.[708]

On the other hand, a court sometimes would cite the great geographic distance between the parents' residences as a justification for joint physical custody, too. The rationale in these cases was that if great geographic distance made regular visitation impractical, then there would be no other alternative but to order joint physical custody.[709] In the case of very young children, though, great geographic distance between the parties' residences tended to be viewed as a reason for denying joint physical custody, not as a reason for granting it.[710]

School attendance

A court was not likely to approve a joint physical custody arrangement if it would require a child to attend two different schools. This is why courts generally disapproved arrangements in which parents divided custody into equal periods of time, but they sometimes could be persuaded to order custody to one parent during the school year and custody to the other during the summer months.[711] Impact on school attendance is still a significant consideration today.

---

[708] Mansfield v. Mansfield, 42 N.W.2d 315 (Minn. 1950); Cross, *supra* note 698.

[709] Ward v. Ward, 353 P.2d 895 (Ariz. 1960); Merrill v. Merrill, 362 P.2d 887 (Idaho 1961); Raw v. Raw, 245 P.2d 431 (Or. 1952); Cross, *supra* note 698. Again, the courts used the terms "divided custody" or "alternating custody" to describe what we today would call joint physical custody.

[710] *See, e.g.,* Brocato v. Walker, 220 So. 2d 340 (Miss. 1969) (psychologically harmful to shuttle two-year-old between residences that are 600 miles apart); Pugh v. Pugh, 56 S.E.2d 901 (W. Va. 1949)

[711] *See, e.g.,* Watson v. Watson, 15 So. 2d 446 (Fla. 1943) (disapproving semiannual division of custody); Newson v. Newson, 146 So. 472 (La. 1933) (same); Wood v. Wood, 400 S.W.2d 431 (Mo. Ct. App. 1966); Ramsden v. Ramsden, 202 P.2d 920 (Wash. 1949) (alternating years); and cases collected in Cross, *supra* note 698 at 724; *see also* M.L. Cross, Annotation, *"Split," "divided," or "alternate" custody of children,* 92 A.L.R.2d 695 (Supp. 2008); *cf.* Drewry v. Drewry, 622 S.W.2d 206 (Ark. Ct. App. 1981) (approving divided custody or equal periods of time, where the parties live in close proximity to each other.)

Frequency of exchanges

Courts regarded frequent shifting of a child from one home to another to be contrary to a child's best interests.[712] For this reason, a school-year/summer arrangement was more likely to be approved than one requiring weekly, monthly or other more frequent exchanges.[713]

The school/summer division of time was not the only way courts accommodated a child's school attendance needs, though. It was not uncommon for a court to approve a divided custody arrangement calling for relatively frequent exchanges if one of the two parents only had custody for brief periods, on days when the child was not in school. Thus, for example, a court might approve an arrangement that called for one parent to have custody for one or two weekends each month, with the other parent having custody the rest of the time.[714]

Parental alienation and disparagement

During the first part of the twentieth century, courts sometimes would award both parents custody rights when one or both of them was guilty of disparagement or alienation of the child from the other parent. This was done in the interest of counteracting the effects of the disparagement or alienation, the idea being that an award of custody to the disparaged or alienated parent would help restore and strengthen the relationship between the child and the disparaged or alienated parent.[715]

---

[712] *See, e.g.*, Rice v. Rice, 231 N.W. 795 (Minn. 1930)

[713] McLemore v. McLemore, 347 S.W.2d 722 (Ky. 1961); Towles v. Towles, 195 S.W. 437 (Ky. 1917); *cf.* Searle v. Searle, 172 P.2d 837 (Colo. 1946); Lambert v. Lambert, 222 S.W.2d 544 (Mo. 1949); Mullen v. Mullen, 49 S.E.2d 349 (Va. 1948); Patrick v. Patrick, 117 N.W.2d 256 (Wis. 1962)

[714] *See, e.g.*, Robertson v. Robertson, 295 P.2d 922 (Cal. Ct. App. 1956); Murnane v. Murnane, 221 N.Y.S.2d 28 (App. Div. 1961); Childers v. Childers, 214 P.2d 722 (Okla. 1950); Campbell v. Campbell, 143 P.2d 534 (Wash. 1943); Cross, *supra* note 698 at 698. Arrangements calling for more than two weekends per month were not as likely to be approved. Some courts deemed a divided custody arrangement giving one parent custody on weekdays and the other parent custody on weekends to be contrary to the child's best interests. Richardson v. Richardson, 236 P.2d 718 (Idaho 1951); Pierce v. Pierce, 35 So. 2d 22 (La. 1948.) A few courts approved such arrangements, though. Grant v. Grant, 286 S.W.2d 349 (Tenn. App. 1954); Flanders v. Flanders, 40 N.W.2d 468 (Iowa 1950).

[715] Weinman, *supra* note 514 at 728 (1944)

Definitional challenges

The early twentieth century expansion of the term *visitation* to include intermittent periods of physical possession of the child (as distinguished from merely visiting with the child while the child was in another person's physical possession) had the effect of obscuring the distinction between visitation and joint physical custody. In *Taylor v. Taylor*, [716] the court found no practical difference between the rights and obligations of a parent with temporary physical custody and those of a parent with possession of a child as an exercise of visitation rights. As a result, some courts in the early- and mid-twentieth century started using the terms interchangeably. Thus, in an arrangement calling for one parent to have the children during the school months and the other parent to have the children during the summer months, a court could elect to call the summer months either "custody" or "visitation." [717] A court might say that one parent will have visitation two weekends per month, while the other will have custody the rest of the time; or it might, to the same effect, say that one parent will have custody two weekends per month, while the other will have custody the rest of the time.

Of course, judicial hostility toward joint physical custody conflicted with the principle that visitation normally is in a child's best interests. Consequently, courts sometimes found themselves struggling to explain the difference between the two concepts.

In some cases, reviewing courts did not even try to explain the difference, conceding that it really was not possible to do that.[718] Rather than admit that there was no real doctrinal basis for asserting that frequent stays in a parent's home is in a child's best interest when it is denominated "visitation" but is detrimental to a child's interests when it is denominated "alternating custody" or "joint custody," these courts adopted an approach similar to that of Justice Potter Stewart in *Jacobellis v. Ohio*.[719] While admitting he could not articulate a definition of obscenity, Justice Stewart nevertheless insisted, "I know it when I see it."[720] Courts could not define

---

[716] 306 Md. 290, 297 (1986)

[717] McDonald v. McDonald, 253 P.2d 249 (Or. 1953); Patrick v. Patrick, 117 N.W. 2d 256 (Wis. 1962)

[718] *See, e.g.,* Doty v. Morrison, 476 S.W. 2d 241, 251 (Ark. 1972)

[719] 378 U.S. 184 (1964) (Stewart, J., concurring.)

[720] *Id.* at 197

the difference between visitation and joint physical custody, either, but they were certain there had to be one, and they were certain that a person could instinctively know the difference simply by looking at an order. Of course, that was not true. What looked like a joint physical custody arrangement to one judge could very easily look like a liberal visitation arrangement to another.[721]

In *Pierce v. Pierce*,[722] the Louisiana Supreme Court struck down the portion of an order purporting to grant "visitation" to a parent on weekends, on the grounds that such frequent periods of parenting time amounted to divided (joint physical) custody, not visitation. At the same time, the court left undisturbed a portion of the order describing a two-month period in the summer as "visitation." Another court might be more inclined to describe weekend periods as visitation, and months-long periods in the summer as joint physical custody.

The only thing that was known for certain was that the difference between visitation and joint physical custody was not quantitative. In *Doty v. Morrison*,[723] for example, the Arkansas Supreme Court held that an arrangement under which a parent would take the child to his home on weekends would be in a child's best interests, and therefore acceptable, if it was called visitation, but that the same arrangement would be considered detrimental to the child's best interests if it was called joint physical custody. Similarly, in *Bush v. Bush*,[724] it was held that a school/summer division of time between the parents would be acceptable if it was called visitation, but it would not be acceptable to the court if it was called joint physical custody.

Sometimes courts attempted to explain the distinction in terms of the reasons for the judicial hostility toward joint physical custody. That hostility originally was an outgrowth of the maternal preference doctrine, i.e., the notion that children need to be raised by their mothers, not by their fathers. The demise of the maternal preference doctrine in the latter half of the

---

[721] *Cf.* McDonald v. McDonald, 253 P.2d 249 (Or. 1953); Patrick v. Patrick, 117 N.W. 2d 256 (Wis. 1962).
[722] 35 So. 2d 22 (La. 1948),
[723] 476 S.W.2d 241 (Ark. 1972)
[724] 163 So. 2d 858 (La. Ct. App. 1964)

century, however, eliminated the possibility of using the judicial reverence for motherhood, or the presumed inferiority of male parenting, as the explicit rationale for distinguishing between visitation and joint physical custody. New justifications for judicial hostility toward joint custody were needed.

The first attempt to articulate a gender-neutral rationale for the judicial aversion to joint physical custody was the argument that frequent shuttling of children between homes exposes children to parental conflict, undercuts a child's need for a single home, and undermines a child's attachment to a single authority figure. None of these arguments is sound.

First, since most courts recognize a distinction between legal and physical custody, the qualitative difference between joint physical custody and visitation cannot have anything to do with the level of authority or control over a child that a parent has a right to exercise. Decision-making authority is an attribute of legal custody, not physical custody.

Next, it is not the case that joint physical custody necessarily entails more "shuttling" between residences than visitation does. In fact, an alternating weekend visitation schedule requires more exchanges between homes than does a joint physical custody arrangement under which a child spends summers with one parent and the school year with the other parent.

The argument about the desirability of a single home is also unavailing. The noncustodial parent's residence is the home for the child when he is there, even if it is only a temporary home, irrespective of whether a court order labels it the home of a joint custodian or the home of a noncustodial parent.

One of the few cases in which a court attempted to provide a reasoned basis for distinguishing visitation from joint physical custody was *Holley v. Holley*,[725] There, the court was called upon to decide whether the division of time between the parents the lower court had ordered amounted to a divided custody arrangement, and therefore was presumptively detrimental to the children, or whether it was visitation, and therefore in their best interests. Acknowledging there could be no quantitative "bright line"

---

[725] 58 So. 2d 620 (La. 1963)

between the two concepts, the court instead analyzed the propriety of the award in terms of whether it was likely to cause the children to "become so confused as to divided authority, or differences in views on the proper way to rear a child, that it would affect their welfare."[726]

The difference between joint physical custody and visitation, then, was an outcome-based one; it was a qualitative rather than a quantitative difference. If a particular allocation of time operated in such a way as to have the effect of confusing a child about parental authority to such an extent as to be detrimental to the child's welfare, then it was a joint custody arrangement. If it did not have that effect, then it was visitation. (The notion that a period of time must be of a particular (albeit arbitrarily-defined) duration in order to qualify as "custodial" rather than "visitorial" is of only very recent origin.)[727]

Of course, defining the terms in this way makes any argument that joint physical custody is detrimental to children a circular one:

Joint physical custody is any visitation that has bad outcomes.
Therefore, joint physical custody has bad outcomes.

In any case, no state has adopted an outcome-based definition of joint physical custody. A few states have attempted to define it in quantitative terms, but most simply say that it means that each parent has a right to spend time with the child.

A more adequate explanation for the judicial preference for labeling the time a child spends with his mother "custody," and the time the child spends with his father "visitation," is that judges know the amount of child support will not be as high if the arrangement is called joint physical custody as it will be if it is called sole physical custody with visitation rights. Judges generally tend to believe higher child support awards are in children's best interests, the assumption being that the custodial parent will use the money for the benefit of the child.

---

[726] *Id.* at 622.

[727] *See, e.g.,* LaRocca v. LaRocca, 135 S.W.3d 522 (Mo. Ct. App. 2004.)

Of course, an award of child support that is set so high that the noncustodial parent cannot afford to maintain a home, furnishings and food for his children when they come to visit him obviously is not in children's best interests, either. Historically, though, judges only concerned themselves with ensuring that mothers had adequate homes and financial resources with which to provide for children while they were in their care. They did not concern themselves with ensuring that noncustodial fathers had adequate resources to maintain homes and care for children during the times they were with them for visitation. The self-support reserve that states have begun building into their child support guidelines did not exist in the twentieth century.

To the extent a particular judge is less averse to using the "joint physical custody" label when the "best interests" factors line up more on a father's side than when they are favorable to a mother, the resulting decision may be seen as a modern application of the maternal preference. On the other hand, if a judge is always averse to joint physical custody, even when the alternative is to award sole physical custody to a father, then the aversion to the "joint physical custody" label has to be attributable to something else. It could be a general desire to maximize the flow of federal money into the state. Or it could be an unreflective belief that the time a parent spends with a child pursuant to a court order that calls it "visitation" time is somehow qualitatively different from the same period of time a parent spends with a child pursuant to a court order that calls it "custodial" time.

Shared parenting

The concept of visitation underwent a transformation in the twentieth century. It began as a judicially granted privilege of access to one's child that was subject to considerable control by the custodial parent. While state laws imposed severe criminal penalties on those who interfered with a custodial parent's rights, there were no criminal penalties for interference with visitation. Numerous laws to help custodial parents protect and enforce their rights were enacted, but it was not until near the end of the century that similar kinds of remedies were made available to noncustodial parents for the protection and enforcement of their visitation rights. Much of the impetus for this change was the U.S. Supreme Court's declaration in *Stanley v. Illinois* in 1972 that parental rights are constitutionally protected fundamental rights even when the parent in question is a father – and a putative one, at that.

Now that visitation has come to be thought of as a parental right rather than a privilege, a judge may – and arguably is constitutionally required to – order it even over the custodial parent's objection, unless some compelling reason is shown for denying it. And a judge may order it to occur at such times and places, and under such conditions, as he decides is best for the child, even if the custodial parent does not agree. Moreover, now that most states prohibit judges from making sex-based decisions, they may no longer simply assume that fatherly care is detrimental to children. Except in those individual cases where a compelling need to protect a child from abuse, neglect or endangerment has been demonstrated, there is no longer any justification for automatically subjecting one parent's time with his child to the other parent's supervision and control.. As a result, there is no longer any supportable qualitative difference between periods of parental joint physical custody and periods of parental visitation anymore.

That being the case, a growing number of policy-makers are reconsidering the entire project of trying to classify some parents as "physical custodians" while relegating others to the status of "visitor." Consequently, there has been a general movement away from the concept of children as property, or as a prize to be won by one, and only one, parent, to a model that views them as people, and treats parenting as a shared responsibility: "shared parenting."

37. GENDER POLARIZATION

The era of equality-oriented feminism that began in the 1970s and resulted in the gender-neutralization of laws in the 1980s was relatively short-lived. It was followed close-upon by a movement opposing equal rights, and demanding, instead, special legislation exclusively for the benefit of women. This movement, at times, has included a demand that even the legislative processes by which such legislation is secured be reserved exclusively for women. For example, men reportedly were not permitted to testify at Congressional hearings when the Violence Against Women Act was under consideration.[728]

The last decade of the twentieth century saw a flurry of special interest legislation, and the trend has continued unabated into the first and second

---

[728] Cathy Young, *The Sexist Violence Against Women Act*, WALL ST. J. A15, March 23, 1994. Objecting to proposed changes to custody laws "because they are deliberately gender neutral," feminists made similar demands for the exclusion of men from legislative hearings on proposed changes to custody laws. Chris Cobb, *Feminists Might Be Granted Own Hearing on Divorce Law*, NATIONAL POST, July 5, 2001; Donna LaFramboise, *When Dad Becomes a Dirty Word*, NATIONAL POST, June 14, 2001; Ontario Women's Network on Custody and Access press release , June 19, 2001.

decades of the twenty-first century.[729] Federal and state governments have

---

[729] In addition to the federal Violence Against Women Act (Title IV, §§ 40001-40703 of the Violent Crime Control and Law Enforcement Act of 1994, Pub. L. 103-322, codified as amended in scattered sections of U.S.C.), other examples of special interest legislation for women include, *inter alia*: programs to educate men and boys not to be violent toward women and girls; programs to address the "heightened vulnerabilities of women and girls to HIV that are targeted specifically at reducing HIV infection rates among women and girls;" mandated use of "gender-specific indicators to monitor progress on outcomes and impacts of" programs designed to reduce women's HIV infection rates; mandates for executive branch participation in "activities to enhance educational, microfinance, and livelihood opportunities for women and girls." 22 U.S.C. § 7611 (2012). Further examples include: laws prohibiting female genital mutilation while encouraging male genital mutilation, *compare* 18 U.S.C. § 116 *and* 22 U.S.C. § 7611 (2011); establishment of an Office of Women's Health within the Centers for Disease Control, 42 U.S.C. § 242S (2011); establishment of an Office of Women's Health within the Health and Human Services Department, 42 U.S.C. § 237a (2011); establishment of an Office of Women's Health and Gender-Based Research, 42 U.S.C. § 299b-24a (2011); establishment of a national data system and clearinghouse on research on women's health, 42 U.S.C. § 287d-1 (2011); establishment of Women's Business Center programs, 15 U.S.C. § 656 (2011); establishment of an Office of Research on Women's Health, 42 U.S.C. § 287d (2011); establishment of an Interagency Committee on Women's Business Enterprise and Women's Business Enterprise Development Council programs, 15 U.S.C. §§ 7101, 7107 (2011); grants to programs and to individual women to further women's educations and advance their careers in science and engineering, 42 U.S.C. § 1885a (2011); state battered women's protection acts; programs for female offenders with children but not for male offenders with children, *see, e.g.*, MINN. STAT. § 241.70 (2012). The Patient Protection and Affordable Care Act of 2010, Public L. 111-148 (codified as amended in scattered sections of U.S.C.) contains a host of special protections exclusively for women. In addition to authorizing grants to private organizations exclusively for the purpose of improving women's health, the Act (as codified at 42 U.S.C. §§ 300gg-13 and 18022 (2012)) requires private health insurance plans to cover "women's health care needs" and to provide no-cost coverage of any preventive care and screenings recommended by the Health Resources and Services Administration ["HRSA."] The HRSA's Required Health Plan Coverage Guidelines require insurers to provide no-cost coverage of "comprehensive preventive services for women," including the following preventive services for which men may be required to continue to pay: HIV screening and counseling; sexually-transmitted infections counseling; contraception (including birth control and sterilization for women; insurers may require men to pay for condoms and vasectomies); domestic violence screening and counseling; and health checkups annually or more frequently as recommended by a doctor. Men may still be required to pay for this coverage out of their own pockets. The cited statutes represent only a tiny fragment of the special interest legislation for the exclusive benefit and protection of women that has been enacted since the

even gone so far as to pass laws directing courts to issue outcomes favorable to specific women in pending custody proceedings regardless of what the judge assigned to the case has determined the facts to be. The Civil Contempt Imprisonment Limitation Act[730] and the Elizabeth Morgan Act,[731] for example, legislatively freed a mother who was illegally concealing a child in violation of the father's court-ordered visitation rights. The legislation directed the court not to enforce its own order.

Men, for their part, got "responsible fatherhood" programs. The objective was said to be to help men to be better fathers. The focus, however, was not on educating men about child development, or teaching them how to raise children. Rather, the stated objective was to enhance the flow of money from male parents to female parents. Responsible Fatherhood grants have been used to fund workshops for unemployed and underemployed fathers, the goal being to increase male compliance with family support orders; to train child support enforcement personnel; and to provide direct grants of millions of dollars to state child support enforcement agencies.[732]

Feminist legislative enactments at the end of the twentieth century and the beginning of the twenty-first century have tended to be premised on stereotypes of men as violent, oppressive, privileged, and irresponsible; and stereotypes of women as passive, nonviolent, instinctively protective of children, dependent, and victimized. It is not surprising, therefore, that arguments for the resurrection of the maternal preference are being advanced.[733]

---

end of the era of equality-feminism. It is not an exhaustive list. *See generally* Nancy Levit, *Feminism for Men: Legal Ideology and the Construction of Maleness*, 43 UCLA L. REV. 1037, 1114 (1996) ("In many ways, current legal doctrines foster a separatist ideology. They reflect and reinforce the sharp separation of the genders.")

[730] Pub. L. 101-97, 103 Stat. 633 (1989)

[731] D.C. CODE § 11-925 (2001). Ultimately, a federal court of appeals struck down the Elizabeth Morgan Act as an unconstitutional bill of attainder. Foretich v. U.S., 351 F.3d 1198 (D.C. Cir. 2003)

[732] *See* 42 U.S.C. § 603 (2011); *see also* U.S. Dep't of Health & Human Services press releases, June 18, 1999; January 2, 2003; May 9, 2003.

[733] *See, e.g.,* MARTHA ALBERTSON FINEMAN, THE NEUTERED MOTHER, THE SEXUAL FAMILY AND OTHER TWENTIETH CENTURY TRAGEDIES 12–28, 176–93 (2002); BARBARA K. ROTHMAN, RECREATING MOTHERHOOD: IDEOLOGY AND TECHNOLOGY IN A PATRIARCHAL SOCIETY (1989); Mary E. Becker, *Double Binds*

Meanwhile, Professor Daniel Amneus, reacting to the historical preference for mothers in custody cases, and to increased marginalization of males in general, published a book in 2000 making the case for the establishment of a preference for fathers in custody cases.[734]

Notwithstanding the trend toward greater polarization of the sexes in the twenty-first century, it does not seem likely that an explicit maternal preference will be fully restored to American custody jurisprudence at any time in the near future. It seems even less likely that a paternal preference as propounded by Professor Amneus will be established. Significantly more women than ever before have chosen to pursue careers outside the home than to devote themselves full-time to nurturing children. In fact, women now outnumber men in managerial and professional occupations, and there are roughly an equal number of women and men in the workforce in general. In 2010, for example, 57.4% of professional positions, 68.9% of sale and office positions, and 56.8% of service jobs were held by women. The unemployment rate is higher now for men than for women. In 2010, the unemployment rate for men was 10.5%; for women, it was 8.6%. In that year, 71.3% of mothers with minor children worked outside the home; and this rate has held steady for several years.[735] Meanwhile, social acceptance of the performance of child-nurturing functions by fathers seems to be increasing, albeit at a somewhat slower rate than the social acceptance of women's performance of traditionally male functions has progressed. These forces, together with the obliteration of any meaningful qualitative difference between parental visitation and joint physical custody

---

Facing Mothers in Abusive Families: Social Support Systems, Custody Outcomes, and Liability for Acts of Others, 2 U. CHI. L. SCH. ROUNDTABLE 13 (1995); Mary Becker, *Maternal Feelings: Myth, Taboo, and Child Custody*, 1 REV. L. &WOMEN'S STUD. 133, 139 (1992) (asserting that "judges should defer to the fit mother's judgment of the custodial arrangement that would be best"); Mary Becker, *Strength in Diversity: Feminist Theoretical Approaches to Child Custody and Same-Sex Relationships*, 23 STETSON L. REV. 701 (1994); Nancy S. Erickson, *The Feminist Dilemma Over Unwed Parents' Custody Rights: The Mother's Rights Must Take Priority*, 2 LAW & INEQ. J. 447 (1984); Martha Fineman, *Dominant Discourse, Professional Language, and Legal Change in Child Custody Decisionmaking*, 101 HARV. L. REV. 727 (1988); Mary Ann Mason, *Motherhood v. Equal Treatment*, 29 J. FAM. L. 1 (1990).

[734] DANIEL AMNEUS, THE CASE FOR FATHER CUSTODY (2000)

[735] BUREAU OF LABOR STATISTICS, U.S. DEP'T OF LABOR, REP. 1034, WOMEN IN THE LABOR FORCE: A DATABOOK 1, 8-9 Table 2, 18. Table 7, 28-38 Table 11 (2011). *Id.* at 1, 18 Table 7 (2011).

rights, have contributed to a general movement toward shared parenting and equality as the paradigms for child custody outcomes.

Of course, it is never possible to predict the future with absolute certainty. It seems likely, though, that the momentum for shared parenting will operate, at least for the time being, as a counterbalance to any movement for the resurrection of sex-based preferences in custody law.

As the battles for sole ownership of children rage on, it may be hoped that some day, when the dust has cleared, somebody will notice that the children have been there all along, watching. They are waiting for adults to think about – to really think about – what is in their best interest.

ABOUT THE AUTHOR

Tom James is the father of two sons. He holds degrees in law and philosophy from the University of California at Berkeley and Southwestern University, and practices family law in Minnesota. For more information, visit his website

www.tomjameslaw.com

Read more about child custody and other law-related topics at:

www.tomjameslaw.com/blog

BIBLIOGRAPHY

Abel-Smith, Brian and Robert Stevens. *Lawyers and the Courts: A Sociological Study of the English Legal System, 1750-1965.* London: Heinemann, 1967.

Adams, Norma. "*Nullius Filius:* A Study of the Exception of Bastardy in the Law Courts of Medieval England." *University of Toronto Law Journal* 6 1946: 361-84.

Addison, C.G. *A Treatise on the Law of Torts.* New York: James Cockcroft, 1876.

Akaddaf, Fatima. "Application of the United Nations Convention on Contracts for the International Sale of Goods (CISG) to Arab Islamic Countries: Is the CISG Compatible with Islamic Law Principles?" *Pace International Law Review* 13 2001:1-58.

Akins, William. "Why Georgia's Child Support Guidelines Are Unconstitutional." 6 *Georgia Bar Journal* 6 2000:8-14, 54-57.

Al Shafi'i. *Kitab Al Umm* 8. n.d.

al-Misri, Ahman ibd Naqib. *Reliance of the Traveler* Ed. & trans. Nuh Ha Mim Keller. 1994.

Ali, Ameer. *Treatise on the Muhammadan Law* 2. 3d ed. n.d.

American Bar Association. *Guide to Marriage, Divorce, & Families.* New York: Random House, 2006.

American Humane Association and Vincent De Francis. *Child Protective Services: A National Survey.* Englewood, Colo.: American Humane Association, 1967.

American Law Institute. *Principles of the Law of Family Dissolution.* Philadelphia: American Law Institute, 2000.

American Psychiatric Association. *Diagnostic and Statistical Manual of Mental Disorders: DMS-IV-TR.* 4th ed. Washington, D.C.: American Psychiatric Association, 2000.

Amneus, Daniel. *The Case for Father Custody.* Alhambra, Calif.: Primrose Press, 2000.

Ancient Charters and Laws of Massachusetts Bay. 1642.

Anitei, Stefan. "Mosuo, One of the Last Matriarchal Societies." September 23, 2006. Softpedia.com. April 1, 2014 <http://news.softpedia.com/news/Mosuo-One-of-the-Last-Matriarchal-Societies-36321.shtml>

Annotation. "Right of Mother to Custody of Illegitimate Child." *American Law Reports 2d* 98. Rochester, N.Y.: Lawyers Co-operative Publishing Co., 1964:417.

Ariès, Philippe. *L'Enfant et la vie familiale sous l'ancien régime.* Trans. Robert Baldick. New York: Knopf, 1962.

Aristotle and Xenophon on Democracy and Oligarchy. Trans. J.M. Moore. Berkeley: University of California Press, 1975.

Atkins, Susan and Brenda Hoggett. *Women and the Law.* New York: B Blackwell, 1984.

Atkinson, Jeff. *Modern Child Custody Practice* 2. New York: Kluwer Law Book Publishers, 1986.

_____. *Modern Child Custody Practice.* 2d ed. New York: LEXIS, 2004.

Attreed, Lorraine C. "From Pearl Maiden to Tower Princes: Towards a New History of Medieval Childhood." *Journal of Medieval History* 9 1983:43-58.

Bachofen, Johann J. *Das Mutterrecht.* Stuttgart: Krais & Hoffmann, 1861.

Baker, John H. *An Introduction to English Legal History.* London: Butterworths LexisNexis, 2002.

Baskerville, Stephen. *Taken Into Custody: The War Against Fathers, Marriage, and the Family.* Nashville, Tenn.: Cumberland House, 2007.

Bastardy and its Comparative History. Ed. Peter Laslett et al. Cambridge, Mass.: Harvard University Press, 1980.

Beale, Ross W. "The Child in Seventeenth-Century America." *American Childhood: A Research Guide and Historical Handbook.* Ed. Joseph M. Hawes and N. Ray Hiner. 1985

Beard, Mary R. *Woman as a Force in History: A Study in Traditions and Realities.* New York: Macmillan, 1962.

Becker, Mary. "Double Binds Facing Mothers in Abusive Families: Social Support Systems, Custody Outcomes, and Liability for Acts of Others." *University of Chicago Law School Roundtable* 2 1995:13-32.

_____. "Maternal Feelings: Myth, Taboo, and Child Custody." *Southern California Review of Law and Women's Studies* 1 1992:133-224.

_____. "Strength in Diversity: Feminist Theoretical Approaches to Child Custody and Same-Sex Relationships." *Stetson Law Review* 23 1994:701-43.

Behrman, R. and L. Quinn. "Children and Divorce: Overview and Analysis." *The Future of Children* 4. Spring/Summer 1994: 4-14.

Bell, Henry E. *An Introduction to the History and Records of the Court of Wards and Liveries.* Cambridge: University Press, 1953.

Bennett-Smith, Meredith. "Ancient Priestess Unearthed in Peru; Tomb Suggests Women Ruled Mysterious, Brutal Culture." *Huffington Post* August 24, 2013

Beschle, Donald L. "God Bless the Child: The Use of Religion as a Factor in Child Custody and Adoption Proceedings." *Fordham Law Review* 58 1989:383-426.

Bishop, Joel. *Commentaries on the Law of Marriage and Divorce.* Boston: Little, Brown & Co., 1852.

_____. *Commentaries on the law of marriage and divorce, of separation without divorce, and the evidence of marriage in all issues* 2. Boston: Little, Brown, 1864.

Black's Law Dictionary. 2d Pocket Ed. 2001.

Blackstone, William. *Commentaries on the Laws of England.* Oxford: Clarendon Press 1765.

_____. *Commentaries on the Law of England* 3. 12th ed. Dublin: White, Jones and Rice, 1794.

_____. *Commentaries On The Laws of England.* 19th ed. London: John Murray, 1857.

_____. *Commentaries on the Laws of England* 1. Ed. William Jones. San Francisco: Bancroft-Whitney, 1915.

Blake, Nelson. *The Road to Reno: A History of Divorce in the United States.* New York: Macmillan, 1962.

Blakesley, Christopher L. "Child Custody and Parental Authority in France, Louisiana and Other States of the United States: A Comparative Analysis." *Boston College International and Comparative Law Review* 4 1981:283-359.

Blankenhorn, David. *Fatherless America: Confronting our most urgent social problem.* New York: Basic Books, 1995.

Blume, F. *Annotated Justinian Code.* 2d ed. 2009. University of Wyoming. 2012 <https://uwacadweb.uwyo.edu/blume&justinian/>

Breen, Claire. *The Standard of the Best Interests of the Child: A Western Tradition in International and Comparative Law.* The Hague: M. Nijhoff Publishers, 2002.

Breiner, Sander J. *Slaughter of the Innocents: Child Abuse Through the Ages and Today.* New York: Plenum Press, 1990.

Bright, John E. *A Treatise on the Law of Husband and Wife as Respects Property* 2. London: W. Benning & Co., 1849.

Brown, Elizabeth. *British Statutes in American Law, 1776-1836.* Ann Arbor: University of Michigan Law School, 1964.

Brown, Kenneth. "Customary rules and the welfare principle: Post-independence custody cases in Solomon Islands and Vanuatu." *Journal of Pacific Studies* 21 1997: 83-101.

Browning, William E. *The Practice and Procedure of the Court for Divorce and Matrimonial Causes.* London: Butterworths, 1862.

Brundage, James A. *Law, Sex, and Christian Society in Medieval Europe.* Chicago: University of Chicago Press, 1987.

Bryant, Anita. *The Anita Bryant Story: The survival of our nation's families and the threat of militant homosexuality.* Old Tappan, N.J.: Revell, 1977.

Bryce, Trevor. *Life and Society in the Hittite World.* New York: Oxford University Press, 2002.

Buckingham, Clyde E. "Early American Orphanages: Ebenezer and Bethesda." *Social Forces* 26 1948:311-21.

Buehler, C. and J.M. Gerard. "Divorce law in the United States: A focus on child custody." *Family Relations* 44 1995:439-58.

Burnham, Margaret A. "An Impossible Marriage: Slave Law and Family Law." *Law and Inequality* 5 July 1987:187-225.

Butler, Sara M. *Divorce in Medieval England: From One to Two Persons in Law.* New York: Routledge, 2013.

Camp, Anthony. "Records of illegitimate children." *Family Tree Magazine* 17 May 2001:7-9.

Campbell, John. *Lives of the Lords Chancellors* 4. Philadelphia: Blanchard & Lea, 1846.

Carroll, John T. "Children in the Bible." *Interpretation* 55. April 2001:121-34.

Carter, Kari J. Note. "The Best Interest Test and Child Custody: Why Transgender Should Not Be a Factor in Custody Determinations." *Health Matrix* 16 2006:209-36.

Cengage, G. *Encyclopedia of Everyday Law.* 2003. May 11, 2012 <www.enotes.com/family-law-reference/child-support-custody>

Chambers, David. "Rethinking the Substantive Rule for Custody Disputes in Divorce." *Michigan Law Review* 83 1984:477-569.

Chandler-Gilbert Community College. "Overview of 1600's/1700's." *Women Leaders and Activists: Experiences of Women Leaders and Activists as told by CGCC Students in partnership with Chandler Museum's Community History Program.* Chandler-Gilbert Community College. August 22, 2011 <http://www.cgc.maricopa.edu/Library/communityHistory/WomenActivists/index-2.2.shtml.html>

Chang, Jianhua. "Review of Theories on Patriarchal Clan Systems Since Song and Ming Dynasties (Song Ming Yi Lai Zong Zu Zhi Xing Cheng Li Lun Bian Xi)" *Anhui Historical Study* 1 2007:75-87.

Chauncey, George, Jr. "From Sexual Inversion to Homosexuality: Medicine and the Changing Conceptualization of Female 'Deviance.'" *Salmagundi* no. 58-59 Fall 1982/Winter 1983":114-46.

"Child Support Enforcement Incentive Funding." Report to the House of Representatives Committee on Ways and Means and the Senate Committee on Finance. Washington, D.C.: Government Printing Office, February 1997.

Chisholm, H. "Divorce." *Encyclopedia Britannica.* 11th ed. 1910.

Christian, George L. and Frank W. "Christian Slave-Marriages." *Virginia Law Journal* 1 November 1877: 641-52.

Cicero. "De Officiis." *Abolition of Man.* Ed. C.S. Lewis. London: Oxford University Press, 1944. App. 101.

Clancy, James. *A Treatise of the Rights, Duties and Liabilities of Husband and Wife, at Law and in Equity.* 2d Amer. ed. New York: Law Press, 1837.

Clarke, Elaine. "City Orphans and Custody Laws in Medieval England." *American Journal of Legal History* 34 1990:168-87.

_____. "The Custody of Children in English Manor Courts." *Law and History Review* 3 1985:333-48

Clark, Homer. *The Law of Domestic Relations in the United States* 2. 2d ed. St. Paul, Minn.: West Publishing, 1987.

Cobb, Chris. "Feminists Might Be Granted Own Hearing on Divorce Law." *National Post* July 5 2001

Cohen, Ed. "Legislating the Norm: From Sodomy to Gross Indecency." *South Atlantic Quarterly* 88 1989:181-217.

Cohen, Felix. *Handbook of federal Indian law, with reference tables, and index.* New York: AMS Press, 1972.

Collins, Billie Jean. *The Hittites and Their World.* Atlanta, Ga.: Society of Biblical Literature, 2007.

Colón, A.R. and P.A. Colón. *A History of Children: A Socio-cultural Survey Across Millennia.* Westport, Connecticut: Greenwood Press, 2001.

Commission on Gender Bias in the Judicial System. *Gender and Justice in the Courts: A Report to the Supreme Court of Georgia.* 1991.

"Common Program of the Chinese People's Political Consultative Conference." *The Important Documents of the First Plenary Session of the Chinese People's Political Consultative Conference.* Peking: Foreign Languages Press, 1949.

Coontz, Stephanie. *Marriage: A History: From obedience to intimacy or how love conquered marriage.* New York: Viking, 2005.

Corbier, M. "Divorce and Adoption as Familial Strategies." *Marriage, Divorce, and Children in Ancient Rome.* Ed. Beryl Rawson. New York: Oxford University Press, 1991. 47-78.

Cott, Nancy F. "Eighteenth Century Family and Social Life Revealed in Massachusetts Divorce Records." *Journal of Social History* 10 Autumn 1976: 20-43.

Crawford, Sally. *Childhood in Anglo-Saxon England.* Gloucestershire, U.K.: Sutton Publishing, 1999.

Cross, M.L. Annotation. "'Split,' 'divided,' or 'alternate' custody of children." *American Law Reports 2d* 92. Rochester, N.Y.: Lawyers Co-operative Pub. Co., 1963. 695.

Cyclopedia of Law and Procedure 21. Ed. William Mack. 1906.

Daley, Timothy J. *Homosexuality and Child Sexual Abuse.* Family Research Council. 2002. April 16, 2014 <http://www.frc.org/get.cfm?i=IS02E3>

Dally, Ann. *Inventing Motherhood: The Consequences of an Ideal.* London: Burnett Books, 1982.

Dawes, Henry L. "Have we failed with the Indian?" *Atlantic Monthly* 84 August 1899: 280-85.

Dawud, Sunan Abu. *Kitab al Talaq* 2. Trans. A. Hasan. 2000.

Dayton, Cornelia. *Women Before the Bar: Gender, Law and Society in Connecticut, 1639-1790.* Chapel Hill: University of North Carolina Press, 1979.

de Bracton, Henry. *On the Laws and Customs of England* 2. Trans. Samuel E. Thorne. Cambridge, Mass.: Belknap Press, 1968.

De Francis, Vincent. *Child Protective Services in the United States: Reporting a Nationwide Survey.* Denver, Colo.: American Humane Association, 1956.

de Glanvill, Ranulf. *The Treatise on the Laws and Customs of the Realm of England Commonly Called Glanvill.* Ed. and trans. G. D. G. Hall. Holmes Beach, Fla.: W.W. Gaunt, 1983.

de Mause, Lloyd. "The Evolution of Childhood." *History of Childhood Quarterly: Journal of Psychohistory* 1 1974: 503-75.

———. *The History of Childhood.* New York: Psychohistory Press, 1975.

"The Declaration of Sentiments, Seneca Falls Conference (1848)." *A History of Woman Suffrage* 1. Ed. Elizabeth C. Stanton, et al. Rochester, N.Y.: Susan B. Anthony, 1889.

Deutsch, F.M. and S.E. Saxon. "The double standard of praise and criticism for mothers and fathers." *Psychology of Women Quarterly* 1998:665-83.

Devereus, G. "Greek Pseudo-Homosexuality and the Greek Miracle." *Symbolae Osloenses* 42 1967: 69-92.

Devereus, G. and L.E. Shiner. "The Darker Side of Hellas: Sexuality and Violence in Ancient Greece." *Psychohistory Rev.* 9 1980: 111-35.

Diefendorf, Elizabeth. *The New York Public Library's Books of the Century.* New York: Oxford University Press, 1996.

Doerhoff, Heidi C. Note. "Assessing the Best Interests of the Child: Missouri Declares that a Homosexual Parent is Not Ipso Facto Unfit for Custody *J.A.D. v. F.J.D.*" *Missouri Law Review* 64 Fall 1999:949-85.

Donahue, C. "*Ius Commune,* Canon Law, and Common Law in England." *Tulane Law Review* 60 1992:1745-80.

Dotterweich, Douglas and Michael McKinney. "National Attitudes Regarding Gender Bias in Child Custody Cases." *Family and Conciliation Courts Review* 38 2000:208-23.

Drechsler, C.T. Annotation. "Award of Custody of Child to Parent Against Whom Divorce Is Decreed." *American Law Reports 3d* 23 San Francisco: Bancroft-Whitney, 1969. 15.

Driver, G.R. and J.C. Miles. *The Babylonian Laws.* Oxford: Clarendon Press, 1968.

Durant, Will. *The Story of Civilization.* New York: Simon & Schuster, 1954.

Echols, Alice. *Daring to Be Bad: Radical Feminism in America 1967-1975.* Minneapolis: University of Minnesota Press, 1989.

Edwards, Charles. *Pleasantries About Courts and Lawyers of the State of New York.* New York: Richardson & Co., 1867.

Eichinger-Swainston, Katja M. Note. "*Fox v. Fox*: Redefining the Best Interest of the Child Standard for Lesbian Mothers and Their Families.*" Tulsa Law Journal* 32 1996:57-74

Einhorn., Jay. "Child Custody in Historical Perspective: A Study of Changing Social Perceptions of Divorce and Child Custody in Anglo-American Law." *Behavioral Sciences & the Law* 4 Spring 1986:119-35.

Eller, Cynthia. *The Myth of Matriarchal Prehistory: Why an Invented Past Wont Give Women a Future*. Boston: Beacon Press, 2000.

Erickson, Nancy S. "The Feminist Dilemma over Unwed Parents' Custody Rights: The Mother's Rights Must Take Priority." 2 *Law and Inequality Journal* 2 1984:447-72.

Eskridge, William, Jr. "Law and the Construction of the Closet: American Regulation of Same-Sex Intimacy, 1880-1946." *Iowa Law Review* 82 1997:1007-36.

Eyben, Emile. "Family Planning in Greco-Roman Antiquity." *Ancient Society* 11/12 1980-1981: 5-82.

Falconer, Douglas P. "Child and- Youth Protection." *Social Work Yearbook* 3. Ed. Fred S. Hall. New York: Russell Sage Foundation, 1935. 63-66.

Families in Global and Multicultural Perspective. 2d ed. Ed. B. Ingoldsby and S. Smith. Thousand Oaks, Calif.: Sage Publications, 2006.

Farb, Peter. *Man's Rise to Civilization as Shown by the Indians of North America from Primeval Time to the Coming of the Industrial State*. New York: Dutton, 1968.

Feldman, W. *The Jewish Child: its history, folklore, biology, & sociology*. London: Baillière, Tindall and Cox, 1918.

Fell, Christine et al. *Women in Anglo-Saxon England and the Impact of 1066*. Bloomington: Indiana University Press, 1984.

Feng, Erkang et al. *The History of China's Patriarchal Clan System (Zhong Guo Zong Zu Shi)*. Shanghai: Shanghai Renmin Press, 2009.

Finberg, B. Annotation. "Right of mother to custody of illegitimate child." *American Law Reports 2d* 98 San Francisco: Bancroft-Whitney, 1964. 417.

Fineman, Martha Albertson. "Dominant Discourse, Professional Language, and Legal Change in Child Custody Decisionmaking." *Harvard Law Review* 101 1988:727-74.

Fineman, Martha Albertson. *The Neutered Mother, the Sexual Family and Other Twentieth Century Tragedies*. New York: Routledge, 2002.

Fisher, Sydney G. *Men, Women and Manners in Colonial Times.* Cranbury, N.J.: Scholar's Bookshelf, 2006.

Fordham, Jim and Andrea Fordham. *The Assault on the Sexes.* New Rochelle, N.Y.: Arlington House, 1977.

Forman, Deborah L. *Every Parent's Guide to the Law.* New York: Harcourt Brace, 1998.

Forseth, Ilene H. "Children in Early Medieval Art: Ninth Through Twelfth Centuries." *Journal of Psychohistory* 4. 1976:31-70.

Foster, Henry and Doris Freed. "Life with Father." *Family Law Quarterly* 11 Winter 1978:321-63.

Fox, Vivian and Martin. Quit, *Loving, Parenting, and Dying: The Family Cycle in England and America, Past and Present.* New York: Psychohistory Press, 1980.

Frechette, A.L. Annotation. "Right of Putative Father to Visit Illegitimate Child." *American Law Reports 3d* 15 1967:887

Freedman, David et al. "Children and Adolescents with Transsexual Parents Referred to a Specialist Gender Identity Development Service: A Brief Report of Key Developmental Features." *Clinical Child Psychology and Psychiatry* 7 2002:423-32.

French, Valerie. "Birth Control, Childbirth and Early Childhood." *Civilization of the Ancient Mediterranean: Greece and Rome* 3. Ed. Michael Grant and Rachel Kitzinger. New York: Scribner's, 1988. 1362.

_____. "Children in Antiquity." *Children in Historical and Comparative Perspective: An International Handbook and Research Guide.* Ed. Joseph M. Hawes and N. Ray Hiner. New York: Greenwood Press, 1991. 13-29.

Friedan, Betty. *The Feminine Mystique.* New York: Norton, 1963.

Friedan, Betty. "National Organization for Women's Statement of Purpose." *Up from the Pedestal: selected writings in the history of American feminism.* Ed. Aileen S. Kraditor. Chicago: Quadrangle Books, 1970.

Friedman, Lawrence. *A History of American Law.* New York: Simon and Schuster, 1973.

Frye, Phyllis Randolph. "Facing Discrimination, Organizing for Freedom: The Transgender Community." *Creating Change: Sexuality, Public Policy, and Civil Rights.* Ed. John D'Emilio et al. New York: St. Martin's Press, 2000). 451-68.

Gallaway, Lowell and Richard Vedder. *Poverty, Income Distribution, the Family and Public Policy.* Washington, D.C.: Government Printing Office, 1986.

Ganzfried, Solomon. *Code of Jewish Law*. New York: Star Hebrew Book Co., 1928.

Gelles, Richard J. *The Book of David: How Preserving Families Can Cost Children's Lives*. New York: Basic Books, 1996.

General Laws and Liberties of the Massachusetts Colony (photo. reprint.) Boston: Rockwell and Churchill, 1887.

George, L. "The challenge of permanency planning in a multicultural society." *Journal of Multicultural Social Work* 5 1997:165-75.

Gies, Frances and Joseph Gies. *Marriage and the Family in the Middle Ages*. New York: Harper & Row, 1987.

Gimbutas, Marija. *Gods and Goddesses of Old Europe, 6500-3500 B.C., Myths and Cult Images*. Berkeley: University of California Press, 1982.

Godefroy, Dionysius. *Corpus juris civilis, Pandectis ad Florentinum archetypum expressis, Institutionibus*. Amsterdam: Elzevirs, 1663.

Godefroy, Dionysius, A. Kriegel and E. Osenbrüggen. *Corpus iuris ciuilis*. Lipsiae: Sumtibus Baumgaertneri, 1872.

Godefroy, Dionysius, A. Kriegel and E.R. Pothier. *Pandectæ Justinianeæ in Novum Ordinem Digestæ*. Paris: F. I. Fournier, 1818.

Goldstein, Joseph et al. *Beyond the Best Interests of the Child*. New York: Free Press, 1973.

Grandparent Visitation Disputes: A Legal Resource Manual. Ed. Ellen C. Segal and Naomi Karp. Chicago: American Bar Association, 1989.

Green, R. "Sexual Identity of 37 Children Raised by Transsexual or Homosexual Parents." *American Journal of Psychiatry* 135 June 1978:692.

Greenbook. U.S. House Ways and Means Committee Print. 105th Cong., 2d Sess. Washington, D.C.: Government Printing Office, 1998.

Greer, Germaine. *The Female Eunuch*. New York: McGraw-Hill, 1971.

Gresley, Richard N. *A Treatise on the Law of Evidence in the Courts of Equity*. 2d ed. Harrisburg, Pa.: I. G. McKinley & J. M. G. Lescure, 1848.

Griswold, Robert L. "Ties That Bind and Bonds That Break: Children's Attitudes Toward Fathers, 1900-1930." *Small Worlds: Children & Adolescents in America, 1850-1950*. Ed. Elliott West and Paula Petrik. Lawrence: University Press of Kansas 1992. 255-74.

Guggenheim, Martin et al. *The Rights of Families: the authoritative ACLU guide to the rights of family members today*. Carbondale: Southern Illinois University Press, 1996.

Gurney, O.R. and Samuel N. Kramer. "Two Fragments of Sumerian Laws." *Assyriological Studies* 16 April 21, 1965: 13-19.

Hammurabi. "Code of Laws." *The Oldest Code of Laws in the World: The Code of Laws Promulgated by Hammurabi, King of Babylon, 2285-2242 B.C.* Trans. C.H.W. Johns. Edinburgh: T. & T. Clark, 1903.

Hanawalt, Barbara A. *The Ties That Bound: Peasant Families in Medieval England.* New York: Oxford University Press, 1986.

Haralambie, Ann M. *Handling Child Custody, Abuse and Adoption Cases.* 2d ed. New York: McGraw-Hill, 1993.

Hartog, Hendrik. *Man and Wife in America: A History.* Cambridge, Mass.: Harvard University Press, 2000.

Haskins, George. *Law and Authority in Early Massachusetts.* New York: Macmillan, 1960.

Hastings. Honey C. "Custodial Rights in New Hampshire: History and Current Law." *New Hampshire Bar Journal* 40 December 1999:26-39.

Heanan, Christopher D. "Ancient Egypt." *Scribd.com.* July 23, 2011 <http:www.scribd.com/doc/49116704/Ancient-Egypt>

Helmholz, H.R. "Support Orders, Church Courts, and the Rule of Filius Nullius: A Reassessment of the Common Law." *Virginia Law Review* 63 1977:431-48.

Hening, William W. *Statutes at Large, being a collection of all the laws of Virginia, from the first session of the Legislature in the year 1619.* Richmond, Va.: Samuel Pleasants, 1821.

Herlihy, David. "Medieval Children." *Essays on Medieval Civilization: The Walter Prescott Webb Memorial Lectures.* Ed. Bede Karl Lackner and Kenneth Roy Philip. Austin: University of Texas Press, 1978. 109-41.

Historical Statistics of the United States, Colonial Times to 1970, Bicentennial Edition. Washington, D.C.: Government Printing Office, 1975.

The History of Woman Suffrage. Ed. Susan B. Anthony and Ida Husted Harper. Indianapolis, Ind.: Hollenbeck Press, 1902.

Hoffman, Saul and Greg Duncan. "The Effects of Incomes, Wages, and AFDC Benefits on Marital Disruption." *Journal of Human Resources* 30 195:19-41.

The Holy Bible. New York: AMS Press, 1982.

Houlbrooke, Ralph A. *The English Family, 1450-1700.* London: Longman, 1984.

Hunter, William. *Introduction to Roman Law*. 9th ed. London: Street & Maxwell, 1934.

Hurd, Rollin C. *A Treatise on the Right of Personal Liberty, and on the Writ of Habeas Corpus and the Practice Connected with It: A View of the Law of Extradition of Fugitives*. 2d ed. Albany, N.Y.: W.C. Little & Co., 1876.

Hurstfield, Joel. *The Queen's Wards: Wardship and Marriage under Elizabeth I*. Cambridge: Longman, 1958.

Ibrahim, A. "Custody of Muslim Infants." *Journal of Malaysian and Comparative Law* 4. 1997:19-94.

Illegitimacy in Britain, 1700 – 1920. Ed. Alysa Levene et al. New York: Palgrave Macmillan, 2005.

Inscriptiones Creticae. Ed. M. Guarducci ed. Rome: Libreria dello Stato, 1935-1950.

The Institutes of Justinian. Trans. Thomas C. Sandars. London: J.W. Parker & Son, 1853.

Jacob, Giles. *The Compleat Parish Officer*. London: E. & R. Nutt & R. Gosling, 1723.

Jacobs, Harriet Ann. *Incidents in the Life of a Slave Girl*. Ed. Jennifer Fleischner. Boston: Bedford/St. Martin's, 2010.

Joakimidis, Yuri. *Back to the Best Interests of the Child: Towards a Rebuttable Presumption of Joint Residence*. 2d ed. Policy Monograph. Australia: Joint Parenting Association, n.d.

Jones, B.J. *The Indian Child Welfare Act Handbook: A Legal Guide to the Custody and Adoption of Native American Children*. Chicago: American Bar Association, 1995.

Jong, Erica. *Fear of Flying*. New York: Holt, Rinehart and Winston, 1973.

Jordan, Mark D. *The Invention of Sodomy in Christian Theology*. Chicago: University of Chicago Press, 1997.

_____. *The Silence of Sodom: Homosexuality in Modern Catholicism*. Chicago: University of Chicago Press, 2000.

"Judge Gives Transsexual Father Custody of Children in Florida." *N.Y. Times* February 22, 2003.

Juvenal. *Satire*. n.d.

Karo, Joseph. *Shulḥan 'Aruk*. Trans. S. I. Levin and Edward A. Boyden. New York: Hermon Press, 1965.

Katz, Jonathan Ned. "The Age of Sodomitical Sin, 1607-1740." *Gay/Lesbian Almanac*. New York: Harper & Row, 1983.

Keezer, Frank H. *Keezer on the Law of Marriage and Divorce*. 3d ed. Ed. John W. Morland. Indianapolis: Bobbs-Merrill, 1946.

Kelly, Joan B. "The Determination of Child Custody in the USA." *The Future of Children* 4 Spring 1994: 121-42.

Kempe, C. Henry et al. "The Battered-Child Syndrome." *Journal of the American Medical Association* 181 1962:17-24.

Kent, James. *Commentaries on American Law* 2. 12th ed. Boston: Little, Brown & Co., 1873.

Kerber, Linda. *Women of the Republic: Intellect and Ideology in Revolutionary America*. Chapel Hill: University of North Carolina Press, 1980.

Klaff, Ramsay Laing. "The Tender Years Doctrine: A Defense." *California Law Review* 70 March 1982: 335-872.

Klassen, Albert D. et al. *Sex and Morality in the U.S.: An empirical enquiry under the auspices of the Kinsey Institute*. Middletown, Conn.: Wesleyan University Press, 1989.

Kohm, Lynne Marie. "Tracing the Foundations of the Best Interests of the Child Standard in American Jurisprudence." *Journal of Law and Family Studies* 10 2008: 337-76.

Kramer, Donald T. *Legal Rights of Children* 1. 2d ed. Colorado Springs: Shepard's/McGraw-Hill, 1994.

Krause, Harry D. and David D. Meyer. *Family Law in a Nutshell*. 5th ed. St. Paul, Minn.: Thomson/West, 2007.

Laffin, John. *The Dagger of Islam*. London: Sphere, 1979.

LaFramboise, Donna. "When Dad Becomes a Dirty Word." *National Post* June 14, 2001

Laslett, Peter. *Family Life and Illicit Love in Earlier Generations*. New York: Cambridge University Press, 1977.

The Laws and Liberties of Massachusetts (reprint.) Cambridge, Mass.: Harvard University Press, 1929.

Lehmann, Nancy and Helen Sullinger. *Declaration of Feminism*. 1971.

Lerner, Gerda. *The Creation of Patriarchy*. New York: Oxford University Press, 1986.

Lesley, Susan I. "Foundlings and Deserted Children." *Proceedings of the Eighth Annual Conference of Charities and Correction*. 1881. 282-84.

Levit, Nancy. "Feminism for Men: Legal Ideology and the Construction of Maleness." *UCLA Law Review* 43 1996:1037-116.

Lewis, C.S. *Abolition of Man.* New York: Simon & Schuster, 1996.

Lewis, Judith. *In the Family Way: Child-bearing in the British Aristocracy, 1760-1860.* New Brunswick, N.J.: Rutgers University Press, 1986.

Li, Yuhui. "Women's Movement and Change of Women's Status in China." *Journal of International Women's Studies* 1 2010:30-40. Available at http://vc.bridgew.edu/jiws/vol1/iss1/3

Lincoln, Charles. *The Colonial Laws of New York from the Year 1664 to the Revolution.* Clark, N.J.: Lawbook Exchange, 2006.

Lloyd, Augustus. *A Treatise on the Law of Divorce.* New York: Houghton Mifflin Co., 1887.

Lubman, Stanley B. *Bird in a Cage: Legal Reform in China After Mao.* Stanford, Calif.: Stanford University Press, 1999.

MacQueen, John F. A *Practical Treatise on the Appellate Jurisdiction of the House of Lords and the Privy Council, together with the Practice of Parliamentary Divorce.* London: A. Maxwell & Son, 1842.

_____. *A Practical Treatise on the Law of Marriage, Divorce and Legitimacy.* London: W. Maxwell, 1860.

_____. *The Rights and Liabilities of Husband and Wife.* London: S. Sweet, 1849.

Maidment, Susan. *Child Custody and Divorce: The Law in Social Context.* London: Croom Helm, 1984.

Marasinghe, M.L. "An Empiricist's View of the Chinese Legal System." *Valparaiso Law Review* 15 1981:283-317.

Marvell, Thomas B. "Divorce rates and the fault requirement." *Law and Society Review* 23 1989:543-567.

Maryland Select Committee on Gender Equality. *Retrospective Report.* 2001.

Maryland Special Joint Committee on Gender Bias in the Courts. *Gender Bias Report.* 1989

Mason, Mary Ann. *The Custody Wars: Why children are losing the legal battle, and what we can do about it.* New York: Basic Books, 1999.

_____. *The Equality Trap.* New Brunswick, N.J.: Transaction Publishers, 2002.

_____. *From Father's Property to Children's Rights: The History of Child Custody in the United States.* 2d ed. New York: Columbia University Press, 1994.

_____. "Motherhood v. Equal Treatment." *Journal of Family Law* 29 1990:1-50.

Massachusetts Society for the Prevention of Cruelty to Children. *Second Annual Report.* Boston, 1882.

Maxwell, N. and R. Donner. "The Psychological Consequences of Judicially Imposed Closets in Child Custody and Visitation Disputes Involving Gay or Lesbian Parents." 13 *William and Mary Journal of Women and Law* 13 2006:305-48.

May, Martha. "The 'Problem of Duty': Family Desertion in the Progressive Era." *Social Service Review* 62 March 1988:40-60

Mays, Dorothy A. *Women in Early America: Struggle, Survival and Freedom in a New World.* Santa Barbara, Calif.: ABL-CIO, 2004.

McLaughlin, Mary. "Survivors and surrogates: children and parents from the ninth to the thirteenth centuries." *The History of Childhood.* Ed. Lloyd de Mause. New York: Psychohistory Press, 1975.

McNeely, Cynthia. "Lagging Behind the Times: Parenthood, Custody, and Gender Bias in the Family Court." *Florida State University Law Review* 25 1998:891-956.

McNeely, Robert A. and Cynthia A. McNeely. "Hopelessly Defective: An Examination of the Assumptions Underlying Current Child Support Guidelines." *The Law and Economics of Child Support Payments.* Ed. William S. Comanor. 2004. 170.

Mead, Margaret. "Some Theoretical Considerations of the Problems of Mother-Child Separation." *American Journal of Orthopsychiatry* 24 1954:24.

Menefee, Samuel P. *Wives for Sale: an ethnographic study of British popular divorce.* New York: St. Martin's Press, 1981.

Mercer, Kathryn L. "A Content Analysis of Judicial Decision-Making: How Judges Use Primary Caretaker Standard to Make a Custody Determination." *William and Mary Journal of Women and Law* 5 1998:1-149.

Meyer, David D. "The Constitutional Rights of Noncustodial Parents." *Hofstra Law Review* 35 2006:1461-96.

Meyers, Felicia. Note. "Gay Custody and Adoption: An Unequal Application of the Law." *Whittier Law Review* 14 1993:839-62.

Millett, Kate., *Sexual Politics.* Garden City, N.Y.: Doubleday, 1970.

Minnesota House of Representatives Research Department. *Information Brief: Minnesota's Child Support Laws.* 2011.

Minnesota Supreme Court Task Force For Gender Fairness in the Courts. *Final Report*. 1989.

Moghadam, V. "Global Feminism and Women's Citizenship in the Muslim World: The Cases of Iran, Algeria and Afghanistan." Paper prepared for the Conference on Citizenship, Borders, and Gender: Mobility and Immobility, Yale University, May 8-10, 2003.

Morgan, Edmund S. *The Puritan Family: religion & domestic relations in seventeenth-century New England*. Westport, Conn.: Greenwood Press, 1980.

Morgan, Lewis H. *Ancient Society*. New York: H. Holt, 1871.

Morris, Richard. *Studies in the History of American Law, with Special Reference to the Seventeenth and Eighteenth Centuries*. New York: Columbia University Press, 1930.

Motz, Lotte. *The Faces of the Goddess*. New York: Oxford University Press, 1997.

Muchembled, Robert. *Popular Culture and Elite Culture in France 1400-1750*. Trans. Lydia Cochrane. Baton Rouge: Louisiana State University Press, 1985.

Murrin, John. "'Things Fearful to Name': Bestiality in Early America." *American Sexual Histories*. Ed. Elizabeth Reis. Oxford: Blackwell, 2001. 14-35.

Musawah, an initiative of Sisters of Islam, CEDAW and Muslim Family Laws. 2011.

Myers, John E.B. "A Short History of Child Protection in America." *Family Law Quarterly* 42 2008-2009:449-63.

N.Y. City-Hall Recorder 3. 1818:56.

Namaste, Viviane K. *Invisible Lives: The Erasure of Transsexual and Transgendered People*. Chicago: University of Chicago Press, 2000.

Nasir, Jamal J. *The Islamic Law of Personal Status*. 2d ed. Boston: Graham & Trotman, 1990.

National Conference of Commissioners on Uniform State Laws. *Uniform Marriage and Divorce Act*. Chicago: National Conference of Commissioners on Uniform State Laws, 1970, 1971 and 1973.

Nawawi. *Minhaj Et Talibin: a manual of Muhammadan law according to the school of Shafii*. Trans. E. Howard. Lahore: Law Publishing Co., 1977.

Neumann, Erich. *The Great Mother*. Trans. Ralph Manheim. New York: Pantheon Book, 1955.

Newsweek. March 28, 1960.

Nicholas, David. "Childhood in Medieval Europe." *Children in Historical and Comparative Perspective: An International Handbook and Research Guide.* Ed. Joseph M. Hawes and N. Ray Hiner. Westport, Conn.: Greenwood Press, 1991. 31-52.

Norton, Caroline. *The Separation of the Mother and Child by the Law of "Custody of Infants" Considered.* London: Roake & Varty, 1838.

Oaks, Robert F. "'Things Fearful to Name': Sodomy and Buggery in Seventeenth-century New England." *Journal of Social History* 1978:268- 81.

Offenhauer, P., U.S. Library of Congress. *Women in Islamic Societies: A Selected Review of Social Scientific Literature.* 2005.

Ogders, Blake W. "Changes in the Common Law And In The Law Of Persons, In The Legal Profession, And In Legal Education." *A Century of Law Reform.* New York: Macmillan, 1902.

Old South Leaflets. Boston: Directors of the Old South Work, n.d.

Ontario Women's Network on Custody and Access. Press release. June 19, 2001.

Orme, Nicholas. *Medieval Children.* New Haven: Yale University Press, 2001.

Ozment, Steven. *When Fathers Ruled: Family Life in Reformation Europe.* Cambridge, Mass.: Harvard University Press, 1983.

Paine, Thomas. *Complete Writings of Thomas Paine* 2. Ed. Philip S. Foner. New York: Citadel Press, 1945.

Parmensus, Bernardus. *Glossa Ordinaria.* n.p. 1472.

Peck, Epaphroditus. *The Law of Persons; or Domestic Relations.* Chicago: Callaghan, 1913.

Perkin, Joan. *Women and Marriage in Nineteenth Century England.* Chicago: Lyceum Books, 1989.

Petit, P.H. "Parental Control and Guardianship." *A Century of Family Law 1857-1957.* Ed. R.H. Graveson and F.R. Crane. London: Sweet & Maxwell, 1957.

Phillips, Roderick. *Putting Asunder: A History of Divorce in Western Society.* New York: Cambridge University Press, 1988.

_____. *Untying the Knot: A Short History of Divorce.* New York: Cambridge University Press, 1991.

Pinchbeck, Ivy and Margaret Hewitt. *Children in English Society*. London: Routledge & K. Paul, 1969.

Pinkerton, Sarah. "Custodial Rights of California Mothers and Fathers: A Brief History." *Journal of Contemporary Legal Issues* 16 Spring 2005: 155-64.

Plutarch. *Life of Lycurgus*. n.d.

Podell, Ralph J., et al. "Custody--To Which Parent?" *Marquette Law Review* 56 Fall 1972: 51-68

Pollock, Frederick and Frederic William Maitland. *The History of English Law Before the Time of Edward I* 1. 2d ed. Cambridge: University Press, 1898.

Pollock, Linda. *Forgotten Children: Parent-child relations from 1500 to 1900*. New York: Cambridge University Press, 1983.

Press releases. Washington, D.C.: U.S. Department of Health and Human Services. June 18, 1999; January 2, 2003; May 9, 2003.

Price, Joseph R. Comment. "*Bottoms III*: Visitation Restrictions and Sexual Orientation." *William and Mary Bill of Rights Journal* 5 1997:643-59.

Putney, Albert H. *Popular Law Library* 4. Minneapolis: Cree Publishing Co., 1908.

Qudamah. *Al Mughni*. n.d.

Radical Feminism – "Marriage" Ed. Anne Koedt et al. New York: Quadrangle Books, 1973.

Rafiqul-Haqq, M. and P. Newton. *The Place of Women in Pure Islam*. Pasadena, Calif.: I.F. Publications, 1996.

Ratliff, Jack. "Parens Patriae: An Overview." *Tulane Law Review* 74 2000:1847-58.

Reeve, Tapping. *The law of baron and femme, of parent and child, of guardian and ward, of master and servant, and of the powers of courts of chancery*. New Haven: Oliver Steele, 1816.

_____. *The Law of Baron and Femme, of Parent and Child, Guardian and Ward, Master and Servant, and of the Powers of the Courts of Chancery*. 3d ed. Albany: W Gould, 1862.

Reggio, M. "History of the Death Penalty." *Society's Final Solution: A History and Discussion of the Death Penalty*. Ed. Laura E. Randa. Lanham, Md.: University Press of America, 1997.

Rendleman, Douglas R. "Parens Patriae: From Chancery to the Juvenile Court." *South Carolina Law Review* 23 1975:201-59.

"Report of the Women's Rights Convention, Held at Seneca Falls, N.Y., July 19th and 20th, 1848 (Rochester, 1848)." *Selected Papers of Elizabeth Cady Stanton and Susan B. Anthony* 1. Ed. Ann. D. Gordon. 1997.

Rheinstein, Max. *Marriage, divorce, stability and the law.* Chicago: University of Chicago Press, 1971.

Riley, Glenda. *Divorce: An American Tradition.* New York: Oxford University Press, 1991.

Roberts, J. *Divorce Bills in the Imperial Parliament.* Dublin: J. Falconer, 1906.

The Roman Antiquities of Dionysius Halicarnassensis. Trans. Edward Spelman. London: Booksellers of London and Westminster, 1758.

Roth, Allan. "The tender years presumption in child custody disputes." *Journal of Family Law* 15 1976-77: 423-61.

Rothman, Barbara K. *Recreating Motherhood: Ideology and Technology in a Patriarchal Society.* New York: Norton, 1989.

Ryan, William B. *Infanticide: Its Law, Prevalence, Prevention and History.* London: J. Churchill, 1862).

Schaffer, H. Rudolph and Peggy E. Emerson. "The Development of Social Attachments in Infancy." *Monographs of the Society for Research in Child Development* 29. Serial No. 94. 1964: 1-77.

Schaps, David. *Economic Rights of Women in Ancient Greece.* Edinburgh: Edinburgh University Press, 1979.

Schouler, James. *A Treatise on the Law of The Domestic Relations.* Boston: Little, Brown & Co., 1870.

_____. *A Treatise on the Law of the Domestic Relations.* 4th ed. Boston: Little Brown & Co., 1889.

Scott, S.P. *The Civil Law, including the Twelve tables, the Institutes of Gaius, the Rules of Ulpian, the Opinions of Paulus, the Enactments of Justinian, and the Constitutions of Leo: translated from the original Latin, edited, and compared with all accessible systems of jurisprudence ancient and modern.* Cincinnati: Central Trust Company, 1932.

Shahar, Shulasmith. *Childhood in the Middle Ages.* New York: Routledge, 1990.

Shapiro, Julie. "Custody and Conduct: How the Law Fails Lesbian and Gay Parents and Their Children." *Indiana Law Journal* 71 Summer 1996:623-71.

Shelford, Leonard. *A Practical Treatise of the Law of Marriage and Divorce.* Philadelphia: J.S. Littell, 1841.

Shorter, Edward. *The Making of the Modern Family*. New York: Basic Books, 1975.

Singer, I. "Daughter in Jewish Law." *The Jewish Encyclopedia*. 1901.

Sisterhood Is Powerful: An Anthology of Writings From the Women's Liberation Movement. Ed. Robin Morgan New York: Random House, 1970.

Slack, Paul. *The English Poor Law, 1531 – 1782*. Houndmills Basingstoke Hampshire, U.K.: Macmillan, 1990.

Smith, William C. "Dads Want Their Day: Fathers Charge Legal Bias Toward Moms Hamstrings Them as Full-Time Parents." *American Bar Association Journal* 89 February 2003:38-43.

Solomon-Fears, Carmen. *Child Support Enforcement Program Incentive Payments: Background and Policy Issues*. Congressional Research Service. Washington, D.C.: Government Printing Office, 2013.

Somerville, Siobhan. "Scientific Racism and the Invention of the Homosexual Body." *Queer Studies: a lesbian, gay, bisexual, & transgender anthology*. Ed. Brett Beemyn and Mickey Eliason. New York: New York University Press, 1996. 241-61.

St. Martin in the Fields. *Bastardy and Settlement Examination Books, 1745-1749*. 1746.

Stacey, Judith. *Patriarchy and Socialist Revolution in China*. Berkeley, Calif.: University of California Press, 1983.

Stamps, Leighton. "Maternal Preference in Child Custody Decisions." *Journal of Divorce and Remarriage* 37 2002:1-11.

Stanley, S.E. and J.J. Berman. "Changing from fault to no-fault divorce: An interrupted time series analysis." *Journal of Applied Social Psychology* 7 1977:300-312.

Stanton, Elizabeth Cady. *Elizabeth Cady Stanton as revealed in her letters, diary and reminiscences*. Ed. Theodore Stanton and Harriot Stanton Blatch. New York: Harper, 1922.

Starnes, Cynthia Lee. "Swords in the Hands of Babes: Rethinking Custody Interviews after *Troxel*." *Wisconsin Law Review* 2003:115-69.

"The State v. Henry Day." *American Jurist. Jurist* 20 October 1838:237.

Statistical Abstract of the United States. Washington, D.C.: Government Printing Office, 1984.

Statutes at Large of Pennsylvania from 1682 to 1801, 2. Ed. James T. Mitchell and Harry Flanders. Harrisburg: Clarence M. Busch, State Printer of Pennsylvania, 1896.

Statutes at Large of South Carolina. Ed. Nicholas Trott. 1837.

Steele, Francis R. "The Code of Lipit-Ishtar." *American Journal of Archaeology* 52 July-September 1948: 425-50.

Steinem, Gloria. "Introduction." *Wonder Woman.* Ed. William M. Marston. New York: Holt, Rhinehart and Winston, 1972.

Stenton, Doris M.P. *The English Woman in History.* New York: Macmillan, 1957.

Sternlight, Jean. A Brief History of Family Law in Florida and the United States: Insights Regarding an Attempt to Simplify Divorce Procedures. 1995. MS. Collection of Cynthia McNeely, Florida State University.

Stone, Lawrence. *The Family, Sex and Marriage in England 1500-1800.* London: Weidenfeld & Nicolson, 1977.

_____. *Road to Divorce: England 1530-1987.* New York: Oxford University Press, 1990.

Story, Joseph. *Commentaries on Equity Jurisprudence* 2. Boston: Hilliard, Gray & Co., 1836.

_____. *Commentaries on Equity Jurisprudence as Administered in England and America.* 2d ed. Boston: C.C. Little & J. Brown, 1839.

_____. *Commentaries on Equity Jurisprudence As Administered in England and America.* 13th ed. Ed. Melville M. Bigelow. Boston: Little, Brown and Co., 1886.

_____. *Equity Jurisprudence* 2. 6th ed. Boston: Little, Brown & Co., 1853.

Suetonius. *The Lives of the Twelve Caesars.* Ed. Joseph Gavorse. New York: Modern Library, 1965.

Ta Tsing Leu Lee. Trans. George T. Staunton. London: Strahan and Preston, 1810.

Taylor, Alan. *American Colonies.* New York: Viking, 2001.

Teichman, Jenny. *Illegitimacy: A Philosophical Examination.* Oxford: B. Blackwell, 1982.

Terry, Jennifer. *An American Obsession: Science, Medicine, and Homosexuality in Modern Society.* Chicago: University of Chicago Press, 1999.

Thomson, George. *Studies in Ancient Greek Society.* 1st Amer. ed. New York: Citadel Press, 1965.

Tiffany, Walter C. *Handbook on the Law of Persons and Domestic Relations.* 2d ed. St. Paul, Minn.: West Publishing, 1909.

Toerien, Merran and Andrew Williams. "In Knots: Dilemmas of a Feminist Couple Contemplating Marriage." *Feminism and Psychology* 13 November 2003:432-36.

Tractate Kethuboth. Ed. Isidore Epstein. Brooklyn, N.Y.: Soncino Press, 1989.

Tractate Niddah. Ed. Isidore Epstein. Brooklyn, N.Y.: Soncino Press, 1989.

Trainor, Elizabeth. Annotation. "Initial Award or Denial of child Custody to Homosexual or Lesbian Parent." *American Law Reports 5th* 62 1998:591.

A Treatise of Feme Coverts: Or, the Lady's Law. The Savoy: E. & R. Nutt, & R. Gosling (assigns of B. Sayer, Esq.) for B. Lintot, 1732.

Trenkner, Thomas R. Annotation. "Modern Status of Maternal Preference Rule or Presumption in Child Custody Cases." *American Law Reports 3d* 70 1976:262.

Uhlman, Kristine. "Overview of Shari'a and Prevalent Customs in Islamic Societies – Divorce and Child Custody." *ExpertLaw.* 2004. California State Bar. August 28, 2013 <www.expertlaw.com/library/family_law/islamic_custody.html>

Vernier, Chester G. *American Family Laws* 4. London: Oxford University Press, 1936.

Viner, Charles. *A General Abridgement of Law and Equity* 14. 2d ed. London: G.G.J. & J. Robinson, 1791.

Vlosky, Denese Ashbaugh and Pamela A. Monroe. "The Effective Dates of No-Fault Divorce Laws in the 50 States." *Family Relations* 51. October 2002: 317-324.

Wagner, Sally Roesch. *Sisters in Spirit: Haudenosaunee (Iroquois) Influence on Early American Feminists.* Summertown, Tenn.: Native Voices, 2001.

Walker, Sue S. "Widow and Ward: The Feudal Law of Child Custody in Medieval England." *Feminist Studies* 3 Spring-Summer 1976: 104-16.

Walsh, Thomas J. "In the Interest of a Child: A Comparative Look at the Treatment of Children Under Wisconsin and Minnesota Custody Statutes." *Marquette Law Review* 85 Summer 2002:929-74.

Wardle, Lynn D. and Laurence C. Nolan. *Fundamental Principles of Family Law.* Buffalo, N.Y.: W.S. Hein, 2002.

Warshak, Richard A. *The Custody Revolution: The Father Factor and The Motherhood Mystique.* New York: Poseidon Press, 1992.

Watnik, Webster. *Child Custody Made Simple: Understanding the Laws of Child Custody and Child Support.* Claremont, Calif.: Single Parent Press, 2000.

Wearing, Betsy. *The Ideology of Motherhood: A Study of Sydney Suburban Mothers.* Sydney: G. Allen & Unwin, 1983.

Weinman, Carl A. "The trial judge awards custody." *Law and Contemporary Problems* 10 1944:721-36.

West's Encyclopedia of American Law. 2d ed. Ed. Jeffrey Lehman and Shirelle Phelps. Detroit, Mich.: Thomson/Gale, 2005.

Westminster City Archives 32 F5037.

Wharton, John J.S. *An Exposition of the Laws relating to the Women of England.* London: Longman, Brown, Green, and Longmans, 1853.

Wilde, Oscar. *De Profundis.* 2d ed. Ed. R. Ross. New York: G.P. Putnam's Sons, 1910.

Wilder, Joanne Ross. "Some Current Trends in Child Custody Litigation in the United States." American Academy of Matrimonial Lawyers. May 11, 2012 <www.aaml.org/sites/default/files/some%20current%20-trends%20in%20child-article.pdf>

Williamson, Laila. "Infanticide: An Anthropological Analysis." *Infanticide and the Value of Life.* Ed. Marvin Kohl. Buffalo, New York: Prometheus Books, 1971.

Willis, Robert J. "Child Support and the Problem of Economic Incentives." *The Law and Economics of Child Support Payments.* Ed. William S. Comanor. Northampton: Edward Elgar Publishing, 2004.

Women in the Labor Force: A Databook. U.S. Bureau of Labor Statistics. Washington, D.C.: Government Printing Office, 2011.

Woody, Robert H. *Getting Custody: Winning the Last Battle of the Marital War.* New York: Macmillan, 1973.

Wright, Danaya C. *"De Manneville v. De Manneville:* Rethinking the Birth of Custody Law under Patriarchy." *Law and History Review* 17 Summer 1999: 247-307.

Xenophon. *Constitution of the Lacedaemonians.* n.d.

_____. "Oeconomicus." *Xenophon: Memorabilia, Oeconomicus, Symposium, Apology.* Trans. E.C. Marchant. London: W. Heinemann, 1923.

Yaron, Reuven. *The Laws of Eshnunna.* 2d ed. Jerusalem: Magnes Press, 1988.

Young, Cathy. "The Sexist Violence Against Women Act." *Wall Street Journal* March 23, 1994: A15.

Zhu, Peter. "How China Court Decides Child Custody." *China Law Blog.* April 11, 2012 <http://www.chinalawblog.org/law-topics/divorce/224-child-custody>

Zimmerman, James M. *China Law Deskbook*. Chicago: American Bar Association, 2005.

Zuhaili, Wahbah. *Fiqh al Islami wa Adillatuhu* 7. 1984.

INDEX

Made in the USA
Lexington, KY
27 February 2015